Resource-Based and Evolutionary Theories of the Firm: Towards a Synthesis

On the Cover

The cover of this volume was designed to reflect the impulse toward synthesis that drove the ideas contained in its pages. The gentleman in the photographs is the great 20th Century architect, Frank Lloyd Wright. The images that appear here are selected from a series of shots taken while he used his hands to demonstrate the differences between conventional and organic architecture. It has been noted that as an architect, Frank Lloyd Wright's genius lay in his ability to draw upon areas that were remote from each other in culture and style to produce something truly modern. For having granted us permission to use his images, we are indebted to Pedro E. Guerrero, the photographer who worked with Wright for many years and who took these pictures.

Resource-Based and Evolutionary Theories of the Firm: Towards a Synthesis

Edited by
Cynthia A. Montgomery
Harvard Business School

Kluwer Academic Publishers
Boston/Dordrecht/London

Distributors for North America:
Kluwer Academic Publishers
101 Philip Drive
Assinippi Park
Norwell, Massachusetts 02061 USA

Distributors for all other countries:
Kluwer Academic Publishers Group
Distribution Centre
Post Office Box 322
3300 AH Dordrecht, THE NETHERLANDS

Library of Congress Cataloging-in-Publication Data

Resource-based and evolutionary theories of the firm : towards a
  synthesis / edited by Cynthia A. Montgomery.
     p. cm.
  Papers presented at a colloquium in Snekkersten, Denmark in
August, 1993.
  Includes bibliographical references and index.
  ISBN 0-7923-9562-X
  1. Industrial organization (Economic theory)--Congresses.
2. Strategic planning--Congresses. I. Montgomery, Cynthia A.,
1952- .
HD2326.R47   1995
338.5--dc20   95-3537
                                        CIP

Printed on acid-free paper.

Printed in the United States of America

Contents

v

Preface

This volume is a collection of papers that explore the intersection of evolutionary theories of the firm and an emergent body of research in the field of strategic management that has been broadly referred to as the "resource-based view of the firm." The papers were first presented at a colloquium on the same theme that was held in Snekkersten, Denmark in August, 1993. The meeting was generously sponsored and jointly directed by the Danish Social Science Research Council and the Institute of Industrial Economics and Strategy at the Copenhagen Business School.

The authors, and by association the papers, approach the task from different vantages. This was done by design, and reflects the belief that the respective fields will prosper from this kind of cross-fertilization. Thus, the views expressed in the papers are diverse: they invoke principles of economics, strategic management, and population ecology.

Since the symposium, the papers have undergone further revision to reflect the comments and insights gleaned from that meeting. While cross references reflect the common dialogue of the colloquium, a conscious choice was made to retain the independent voices of the authors.

From beginning to end, the creation of this volume drew on the efforts and contributions of many individuals. Special thanks go to Jacqui Archer, whose dedication to detail and good humor and grace under pressure carried us through the final production phase. Elizabeth Wynne Johnson provided adept editorial assistance. Her contribution and the support provided by the Harvard Business School Division of Research is gratefully acknowledged.

Resource-Based and Evolutionary Theories of the Firm: Towards a Synthesis

1

AN EXPLORATION OF COMMON GROUND: INTEGRATING EVOLUTIONARY AND STRATEGIC THEORIES OF THE FIRM

Nicolai Juul Foss[1]
Christian Knudsen
Institute of Industrial Economics and Strategy
Copenhagen Business School

Cynthia A. Montgomery
Harvard Business School

Introduction

The field of strategy has taken shape around a framework first conceived by Kenneth Andrews in the now-classic book, *The Concept of Corporate Strategy*. Andrews characterized the role of a strategist as one of finding the match between what a firm *can* do (organizational strengths and weaknesses) within the universe of what it *might* do (environmental opportunities and threats). The basic structure of this framework has demonstrated remarkable elasticity as the field has grown internally, and as insights borrowed from other disciplines have stretched its boundaries.

In particular, economic modes of thought have had a profound influence on thinking in the strategy field. These advances have prompted some commentators to proclaim no less than "a minor revolution in strategic management research and writing" (Rumelt, Schendel and Teece

[1]The authors thank Anita McGahan and Robert E. Kennedy for their helpful comments, and Birger Wernerfelt for his contribution to the development of these ideas.

1

1991: 5). We would like to suggest that (at least) three developments can be singled out as having contributed to the economic turn in strategy thinking. First, the modifications of traditional industrial organization economics through the use of game-theoretic entry-barrier models; second, the contractual approach to economic organization associated with R.H. Coase, Oliver Williamson, and many others; and third, the attempts of economists to address in evolutionary terms the consequences of essential diversity among firms.

In this book, we explore potential complementarities between evolutionary economics and an emergent stream of work in the business strategy field, called the resource-based view of the firm. Our purpose will be to contribute to an understanding of how one or both of these views of the firm could be enhanced by exposure to the other. Before beginning this task, we will comment briefly on why we have chosen to focus on this particular intersection.[2]

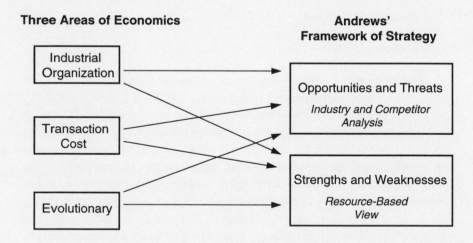

Figure 1 Cross-Fertilization Between Economics and Strategy

---

[2]The authors are indebted to Robert Kennedy at Harvard Business School for having first suggested this diagram.

The Basis for Integration

For the strategy field, we believe that the most important developments in economics are those that recognize differences across firms. The distinguishing characteristic of the evolutionary approach is precisely that it goes to the question of where the differences come from, placing the analysis of organizational capabilities center-stage in understanding firm behavior. As such, it is an invaluable counterpart to industry and competitor analysis. It is this attempt to investigate forces previously left unexplored within the "black box" of the firm that gives the evolutionary approach its particular relevance to strategy thinkers.

In an evolutionary approach the concept of strategy shares much in common with that used by scholars of management. Richard Nelson provided the following description that is consistent with both the evolutionary and management uses of the term:

> It [strategy] connotes a set of brand commitments
> made by a firm that define and rationalize its objectives
> and how it intends to pursue them. Some of this may be
> written down, some may not be but is in the management
> culture of the firm (Nelson 1991: 67).[3]

It is our belief that the evolutionary approach has a great deal to offer as a complement to the still-developing resource-based approach in the field of strategic management. Both stress the existence of fundamental diversity among firms, the recognition of which is an essential starting point for analysis and description. Ultimately, it is a firm's path-dependent, hence "sticky," knowledge endowment that differentiates it from other firms, allowing it to articulate unique profit-seeking strategies. Thus, the notions of routines (Nelson and Winter 1982), capabilities (Teece, Pisano and Shuen 1992; Grant 1991), and [core] competencies (Burgelman and Rosenbloom 1989, Prahalad and Hamel 1990), all have a fundamentally epistemic content, while the notion of resources incorporates knowledge-related resources. From a doctrinal perspective, it is noteworthy that both

---

[3]In contrast, strategy to game theorists is a function which maps the information of a player to its actions. Depending on the application, these actions may be considered either strategic or tactical by a management theorist.

approaches claim an antecedent in Edith Penrose's *The Theory of the Growth of the Firm* (1959).

It is important to note a few examples of how the evolutionary approach shares common space with the resource-based approach in ways that various game-theoretic approaches do not. For example, both resource-based and evolutionary approaches fundamentally take an efficiency approach to firm performance, in contrast to the market power perspective found in many entry deterrence models. On a different note, some of the areas where the game-theoretic approach is strong, and the resource-based perspective is weak, are areas where the evolutionary approach is also strong. We have in mind such areas as technological competition (e.g., patent races and technological first-mover advantages) and inter-temporal choice (e.g., credibility of threats and commitments). Conversely, whereas the relative lack of normative implications for individual firms has been a weakness of the evolutionary approach, the resource-based view is rich with firm-level normative content.

There are other differences between evolutionary and resource-based approaches, although none preclude the opportunities for synthesis that will be explored in the coming chapters. Modern evolutionary theory has grown out of Schumpeterian technology studies, while the resource-based approach stands firmly in the tradition of American strategic management thinking and, perhaps more distantly, in the tradition of Chicago School industrial economics.

Given the existence of both similarities and differences between resource-based and evolutionary approaches, the two may have something meaningful to contribute to one another along several dimensions. We pursue this attempt to blend the two distinct lines of scholarship on the basis of our belief that new insights will come to light as a result. Doing so, however, first requires a comparative discussion that identifies the differences as well as the areas of complementarity. A number of the basic points established here will be explored further in coming chapters. A few will even be challenged.

Evolutionary Approaches

Although evolutionary approaches have had a long history in economics, they have never occupied a formal place in the mainstream of that field. In part, this has to do with the diversity that characterizes evolutionary approaches, and with theorizing that ranges from the level of the individual decision-maker to extremely aggregate Kondratieff cycles or national systems of innovation. It is also a matter of what it means to say that a theory is "evolutionary" in the first place: is the relevant criterion the use of analogies to central concepts from evolutionary biology, or is it something altogether different? And if so, what is the status of such analogies (cf., Penrose 1952)?

On a general level, the kind of evolutionary theory that applies to the field of strategic management provides analogies to the biological concepts of variation, heredity and selection. It attempts to give a real-time account of social and economic phenomena in terms of processes of change. Indeed, process is a crucial element of the evolutionary approach. In a managerial context, the process of technological change is perhaps the most readily obvious analogy to biological concepts of mutation.

To date, perhaps the most important contribution to this kind of evolutionary theory is Richard Nelson and Sidney Winter's *An Evolutionary Theory of Economic Change* (1982). With this publication, the contours of a unified and rigorous evolutionary research program began to take shape. The Nelson and Winter approach stands directly in the tradition of the biological analogy that previously had been best expressed by Armen Alchian (1950). Emphasizing that the biological analogy is just that, Nelson and Winter nevertheless successfully construct an evolutionary framework that incorporates innovation (variation, mutation), the firm as a knowledge-bearing entity (heredity), and market selection.

Within this evolutionary framework, firms have primarily been conceptualized as possessing path-dependent knowledge bases (bundles of hierarchically arranged "routines"). The notion of routines provides a rationale for the relative rigidity that is necessary for the successful application of selection arguments. There has been little interest *per se* in the strategies that individual firms articulate on the basis of these knowledge bases. To use biological terminology, this represents a *phylogenetic* theory, i.e. one that is occupied with explaining evolutionary change in a population. The alternative, *ontogenetic* theory, refers to change in a single organism. In economic terms, the Nelson and Winter theory is primarily, like its neoclassical counterpart, a theory of industries, with less emphasis on the firm, due primarily to the importance it places on the selection environment. Indeed, evolutionary theory in the management context until recently has been predominantly phylogenetic, because it has dealt with understanding the evolution of industries (Hannan and Freeman 1977).

However, firm behavior is also important, since it is on this level that analogies to heredity should be found. Concepts like adaptation,

5

learning, search and path-dependence mostly relate to the level of the firm. A number of attempts have been made to apply evolutionary thinking to firm-level analysis, i.e. to construct more ontogenetic theories. Some of this is reflected in the recent increase in publications dealing with firm-level technology strategy of the firm from an evolutionary perspective (Burgelman and Rosenbloom 1989). The increasing interest that Williamson's version of transaction cost theory has generated among evolutionary theorists (e.g., Dosi, Winter and Teece 1992) is further testimony. Finally, one should mention Richard Nelson's (1991) and Sidney Winter's post-1982 publications (e.g., 1987, 1988), in which the perspective has become more firm-oriented than that in the 1982 book.

The fact that the industry-perspective nonetheless remains dominant in evolutionary theory accounts for our observation that the theory offers only a relatively narrow description of the firm and its resources. The kinds of resources most often discussed are knowledge-related ones, particularly the knowledge aspects of what Nelson and Winter call "routines," viz.". . . the skills of the organization" (1982). Other resources such as physical assets and patents are not factored in to the same extent. But there is no *a priori* reason why they should not be included in a more comprehensive evolutionary theory of the firm. Indeed they should be, as they may contribute to the further enhancement of the theory.

The Resource-Based Approach

As noted earlier, the resource-based approach that is developing within the field of strategic management has two sets of roots: seminal writings on business strategy by Kenneth Andrews, C. Roland Christiansen, and Alfred Chandler among others, and Edith Penrose's (1959) work characterizing the firm as a collection of productive resources.

Managerial writers like Andrews were interested in the functions and responsibilities of senior management and used the concept of strategy as a means for helping them shape the future destiny of their firms. Andrews thought that corporate strategy should define the businesses in which a company will compete, *preferably in a way that focuses resources to convert distinctive competence into competitive advantage* (1980: 18-19) [italics ours].

Authors addressing managerial audiences have tended to treat most variables as discretionary (Nelson 1991). This certainly is true in the early strategy literature, where managers implicitly were viewed as having the power to effect dramatic changes in their firms. While managers were

6

encouraged to develop their firms' resources and adroitly match them with market opportunities, little advice was given on how to assess either the resources themselves or the market opportunities in a systematic manner.

As the field developed and scholars sought a more rigorous approach, they focused first on the exogenous variables in a firm's competitive environment. Drawing on the Bain-Mason paradigm and oligopoly theory (Porter 1980), they examined the structural forces in a firm's environment and how those forces influenced firm performance. These themes dominated the strategy field throughout the 1980s. Strategy scholars interested in these questions are the ones who more recently have turned to game-theoretic industrial organization economics.

More recently, some strategy scholars have returned to Andrews' framework and have begun to address issues pertaining to the firm itself. Operating under the rubric of "the resource-based view," they have brought a more systematic approach to firm-level analysis. In the tradition of Penrose (1959), Wernerfelt (1984) characterized the firm as a collection of resources rather than a set of product-market positions. In a theoretical account, Lippman and Rumelt (1982) showed that "uncertainly imitable" resources may discourage competitors from challenging an incumbent.

Throughout this period, a number of scholars made other contributions that lend themselves to incorporation in the resource-based approach. Barney addressed competitive imperfections in strategic factor markets and argued that first mover advantages and entry barriers exist only under conditions of resource heterogeneity and immobility (1986, 1991). Dierickx and Cool (1989) differentiated between resource stocks and flows and argued that strategic assets, those that are necessary for sustainable competitive advantage, must be developed internally and cannot be purchased on the factor markets. Amit and Schoemaker (1993) described the process through which resources are developed. In their view, boundedly rational managers make imperfect and discretionary decisions through time that culminate in a given set of organizational capabilities.

Other authors used the resource-based view to help explain the growth and development of multi-line firms. Montgomery and Hariharan (1991) showed that a firm's diversified expansion is a function of its extant resource base. Their empirical examination revealed that firms with established capabilities in marketing and R&D were able to vault entry barriers into industries where these were the critical resource requirements. In a separate analysis of corporate diversification, Montgomery and Wernerfelt (1988) distinguished between corporate expansion that relied on less specific and more specific factors.

Like early strategy scholars, these authors are primarily interested in differences across firms. What differentiates them is their use of economic reasoning, notably the economics of Ricardian and Paretian rents. In particular, the question of why some firms earn supernormal profits has received careful scrutiny. While theoretical and empirical research in industrial organization economics has shown that a firm's profits are related to its choice of industry (Schmalensee 1985; Wernerfelt and Montgomery 1988), resource-based reasoning examines this question from the perspective of inter-firm differences.

As noted earlier, the resource-based view tends to see performance differences across firms as the result of differences in efficiency, rather than differences in market power. In explaining these differences, resource-based theorists tend to focus on resources and capabilities that are long-lived and difficult to imitate (Conner 1991). As Peteraf (1991) noted, in the resource-based view "history matters, profits are persistent, and change most often occurs slowly and incrementally" (p. 14).

Despite its considerable progress in a relatively short amount of time, the resource-based view suffers from a number of weaknesses. Theoretical progress has been made in identifying resources and characterizing what makes them "valuable" (Dierickx and Cool 1989). However, when faced with the complexities of a real firm, it is often difficult to identify which of a firm's many "resources," singly or in combination, account for the firm's success. Where such attempts have been made, they have met with criticism for ultimately being tautological. At the very least, the identification process often has a distinctly *ex post* quality: once a firm is recognized as successful, the resources behind the success are labeled as valuable. If observed in another setting, it is not clear the resources would be valued in the same way.

This difficulty in assessing the value of resources might be due to the fact that it is impossible to measure them in isolation. As Porter argued, resources are valuable only if they "allow firms to perform activities that create advantages in particular markets" (1991: 108). Another contextual factor to consider is the presence of complementary assets. The value of an individual resource is likely to be at least partially contingent upon the presence (or absence) of other resources; that is, it may be a system of resources that matters, not the individual resources taken separately. Further, the value of resources will change over time. What was once an advantage may one day become an encumbrance, even though the resource itself has not changed.

8

Not unrelated to the identification and valuation issues discussed above, the resource-based literature uses both equilibrium and process arguments, although the inconsistencies between these are rarely acknowledged. Basic price theory reasoning in neoclassical economics, for example, looms large in many of the more formal resource-based papers. Indeed, one of the central concepts, the concept of sustained competitive advantage, is fundamentally an equilibrium concept. Similarly, the reasoning associated with strategic factor markets (Barney 1986) is fundamentally neoclassical. On the other hand, many of the more application-oriented contributions (Wernerfelt 1989, for example), deal explicitly with process. Teece *et al* (1992) have studied organizational capabilities and openly acknowledge the tension between static and dynamic treatments of resources. We are sympathetic to their argument, and believe there is much more to be done on this issue.

The next step in our brief introduction to the evolutionary and resource-based concepts is to place them side by side. In so doing, we hope to suggest possible areas for cross-fertilization.

The Two Schools of Thought Compared

As noted earlier, both the resource-based and the evolutionary approaches share a common doctrinal antecedent in Edith Penrose's seminal work of the 1950s, although each draws upon distinct elements of her analysis. Briefly, one may see the evolutionary approach as having developed the dynamic aspects of Penrose's theory (her view of the process of firm growth as a continuous and cumulative "unfolding" process), while the resource-based approach has been more pertinent to the analysis of the resources themselves. Another way to compare the approaches is to point to the different levels of analysis on which they operate.

Table 1 is a preliminary attempt to identify the differences as well as some points of convergence between the evolutionary and resource-based perspectives. To be meaningful, synthesizing the two must imply, first, that they supplement each other in some vital dimensions and, second, that new insights may be expected to appear.

Emerging Issues

The potential for inquiry inspired by a juxtaposition of evolutionary and resource-based approaches goes well beyond what will be presented here. Nevertheless, we offer our own thoughts as to some appropriate avenues for exploration.

	Evolutionary Theory	Resource-based Theory
Underlying Economic Theory	Process oriented	Equilibrium oriented
Level of Analysis	Primarily industry	Firm
Units of Analysis	Routines	Resources
Intellectual Heritage	Schumpeter, Alchian	Penrose, strategic management tradition; Chicago industrial economics
Selected Contributors	Nelson/Winter; Metcalfe/Gibbons	Wernerfelt, Barney; Dierickx/Cool, Rumelt
Primary Object of Explanation	Technological evolution and competition	Sources of competitive advantage, diversification
Central Resources	Primarily intangible resources	In principle: all resources
Concept of Strategy	Articulation of routines in a profit-seeking way (generally not well-described)	The quest for Ricardian rents through the accumulation and deployment of non-imitable resources

Table 1 Evolutionary and Resource-based Approaches: A Juxtaposition

Equilibrium or process?

Equilibrium constructs are, of course, the cornerstone of most economic thinking; they are a straightforward way in which to model competition, they organize thought, and they permit predictions as to how the market will move. But it is also important to be aware of the limitations of equilibrium constructs. Economic equilibrium generally means that all known possibilities for trade have been exploited; it is an end-state of a process of opportunity discovery.

But can we safely neglect the disequilibrium process when thinking about strategy? The roots of the resource-based view of the firm stretch back to Penrose (1959), who characterized firms as collections of productive resources that never reach an equilibrium state:

> The attainment of such a "state of rest" is precluded by three significant obstacles: those arising from the familiar difficulties posed by the indivisibility of resources; those arising from the fact that the same resources can be used differently under different circumstances, and in particular, in a "specialized" manner; and those arising because in the ordinary processes of operation and expansion new productive services are continually being created (1959: 68).

The resource-based view holds that valuable resources are those that competitors cannot immediately imitate. Innovations, whether protected by a patent or not, often fall into this category. Schumpeterian competition that describes the process through which innovations are imitated is inherently non-equilibrium in nature.

These would appear to be compelling reasons for resource-based theorists to reconsider the equilibrium requirement. Perhaps a compromise position, preserving some element of dynamic rather than static equilibrium, would be possible. Such a model could, for example, allow for learning, uncertainty, and shocks, elements that are often present in strategic settings.

Technology

There is perhaps no better example of disequilibrium than the upheavals brought about by changes in technology. The resource-based view has given little attention to technology issues, but these concerns have occupied center stage in the evolutionary approach. In addressing these questions, evolutionary theorists have tended to focus on the industry or sector level (e.g., dominant designs, design configurations, technological paradigms, regimes, trajectories), and have had little to say about the firm itself. However, the implications of significant shifts in technology are immense at the firm level and give us a particularly good window through which we can observe the effect of major discontinuities.

If accompanied by high levels of uncertainty, shifts in technology confront firms with difficult investment choices. This setting represents an extreme case of the more general question of how managers make decisions about the resources in which their firms will invest. How, *ex ante*, are those choices made?

Shifts in technology also are important because they are likely to have a cascading impact on the value of a firm's extant resource base. This is true whether the firm itself is the innovator, displaced follower, or somewhere in between. Because technologies exist in a broader system of complementary assets (Teece 1986), shifts in technology are likely to induce changes in the value of supporting or complementary assets. Given that the health or value of a firm's resource portfolio is a primary concern of the resource-based view, closer attention to conditions that impact that portfolio, sometimes in dramatic ways, would seem to be in order.

What behavioral assumptions?

The above points are closely related to the problem of behavioral assumptions, since such assumptions are typically dependent on whether one uses a process or an equilibrium framework. However, an integrated program should be based on common behavioral assumptions. The resource-based approach relies on rationality, while the evolutionary approach bypasses it.

What behavioral foundations should appear in a synthesis? Specifically, how much intentionality should be ascribed to individual managers? Such foundational questions are important because they ultimately shape our views about, for example, how proactive successful strategic behavior may be. Whereas Penrose (1959) saw strategy as having a strongly intentional element, evolutionary theorists have traditionally been much more "pessimistic" about the possibilities for significant, proactive change.

Amit and Schoemaker (1993) link elements of behavioral decision-making with the development and deployment of organizational resources through time. Examinations like this are critical because they trace the evolution of asymmetry among firms. Such inquiries also raise a host of fundamental questions about the value of strategic analysis, and the extent

12

to which managers can influence the destinies of their firms, and also because they blend the analytical with the behavioral. In most simple models with rational players, there is a unique outcome associated with every set of initial conditions. When noise and bounded rationality are introduced into that model, the uniqueness is lost, thereby creating the basis for a richer theory. We believe more work of this kind should be encouraged.

Problems in purposive development of resources

The question of intentionality becomes particularly salient when considering how a firm sets out to build a given set of capabilities. Because resources that support a competitive advantage are by definition inimitable, and unidentifiability is a sufficient condition for inimitability, it is difficult to say how one should invest to build a competitive advantage. On the other hand, the view that one cannot make such investments purposively is not satisfactory either. Is there a way out of this conundrum?

Level of analysis

As noted earlier, the resource-based approach operates almost exclusively at the level of the firm, while the evolutionary approach tends to operate at the level of the industry. Nonetheless, the two are not mutually exclusive. Indeed, an understanding of the industry-level forces behind the appearance and disappearance of entire populations of firms should be helpful to those who are interested in the destinies of individual firms. It should also be useful for those interested in population-level movements to understand the firm-level characteristics of those who survived and those who did not.

It remains to be determined whether the firm-level and industry-level foci can be merged in some way. As a consequence, it is difficult to predict how such a two-level theory would look. What would be its important elements? What would be its benefits?

The problem of coherence

A central problem in recent evolutionary thinking on firm behavior is the problem of coherence (Dosi, Winter and Teece 1992). This question has to do with what it is that fundamentally distinguishes the viable firm as a historical entity, rather than just an arbitrary collection of businesses held together by the thin glue of transaction cost minimization. In Nelson and Winter (1982), part of the answer is provided by the concept of routines, whereas in the classic business strategy, top management occupied center-stage in an explanation. While each of these views provides a partial answer, surely a theory of coherence must involve something more. There are a number of intriguing problems related to questions of coherence, such as: What are the respective roles of "local" and "global" (management) knowledge in the production of coherence? Is the knowledge on which coherence rests ultimately a resource or rather "something" that integrates resources? How fragile is coherence? How transferable?

In an evolutionary reading, we see coherence as the central aspect of the firm's "heritage," how knowledge is contained and transmitted over time. A firm-level theory of "ontogenesis", the mechanisms underlying the transmission of knowledge as well as how it is utilized, implies coming to grips with the economic meaning and implications of coherence. Theories of commitment, path-dependency, coordination costs, and adaptation may supply some of the economic insights needed. So, too, may organizational economics.

Transaction costs

Recently, there have been some attempts to incorporate insights from transaction-cost analysis in evolutionary economics (Dosi, Winter and Teece 1992; Langlois 1991), and in the resource-based literature as well (Gabel 1984; Dierickx and Cool 1989) (see Figure 1). However, there has been very little systematic work on the precise relations between the resource and evolutionary approaches on the one hand and transaction costs on the other. Nonetheless, it seems evident that transaction costs are relevant to evolutionary and resource approaches, and therefore to their integration. For example, there are rather direct correlations between rent-earning resources and specific assets. Further, transaction costs surely influence the accumulation of resources and are therefore pertinent to the questions of coherence via, for example, the incentives of hierarchical organization and regimes of appropriability.

Stage of development

Although the fledgling organization is easily addressed by evolutionary approaches, the resource-based view has relatively little to say about it. If the set of existing resources is small, the random developments

14

that evolutionary theory highlights play a much more powerful role than they would in larger established organizations. In contrast, where the set of resources is small, the resource-based view has little predictive ability. Not surprisingly, most successful applications of this view have been to diversified or well-established companies. Is there a way to combine the relative merits of each approach?

A Focused Dialogue

The purpose of this introduction has been to outline the domain of the discussion, articulating a basis for a synthesis of evolutionary and resource-based thinking. The chapters that follow approach the challenge in a variety of ways, each focusing on specific avenues within the domain. There remain any number of roads not taken. The book as whole is intended to spark the kind of dialogue that will lead to their discovery.

References

Alchian, A.A. 1950. Uncertainty, evolution and economic theory. In idem, 1977. *Economic forces at work.* Indianapolis: Liberty Press.
Amit, R., and Schoemaker, P. 1993. "Strategic assets and organizational rent." *Strategic Management Journal* 14: 33-46.
Andrews, K. 1980. *The concept of corporate strategy.* Homewood, Ill.: Richard D. Irwin.
Barney, J.B. 1991. "Firm resources and sustained competitive advantage." *Journal of Management* 17: 99-120.
Barney, J.B. 1986. "Strategic factor markets." *Management Science* 32: 1231-1241.
Burgelman, R., and Rosenbloom, R. 1989. Technology strategy: an evolutionary process perspective. In idem (eds.) 1989. *Research on technological innovation, management and policy* 4: 1-23.
Castanias, R.P., and Helfat, C.E. 1991. "Managerial resources and rents." *Journal of Management* 17: 155-171.
Conner, K. 1991. "A historical comparison of resource-based theory and five schools of thought within industrial organization economics: do we have a new theory of the firm?" *Journal of Management* 17: 121-154.

Demsetz, H. 1988. "The theory of the firm revisited. *Journal of Law, Economics and Organization* 4: 141-162.

Dierickx, I., and Cool, K. 1989. "Asset stock accumulation and sustainability of competitive advantage." *Management Science* 35: 1504-1511.

Dosi, G., Winter, S.G., and Teece, D.J. 1992. Towards a theory of corporate coherence: preliminary remarks. In G. Dosi, R. Giannetti and P.A. Toninelli (eds.) 1992. *Technology and enterprise in a historical perspective.* Oxford: Clarendon Press.

Gabel, H.L. 1984. "The microfoundations of competitive strategy." Mimeo, INSEAD.

Grant, R.M. 1991. "The resource-based theory of competitive advantage: implications for strategy formulation." *California Management Review* 33: 114-135.

Hannan, M.T., and Freeman, J. 1977. "The population ecology of organizations." *American Journal of Sociology* 82: 929-964.

Langlois, R.N. 1991. "Transaction cost economics in real time." *Industrial and Corporate Change* 1: 99-127.

Lippman, S.A., and Rumelt, R.P. 1982. "Uncertain imitability: an analysis of interfirm differences in efficiency under competition." *The Bell Journal of Economics* 13: 418-438.

Metcalfe, J.S., and Gibbons, M. 1989. "Technology, variety and organization." *Research on Technological Innovation, Management and Policy* 4: 153-193.

Montgomery, C.A., and Hariharan, S. 1991. "Diversified expansion by large established firms." *Journal of Economic Behavior and Organization* 15: 71-89.

Montgomery, C.A., and Wernerfelt, B. 1988. "Diversification, Ricardian rents, and Tobin's q." *RAND Journal of Economics* 19: 623-632.

Nelson, R.R. 1991. "Why do firms differ, and how does it matter?" *Strategic Management Journal* 12: 61-74.

Nelson, R.R., and Winter, S.G. 1982. *An evolutionary theory of economic change.* Cambridge, Mass.: Belknap Press.

Penrose, E.T. 1952. "Biological analogies in the theory of the firm." *American Economic Review* 52: 804-819.

Penrose, E.T. 1959. *The theory of the growth of the firm.* Oxford: Oxford University Press.

Peteraf, M. 1991. "The resource-based model: an emerging paradigm for strategic management." Discussion paper. J.L. Kellogg Graduate School of Management, Northwestern University.

Porter, M.E. 1980. *Competitive strategy.* New York: Free Press.

Porter, M.E. 1991. "Towards a dynamic theory of strategy." *Strategic Management Journal* 12 (Winter 1991): 95-117.

Prahalad, C.K., and Hamel, G. 1990. "The core competence of the corporation." *Harvard Business Review* 66: 79-91.

Rumelt, R.P. 1984. "Towards a strategic theory of the firm." In R.D. Lamb. 1984. *Competitive strategic management.* New Jersey: Englewood Cliffs.

Rumelt, R.P. 1991. "How much does industry matter?" *Strategic Management Journal* 12: 167-185.

Rumelt, R.P., Schendel, D., and Teece, D.J. 1991. "Strategic management and economics." *Strategic Management Journal* 12: 5-29.

Schmalensee, R. "Do markets differ much?" *The American Economic Review* 75: 341-351.

Teece, D.J. "Profiting from technological innovation: implications for integration, collaboration, licensing and public policy." *Research Policy* 15: 285-306.

Teece, D.J., Pisano, G., and Shuen, A. 1992. "Dynamic capabilities and strategic management." Working paper, Consortium on Competitiveness and Cooperation, University of California at Berkeley.

Wernerfelt, B. 1984. "A resource-based view of the firm." *Strategic Management Journal* 5: 171-180.

Wernerfelt, B. 1989. "From critical resources to corporate strategy." *Journal of General Management* 14 (Spring): 4-12.

Wernerfelt, B., and Montgomery, C.A. 1988. "Tobin's q and the importance of focus in firm performance." *The American Economic Review* 78: 246-250.

Winter, S.G. 1987. "Knowledge and competence as strategic assets." In D.J. Teece (ed.) *The competitive challenge.* Cambridge: Ballinger.

Winter, S.G. 1988. "On Coase, competence and the corporation." *Journal of Law, Economics and Organization* 4: 163-180.

17

2

STRATEGIC MANAGEMENT AND THE EXPLORATION OF DIVERSITY

Daniel A. Levinthal[1]
Wharton School
University of Pennsylvania

The field of Strategic Management has had as a primary mission the analysis of diversity of performance among firms. While most research in the field has shared this common agenda, the approach taken has varied. Researchers have tended to be divided by the level of analysis with which they approach the issue and by their assumptions about the rationality of individuals and firms. This essay applies an evolutionary perspective to explore this question of diversity. It is suggested that such a perspective not only is an useful means with which to approach this question, but that as a by-product it may help to unify the strategy literature which has faced these methodological divisions based on level of analysis and assumptions of individual and firm rationality.

[1]This research was supported by the Sol C. Snider Entrepreneurial Center at the Wharton School and by a grant from the Sloan Foundation to the Financial Institutions Center, also at the Wharton School. I thank Cynthia Montgomery for comments on a prior draft.

Level of Analysis

In early work, the focus was on distinctive competencies among organizations (Selznick 1957; Andrews 1971). As the field began to relabel itself Strategic Management, the primary interest became diversity across industries (Porter 1980). The field is now in the process of re-adjusting its focus to firm-level differences under the rubric of the resource view of the firm.

This ebb and flow of level of analysis may, in part, reflect the efforts of academics to distinguish themselves from their immediate predecessors, but it is also driven by emerging empirical findings and changes in markets. The movement to the industry level of analysis resulted from the successful application of the techniques of industrial organization economics to questions of competitive strategy (Porter 1981). This line of argument has been embellished in recent years by more formal applications of game theory to questions of strategic interaction (Shapiro 1989; Saloner 1991; Camerer 1991).

The movement back to the firm-level of analysis seems to have been driven more by empirical anomalies and the challenges of managerial practice then the "technological opportunity" represented by the availability of powerful analytic techniques. One of the more prominent of these issues is the question of firm diversification. An exclusive focus on an industry level of analysis would imply that the question of the appropriate diversification policy of a firm could be reposed as a question of "what is an attractive industry?" The limitations of such a singular focus have been demonstrated both by individual firm failures and more systematic empirical accounts (Rumelt 1974; Porter 1987).

The other basic empirical challenge to the industry level of analysis is the finding that industry identity accounts for only a modest fraction of the variation in performance differences among firms (Rumelt 1991). Furthermore, the increasingly global nature of competition and, in turn, the broader number of players within a given industry mitigate the importance of implicit collusion and coordination, factors that are central to industry analysis and models of strategic interaction. For instance, in the 1950s the automobile industry was fertile ground for examining price collusion (Bresnahan 1987), whereas current analysis of the industry focuses on variation in manufacturing systems (Womack, Jones, and Ross 1990) and product development efforts (Clark and Fujimoto 1991).

These empirical findings have caused researchers to reframe the issue of diversification from what is an attractive industry to what are a firm's core competencies (Prahalad and Hamel 1990). Instead of searching for entry barriers to an industry, researchers now attempt to unearth what constitutes those scarce, valuable, and difficult to imitate firm capabilities that account for variation in firm performance (Barney 1991). The emergence of the resource view of the firm in the academic literature is a manifestation of this shift in the level of analysis of strategy researchers.

Behavioral and Economic Traditions

Not only has strategy research differed in level of analysis, but historically the strategy field has divided itself into two basic camps of academic discourse on the basis of differing assumptions about the rationality of decision making. One group of academic warriors have focused on what is termed issues of strategy content (Montgomery 1988). These researchers draw their intellectual heritage from economics and are concerned with well-defined firm decisions, such as diversification choices, and observable performance outcomes.

The other camp of warriors operate under the banner of process research (Chakravthy and Doz 1992). Their intellectual roots lie in the behavior sciences. For them, strategy does not consist of discrete choices but of a complex stream of decisions that, when taken as a whole, might be interpreted, though in their view often incorrectly, as constituting a firm's strategy (Mintzberg 1978).

As the use of the term warriors suggests, these cohabitants of the academy have not always lived at peace with one another. There is a tendency for members of the content camp to view process research as lacking in rigor; while process researchers sometimes question the relevance of large sample empirical research and theoretical modeling to the problems of strategic management.

The leaders of the revival of the study of the firm-level differences in capabilities, termed the resource view, (cf., Rumelt 1984; Barney 1991; Wernerfelt 1984; Montgomery and Wernerfelt 1988; Teece 1980) are deeply steeped in the traditions of economic research and the content camp of strategy research. There is a certain irony in this. An irony that holds some promise for greater unification of the research streams within the strategy field.

In an ex-post analysis of firm-level performance differences, there are a variety of viable candidate explanations. Many of them, such as property rights around a valued technology or brand name, proprietary access to a distribution channel, or economies of scale and scope, are readily appealing to a content researcher. However, traditional economic tools, which form the basis of much content research, do not readily lend themselves to an understanding of how these distinct positions emerge. Furthermore, to the extent that the firm's competitive environment changes, the advantages identified by a traditional resource analysis at a prior point in time may not lend themselves to a competitive advantage in subsequent time periods.

Thus, the emergence of diversity and, to some extent, the sustainability of diversity over time are not adequately handled by traditional "content" variables. As research under the resource view continues, it is beginning to enter the murky waters of such process issues as organizational culture (Barney 1986b). This is not accidental. In order to understand the emergence of diversity and, over long periods, its sustainability, one is virtually forced to consider more process-like variables. A particularly strong statement of this is Senge's (1990) comment that "the only enduring source of competitive advantage is the ability to learn."

Resource View as a Bridge

A prime impetus behind the resource view of the firm is the felt need to focus greater attention in the strategy field on issues of firm level differences. As a result, work in the resource view of the firm has not been directed at bridging levels of analysis between firms and industries but rather to redress an imbalance in the literature by its focus on the firm. While this re-direction of attention has been an important contribution, looking forward, research in this area must reconnect with market level perspectives on competition. To the extent that market considerations enter the discussion, they tend to be factor markets not product markets. However, if one is interested in understanding the diversity in a population of firms, the selection forces represented by product market competition are critical. There are some important exceptions in the literature that address forces guiding diversity both at the level of the firm and market, such as Lippman and Rumelt (1982), Wernerfelt and Montgomery (1986), and more recently Teece, Pisano and Shuen (1990). These efforts, however, are relative islands in a sea of core competencies.

As suggested above, practitioners of the resource view of the firm are finding themselves, despite their roots in economics, facing issues of organizational behavior. However, how this work relates to the behavioral traditions within strategy research depends upon which variant of the literature on the resource view of the firm to which one refers. One branch of this literature, which I will term the "High Church," bases its analysis on two critical assumptions. At the level of firms (and individuals within firms), there is the assumption of rational choice. Firms and individuals maximize their payoffs, given the constraints of their existing resources. The other assumption is an equilibrium notion of some sort. In many respects, the equilibrium property falls immediately out of the assumption of maximizing behavior. Profit maximizing firms will not leave profits on the table. In analyses of strategic interaction, the equilibrium notion poses a further requirement of a set of mutually consistent expectations among the actors.

The other branch of the resource-based literature, which I term "Low Church," rejects these two assumptions. For these authors, the resource perspective seems to have two defining elements. One is simply an issue of the appropriate level of analysis with which to explore strategy issues. Heterogeneity across firms is of greater interest than heterogeneity across markets. A second, and related attribute, is that for the firm attributes that account for variation in profitability, factor inputs must be highly imperfect.

These properties are not at odds with what I have termed the High Church of the resource view of the firm. The differences between the two branches of this literature lie in the degree of adherence to the dual assumptions of rationality and equilibria. This discrepancy is effectively illustrated by the exchange between Barney and Dierickx and Cool (Barney 1986a; Dierickx and Cool 1989; Barney 1989). While Barney does not formally model the dual assumptions of rationality and equilibrium, they are critical drivers of his arguments. It is these properties that lead him to the conclusion that only differences in *ex ante* information sets or chance can account for differences in firm performance. Absent either of these two conditions, the price of resource acquisition should fully reflect its value.

Dierickx and Cool do not wish to follow Barney to the primordial state of differences in initial information sets. They, implicitly, prefer to start with substantive resource differences across firms and argue why these differences are not readily eliminated either by factor market activity or internal development efforts. Barney does not disagree with these later arguments, but, driven by the engines of rational choice and equilibrium concepts, engages in the infinite recursion to an hypothetical world of no resource differences.[2]

Evolutionary Arguments as a Bridge

An evolutionary perspective may serve to bridge the chasms that divide the strategy field along the "fault lines" of assumptions of rationality and level of analysis. An evolutionary approach, at least in the tradition of Nelson and Winter (1982), takes as a foundational assumption the notion of bounded rationality. In that respect, such an approach relates most closely to the behavioral strands of the literature and, what I have termed, the "Low Church" of the resource view of the firm. However, at the market level, central to the analysis is the impact of the competitive forces of market selection. In that sense, Nelson and Winter straddle the behavioral and economic camps of the strategy literature; they are sensitive to the limitations of individual rationality but are equally sensitive to the collective intelligence of markets. As this argument suggests, the evolutionary approach as exemplified by Nelson and Winter is an effective means of linking discussions of firm capabilities and industry dynamics. Lastly, evolutionary arguments have as their defining characteristic a concern with the past and, in particular, the degree to which past forms influence present ones. Thus, unlike some accounts of firm differences from a resource perspective, evolutionary arguments do not suffer from the problem of retrospective attribution. Descent with modification is the cornerstone of evolutionary arguments.

For these reasons, evolutionary economics offers a promising basis with which to explore the diversity in performance among firms. Useful not only as a tool to examine the question of diversity, but also for the potential "by-product" of helping to unify the various strands of the strategy field.

If one is to adopt an evolutionary perspective, the issue remains as to what forces drive the evolutionary process. The basic elements of an evolutionary process are variation, selection, and retention (Campbell 1965). The following discussion applies these basic concepts of evolutionary systems to explore the sources of diversity among firms.

---

[2]Indeed, one could push the logical recursion back further and argue that differences in beliefs are themselves the result of investment activities, whether general human capital (Becker 1962) or more direct efforts (Cohen and Levinthal 1994).

Variation

While the occurrence of variation is critical in biological models of evolution, it tends to be treated as random event, a mutation. Strategy researchers and organizational theorists, operating in a tradition which places a strong value of the role and efficacy of managerial action have devoted considerable energy exploring the nature of variation inducing mechanisms.

Variation generation and incentive mechanisms

In a capitalist system, the entrepreneurial motive for profit is a primary force of variation generation (Schumpeter 1934, 1954; Baumol 1993). Entrepreneurial efforts may or may not payoff for individual entrepreneurs, and in some cases may not even be attractive *ex ante* gambles; however, from a societal perspective they serve an important role of introducing variation in the population of organizations.

As Burgelman and Sayles (1986) and Block and MacMillan (1993) point out, entrepreneurial activity can occur within the context of established firms as well as be associated with the founding of new enterprises. From the perspective of corporate entrepreneurship, the critical managerial issues lie in the specification of incentive systems that induce variation generating behaviors as well as in the development of internal selection mechanisms to sort out favorable from less favorable variants (Burgelman 1990).

In recent years, there has been considerable interest in learning and innovative activity at relatively low-levels of organizational hierarchies. These initiatives have gone by labels such as quality circles and continuous learning. Such efforts are attempts to induce front-line operating personnel to engage in variation creating organizational experiments (Miner 1994; Winter 1994). Ghemawat (1992) provides a detailed illustration of the impact of incentive systems on process improvements by operating personnel.

Organizational search

One of the initial discussions of variation generating mechanisms occurs in the work of March and Simon (1958). In particular, they developed the notion of organizational search. A critical feature of organizational search is that it tends to be local. Organizations search for solutions in the neighborhood of current alternatives (March and Simon 1958; Cyert and March 1963). By implication, if capabilities are enhanced via a search process, then the capabilities that emerge will be, to an important extent, path- or history-dependent.

Levinthal (1994) provides some insight into the impact on firm evolution of such local search processes. Consider a setting in which the impact of particular organizational attributes on overall organizational effectiveness are highly interdependent with one another. What would the mapping from organizational attributes to organizational effectiveness look like under such a setting? With a high level of interaction effects, there is unlikely to be an unique optimum to the problem of organizational design and strategy choice. Rather, this mapping from attributes to outcomes will tend to constitute a "rugged landscape" (Kauffman 1989). That is, there will be many local optima in such a space, with valleys of varying depth and width separating these local optima. Local search will tend to identify a particular local optimum; furthermore, the local optimum at which one arrives will be largely determined by the starting point of one's search process. As a result, when the impact on organizational effectiveness of individual attributes is highly interdependent, what geneticists term epistatic effects (Smith 1989), search processes will tend to be very path- or history-dependent (Levinthal 1994).

As a result, the observed distribution of organizational forms in a population may reflect heterogeneity in the population of organizations at an earlier point in time rather than variation in niches in the environment, as suggested by ecological analyses (Hannan and Freeman 1977), or a set of distinct external conditions, as suggested by contingency theories (Lawrence and Lorsch 1967). Contingency theory argues for a correspondence between facets of organizations and features of the environment in which organizations function (Lawrence and Lorsch 1967). However, even if all organizations face the same environment, they may be led, as a result of these different starting points, to adopt distinct organizational forms. These distinct forms do not reflect a response to a different set of environmental conditions, but merely a different starting point for the evolution of the firm's organizational form.[3]

Thus, observed differences in organizational form may in large part reflect variation in founding conditions (Stinchcombe 1965) in conjunction

---

[3]Bartlett and Ghoshal's (1989) argument regarding the role, of what they term, administrative heritage, is very much in this spirit.

with local search on a rugged landscape (Levinthal 1994). Consider the contrast between United Parcel Services and Federal Express (Cappelli and Crocker-Hefher 1993). United Parcel Services was founded at a time when Taylorism and the principles of scientific management were dominant. Federal Express was developed in more recent years and the organization reflects the emphasis in recent years on information technology and employee empowerment. From their different starting points, UPS and Federal Express have developed distinct sets of management policies and organizational structures. Despite the fact that the two organizations compete in the same product market and the two organizational "solutions" are radically different, they are both quite effective. The possibility of such equafinality for complex systems such as organizations suggests important limitations for both ecological and contingency analyses.

Co-evolution of capabilities and industry

The evaluation of a firm's capabilities is intimately linked with the evaluation of the markets it serves. This coupling is not merely the result of financial flows derived from profitable markets providing the basis for investment resources. There are clearly instances in which such a coupling is important, but the presence of well-developed capital markets in Western economies tends to mitigate the importance of purely financial couplings. More importantly, many organizational capabilities emerge, are refined, or decay as a result of, or an absence of, product market activity. Therefore, the particular submarkets a firm serves will engender a distinctive, though not necessarily unique, set of capabilities. Certainly, many capabilities, particularly technological knowledge, do not follow directly from current operations. However, even with regard to such investments, the incentives that a firm has to make such investments and the political forces internal to the firm that may influence such decisions are not independent of its current product market activities.

The fate of a firm's capabilities, however, are not purely a deterministic outcome of such couplings. Indeed, the couplings themselves are a critical management decision. What markets should the firm serve? What activities should be performed within the firm and what sorts of external linkages should the firm make? These choices provide managerial discretion over the evolutionary path that the firm's capability set takes. The framework suggested here is somewhat akin to the distinction Argyris and Schon (1978) make between first-order and second-order learning processes. The impact on capabilities of serving particular markets is analogous to a first-order learning process. While not automatic, first-order learning processes are a direct outcome of the existing structure. By establishing a new set of linkages, whether by choice of a new submarket to serve, a new set of customer relations, or a new internal organizational structure, management sets in motion a new direction for the development of the firm's capabilities.

Feedback. Feedback effects can greatly amplify the existing heterogeneity in a population of organizations. A prominent example of such feedback effects in the strategy literature revolves around the re-enforcing advantages of market position (Rumelt 1984). In particular, the notion of a learning or experience curve implies that greater market share will lead to lower costs, which in turn will tend to enhance the firm's market share (Boston Consulting Group 1972). The notion of absorptive capacity (Cohen and Levinthal 1989, 1990) has a similar implication. Organizations with more expertise in a particular technical domain will more readily acquire subsequent knowledge in that domain. Market position advantages associated with a firm's scale of operations may also be self-reinforcing. As Cohen and Klepper (1992) argue in the context of firms' investment in research and development activity, the ability of firms to appropriate the returns to such investments is often a function of their existing sales base.

The notion of brand equity (Aaker 1991) offers another illustration of such market position advantages. Not only does a strong brand name enhance the margins a firm receives on a particular product, but the ability of a firm to place that brand name on other related products enhances the ability of the firm to extend its product line. In addition, the introduction of product extensions that share the established name results in a higher level of brand awareness, further enhancing the brand equity.

An important caveat to these market positional advantages is that they are self-reinforcing in competitive environments in which the bases of competitive advantage are stable. Conversely, in changing environments, these same self-reinforcing mechanisms may lead to a decline in a firm's competitive position. Environmental change occurs for several reasons. The needs of existing customers may change or the subfields and customers the firm serves may decline. On a more macro level, the drivers of success may change (Abernathy and Clark 1985).

Feedback effects tend to reduce the likelihood that a firm will successfully adapt to these changes. For instance, an established firm may have more incentive to invest in incremental changes in a current technology than in exploring more radical innovations. More generally, Levinthal and March (1993) argue that myopia tends to be an important property of many organizational learning processes. The returns to exploiting existing knowledge and capabilities tend to more certain and immediate then the returns to the exploration of novel capabilities and opportunities. Furthermore, the past exploitation activities in a given domain tend to make further exploitation in that domain even more attractive due to various sorts of competency learning. This positive reinforcement of activities in the current domain in which returns are relatively certain and favorable tends to drive out search for alternative bases of action.[4]

Feedforward. These feedback effects that amplify heterogeneity among firms may also influence firms' current activities. Prescient managers look ahead, anticipating such feedback effects when making decisions about what industries or emerging subfields to enter and which clients may help further the firm's development. Thus, in making a choice about what markets to serve, a firm is making a bet on a co-evolutionary process. The firm is, or should, not only be concerned about its current capability to compete within that domain, but also with how participating in that particular industry or subfield will effect the firm's future capabilities.

Perhaps the most basic attribute of the markets and customers served that will impact the development of the firm's capabilities is their growth rate. Is the firm serving customers and market segments that are growing rapidly, thereby providing a basis for significant productivity advances of its own. In addition, leading edge customers may expose the firm to advances in technology (Von Hippel 1988) and product offerings.

For instance, consider a firm that wishes to participate in the mutual fund industry. One of the critical choices that such a firm must make is its mode of distribution. Will the firm rely on direct sales or selling through a financial intermediary such as a bank or independent financial agents? The firm's choice of distribution system may set it on either a constructive or destructive co-evolutionary process. The firm must both assess the market penetration of that mode of distribution as well as the feedback effects of serving that market.

---

[4]Christensen and Bower (1994) provide a compelling example of this phenomenon in the context of the disk drive industry. Strong existing customer relations provide an incentive to advance the existing technological trajectory; however, when new technological opportunities do not correspond to current customer needs they tend not to be pursued.

Similarly, consider the co-evolution of a firm's capabilities and industry when the industry is in decline. As markets shrink, so does re-investment in equipment. This yields a vintage effect on the firm's production capabilities. Indirectly, this has further implications for a firm's engineering capabilities. Top flight engineers value being able to work on the latest equipment and the associated technical challenges; therefore, as the equipment begins to become dated the firm begins to lose some of its most valuable engineering talent.

Certain subfields impose more or less technical demands on a firm than others. For instance, in printed circuit boards, if a firm only participates in the defense sector, it will not develop the technical competence to deal with the high density requirement of commercial markets. Thus, serving leading commercial markets is a critical means of developing new capabilities within PC Board manufacturing.

Along the same lines, certain customers may drive the firm to enhance their capabilities. For instance, State Street Bank, within the mutual fund industry, has such a large proportion of the market for mutual fund processing that it is likely to experience first any new demand associated with new instruments, such as financial derivatives, or new services. In the process of serving this demand for a new service, the firm enhances its capabilities relative to competitors. Similarly, R.R. Donnelley, a commercial printing firm which traditionally focused exclusively on the U.S. market, has developed significant foreign operations as it follows its client telecommunication companies overseas (Carey 1993). Along the same lines, serving the computer industry was the catalyst for Donnelley learning about emerging technologies (Carey 1993).

The role suggested here of leading edge customers is analogous to Porter's (1990) discussion of demand factors associated with industry performance across nations. Porter (1990) points to two critical attributes of home country demand. One is timing: does the home country tend to be early or late in its demand for a particular class of new products or services? The other is the level of sophistication and the degree to which customers are demanding in their quality requirements. These factors influence the speed and direction with which organizations proceed along their evolutionary trajectories.

Focusing forces. The notion of feedforward suggests a significant role for managerial discretion. By its choice of customers and submarkets, top management has an important role in influencing the evolution of the firm's capability set. These choices about external linkages, however, may be constrained by the internal attributes of the firm. Obviously, the existing capability set determines what external linkages are competitively viable. As Teece, Pisano, and Shuen (1990) suggest in their discussion of dynamic capabilities there are a variety of focusing forces that tend to constrain a firm to a particular capability trajectory.

Perversely, learning process may serve to constrain the range of organizational activities (Levinthal and March 1993). As noted earlier, rapid learning may result in a competency trap, whereby increasing skill at the current procedures makes experimentation with alternatives progressively less attractive. Along similar lines, Cohen and Levinthal (1989 and 1990) argue that a firm's "absorptive capacity"—that is, the ability of firms to evaluate and utilize outside knowledge is a function of their prior related knowledge. As a result, firms will tend to confine themselves to a limited set of technological domains and have difficulty responding to developments outside those areas.

Teece et al. (1990) point out that the presence of co-specialized assets (Teece 1985) will also act as a constraining force on the development of firm capabilities. They suggest that complementary or co-specialized assets whose value is enhanced by a particular class of innovative activities will steer the firm's resources in that direction. One can think of this argument in the context of Sutton's (1991) work on the effect of sunk costs on firm and industry development. A pre-existing co-specialized asset is a sunk cost, which can then influence the firm's subsequent investment decisions. Thomas (1993) has developed these ideas in the context of the impact of brand equity on subsequent decisions regarding product extensions.

The political structure of a firm is another important class of constraining forces. There is a large literature in the management field (cf., Hambrick and Finkelstein 1987; Tushman and Romanelli 1985) concerned with the role of top management in both inhibiting and facilitating organizational change. A particular form of this argument is that incumbent executives tend to be committed to the company's current course of action. Some variants of this argument are psychological, either associated with psychological commitment (Staw 1981) or cognitive blinders that restrict the management's awareness of alternative courses of action (Daft and Weick 1984; Dutton and Dukerich 1991). Other variants revolve around issues of organizational politics (Boeker 1989). A switch in strategy may change the importance of particular units of the organization and, thereby, threaten existing power bases.

Selection

Level of analysis

Researchers have tended to assume that selection operates at the level of the organization, or what biologists would term the phenotypic level. For many purposes, this may be an appropriate unit of analysis. If, however, one is interested in the issue of organizational capabilities, a focus on phenotypic selection pressures may be misleading. Selection pressures at the level of the phenotype (i.e., organizational level) need not be so intense as to have strong implications for fitness at the level of the genotype (e.g., routines in Nelson and Winter's framework). There are a number of reasons for this. First, selection pressures at one level need not be reflected at lower levels. Secondly, to the extent that overall organizational effectiveness is the result of complex interactions among the various attributes of the organization, the relationship between phenotypic selection and genetic selection becomes further blurred.

If the unit of selection is the firm, one may still observe considerable heterogeneity across firms with regard to the effectiveness of a particular function. For instance, banks vary widely in the efficiency of their operations (Berger, Hancock, and Humphrey 1993). This variation in efficiency is not readily eliminated by competitive processes as sometimes suggested by simplistic evolutionary arguments. Since the firm as a whole is subjected to selection pressures not the individual functions, the firm may persist in the market if other attributes are of sufficient value, such as a strong retail presence in the case of a bank.

The recent interest in outsourcing in the strategy literature would seem to stem from increasing selection pressures at the firm level that are forcing management to evaluate the viability of individual functions within the firm. Indeed, one could interpret the recent efforts at benchmarking that are becoming widely adopted by firms as changing the unit of selection from the firm to the underlying activity. Benchmarking forces a firm to examine the competitive viability of a particular activity rather than the aggregate statistic of the viability of the firm as a whole.

Furthermore, if organizational effectiveness is highly interactive, it doesn't make much sense to speak of fitness of a particular genotype. Organizations are complex social systems and, as a result, are likely to be subject to a large number of epistatic interactions. This suggests that the mapping from the various facets of an organization to an effectiveness measure, whether the measure is survival rates as in ecological analysis or financial performance as in the case of many applications of contingency theory, may be exceedingly complex.

Perhaps the most prominent example of such interdependence in the strategy literature is Chandler's (1962) work on the relationship between a firm's strategy and its organizational structure. Recent work in the economics literature by Milgrom and Roberts (1990) also points to the need to examine "complements" among a firm's choices of product lines, production strategies, and technology. The McKinsey consulting group's 7S framework is a well-known application of this idea that it is important to consider the degree to which the various facets of an organization's policies are mutually reinforcing (Waterman, Peters, and Philips 1980). In such a setting, it is difficult to speak of the superiority of a particular capability or process, whether it be the virtues of a high commitment workforce or a novel information technology.

In evolutionary accounts of firm diversity, this distinction in level of analysis between the unit of selection and the underlying units that constitute a firm's capabilities (eg., routines in the case of Nelson and Winter (1982)) tends to be undeveloped. Addressing this deficiency is particularly important if evolutionary theories are to speak effectively to the emergence of firm capabilities.

Selection environments: natural and artificial

In considering the survival of business enterprises, the selection environment tends to be either implicitly or explicitly defined as a competitive market in which less effective organizations are ultimately driven out of business. Organizations, however, operate in a variety of selection environments. Environments in which such fitness based selection occurs can be thought of as natural selection environments (Levinthal 1992). Selection pressures, however, need not reflect efficiency or other traditional performance measures (Meyer and Zucker 1989).

Organizations may be buffered from such "natural" selection pressures by a variety of mechanisms. For instance, product markets may be shielded from competitive forces by government actions. In addition, financial capital need not be allocated by pure market forces. Following the distinction made by Dosi (1990), capital markets can be characterized as being either competitive or institutional. In the former, capital is raised in competitive financial markets; while in the latter, capital is obtained by direct institutional sources. With institutional sources of capital, firms may be buffered from the selection pressures of capital markets. As a result, consistent with Meyer and Zucker's (1989) arguments regarding permanently failing organizations, a firm may be in an uncompetitive position in product markets, but still survive for a considerable period of time.

An important form of such insulation from competitive capital markets are business units within large corporations; in particular, as pointed out by Marris (1963) corporations with significant levels of retained earnings. The investment decisions of such a firm may reflect the discretionary judgements and preferences of its management (Baumol 1967; Marris 1963; Jensen 1986), more so than the demands of profit maximization or fitness based selection pressures.

Endogenous nature of selection pressure

Selection criteria change over time. The strategy literature has tended to focus on exogenous changes, particularly technological changes (Tushman and Anderson 1986). Many changes in selection criteria, however, are endogenous to the evolutionary system itself. The most basic of these endogenous changes are changes in population demographics which, in turn, change the likelihood of survival for individual members of the population (Hannan and Carroll 1992). The most dramatic of this sort of change is what Eldridge and Gould (1972) refer to as a punctuated equilibrium. As the result of the emergence of an new form in the population, survival rates for existing entities may decline markedly. This speciation event may lead to a radical shift in the distribution of forms within the population.

Carroll (1985) has explored some of the implications of an endogenous selection criteria in his work on resource partitioning. As competition within an industry leads to the dominance of a few large, generalist firms, the industry becomes open to the entry of small specialist organizations. To use the example of the brewing industry, as the industry consolidated and the mid-size regional brewers either where acquired or expanded to national coverage, microbreweries began to proliferate. Carroll suggests that these microbreweries were only viable subsequent to the consolidation of the industry.

Arthur (1989, 1990) has done some important theoretical work highlighting the path-dependent nature of industry evolution. Arthur explores these issues in settings in which there are network externalities. For some products consumer preferences for a particular product depend in part on the number of other consumers who have already purchased the product. The battle between Beta and VHS format video recorders has become a classic illustration of such dynamics (Cusumano, Mylonadis, and Rosenbloom 1992). In such settings, stochastic effects that influence early purchase decisions may have an enduring effect on the firm and industry dynamics. Once a product class develops an early lead in market share, this advantage becomes self-reinforcing as a result of the presence of positive network externalities.

Some sociological research points to the considerable ability of powerful organizations to influence the selection environment under which they operate (Perrow 1986; Hirsch 1975). For instance, resource dependence theory (Pfeffer and Salancik 1978) examines "the various strategies of organizations and their managers to cope with external constraints resulting from resource interdependence" (Pfeffer 1982: 193). Pfeffer (1982) offers the particular example of small retailers in the United States obtaining passage of resale price maintenance legislation in the 1930s that inhibited competition from larger firms and substantially changed the selection environment for retailers.

Retention

Within biological models of evolution, retention constitutes the mechanism for the preservation, duplication, or propagation of positively selected forms (Campbell 1965). Within the Nelson and Winter (1982) framework, this role is carried out by organizational routines. Iwai (1984) and Winter (1984) extend this work by considering the duplication, or imitation, of routines within a population of organizations as another force influencing the observed pattern of diversity.

Somewhat paradoxically, within the writings on the resource view of the firm the focus has been not on the retention of a particular capability across time within a firm but the persistence of the uniqueness of a particular capability within a population of organizations across time (Rumelt 1984). Thus, the concern in this literature is with the barriers to imitation of a firm's capability. Concepts such as causal ambiguity (Rumelt 1984; Lippman and Rumelt 1982), tacitness (Winter 1987), and appropriability (Teece 1986) have been used to explain the persistence of firm-level differences.

In this sense, the notion of retention in the biological literature on evolution is at cross-purposes to the meaning of this term in the context of resource theories of the firm. From a biological perspective, the persistence of the uniqueness of a trait within a particular entity poses the risk of extinction of that trait in the population. In contrast, from the perspective of resource theory, the continued uniqueness of a positive trait enhances the competitive viability of the particular organization possessing it. Clearly, the different level of analysis at which these theories operate leads to these vastly different perspectives on the notion of retention.

One of the few examples of writing within the tradition of the resource view of the firm that addresses retention in a manner similar in spirit to the role retention plays in evolutionary arguments is Penrose's discussion of the limits to the growth of the firm (Penrose 1959). Penrose argues that it takes time for an organization to assimilate new managers. This assimilation consists of both socialization processes as well as the passing on of substantive knowledge. Penrose's arguments suggest that rapid growth may act as a threat to the persistence of some distinctive firm attributes. For instance, if, as Barney (1986b) suggests, organizational culture can act as a important firm-specific resource, then the rapid introduction of new employees into the firm could threaten the integrity of this culture and thereby diminish this resource advantage.

One could postulate analogous arguments premised on a rapid decline in organizational growth. A rapidly growing organization is likely to generate tremendous opportunities for internal advancement. These opportunities for personal advancement provide a powerful incentive for employees. The decline in growth, which in turn would reduce these opportunities for individual advancement and, thereby, reduce incentives associated with the firm's internal labor market. As a result, firms whose growth rate declines may be forced to rely on incentive structures based on measures of operating performance. Such objective measures may not be as effective in capturing the benefits of employee actions that contribute to other units within the firm (i.e., more distant in "space") or outcomes with longer term payoffs (i.e., more distant in time).

A particular variant of this phenomenon is the threat to systems of life time employment posed by dramatic and sustained changes in a firm's competitive position. Influenced in particular by the commercial success of Japanese firms, a considerable body of management literature has extolled the virtues of systems of lifetime employment. Such employment relations provide an incentive on both the firm's part and the individual's for workers to develop a high degree of firm-specific human capital. However, in the presence of excess capacity, a commitment to lifetime employment becomes increasingly costly and may, as in the case of IBM and Kodak, cause the firm to change its human resource policies.

36

Conclusion

Organizational capabilities are part of a broader system, one that consists of a variety of features of organizational context as well as the competitive environment in which the firm operates. To understand the emergence and possible decline of these capabilities, it is important to consider the linkages among these various elements. Strategy research, however, in its effort to understand the sources of firm diversity has tended to focus one element of this broader system while neglecting others. In one study the focus may be industry differences, while in another work firm differences loom large.

In many respects such a research strategy has much to commend it. Parsimony in one's theories is a virtue. However, by modeling the interrelationship among some of these forces influencing diversity at the level of both the firm and industry, one may generate novel insights. Dosi et al.'s (1994) work on firm diversification provides a good illustration of this. Diversification is in part a function of the learning dynamics of the firm and in part the outcome of the selection environment in which the firm operates. Such efforts, by linking firm and industry levels of analysis and bridging the behavioral and economic traditions of the field, would have the attractive side benefit of providing greater coherence to the confusing mosaic of strategy research.

References

Aaker, D.A. 1991. *Managing brand equity*. New York: Free Press.

Abernathy, W.J., and Clark, K.B. 1985. Innovation: Mapping the winds of creative destruction. *Research Policy*, 14: 3-22.

Andrews, K.R. 1971. *The concept of corporate strategy*. Homewood, IL: Richard D. Irwin.

Argyris, C. and Schon, D. 1978. *Organizational learning*. Reading, MA: Addison-Wesley.

Arthur, W.B. 1989. "Competing technologies, increasing returns, and lock-in by historical events." *Economic Journal* 99: 116-131.

Arthur, W.B. 1990. Positive feedbacks in the economy. *Scientific American*: 92-99.

Barney, J.B. 1986a. Strategic factor markets: expectations, luck, and business strategy. *Management Science* 42: 1231-1241.

Barney, J.B. 1986b. Organizational culture: can it be a source of competitive advantage? *Academy of Management Review* 11: 656-665.

Barney, J.B. 1989. Asset stock accumulation and sustained competitive advantage: A comment. *Management Science* 35: 1511-1513.

Barney, J.B. 1991. "Firm resources and sustained competitive advantage." *Journal of Management* 17: 99-120.

Bartlett, C.A., and Ghoshal, S. 1989. *Managing across borders: The transnational solution.* Boston, MA: Harvard Business School Press.

Baumol, W.J. 1967. *Business behavior, value and growth.* New York: Harcourt, Brace and World.

Baumol, W.J. 1993. *Entrepreneurship, management, and the structure of payoffs.* Cambridge, MA: MIT Press.

Becker, G.S. 1975. *Human capital.* Chicago, IL: University of Chicago Press.

Berger, A., Hancock, D., and Humphrey, D. 1993. Bank efficiency derived from the profit function. *Journal of Banking and Finance*, 17: 317-347.

Block, Z., and MacMillan, I.C. 1993. *Corporate venturing.* Cambridge, MA: Harvard Business School Press.

Boeker, W. 1989. The development and institutionalization of subunit power in organizations. *Administrative Science Quarterly*, 34: 388-410.

Boston Consulting Group. 1972. *Perspectives on experience.* Boston, MA: Boston Consulting Group, Inc.

Bresnahan, T.F. 1987. Competition and collusion in the American automobile industry: The 1955 price war. *Journal of Industrial Economics*, 35: 457-82.

Burgelman, R.A., and Sayles, L. 1986. *Inside corporate innovation.* New York: Free Press.

Burgelman, R.A. 1990. Strategy-making and organizational ecology: a conceptual integration. In J. V. Singh (Ed.), *Organizational Evolution: New Directions.* Newbury Park, CA: Sage Publications.

Camerer, C.F. 1991. Does strategy need game theory. *Strategic Management Review*, 12: 137-152.

Campbell, D.T. 1965. Variation and selective retention in socio-cultural evolution. In Herbert R. Barringer, George I. Blanksten, and Raymond W. Mack (eds.) Social change in developing areas. Cambridge, MA: Schenkman Publishing Company.

Cappelli, P., and Crocker-Hefher, A. 1993. "No more 'best practices' in managing employees: Distinctive human resources create the core competence of firms." Unpublished Working Paper, Wharton School University of Pennsylvania.

Carey, S. 1993. Donnelley follows its customers around the world. *Wall Street Journal.* July 1.

Carroll, G.R. 1985. Concentration and specialization: dynamics of niche width in populations of organizations. *American Journal of Sociology*, 90: 1265-1283.

Chakravarthy, B.S., and Doz, Y. 1992. Strategy process research: focusing on corporate self-renewal. *Strategic Management Journal*. 13: 5-14.

Chandler, A. 1962. *Strategy and structure: chapters in the history of the American industrial enterprise*. Cambridge, MA: MIT Press.

Christensen, C.M., and Bower, J.L. 1994. Catching the next wave: why good customers make it hard. Unpublished manuscript. Graduate School of Business, Harvard University.

Clark, K.B., and Fujimoto, T. 1991. *Product development performance: strategy, organization, and management in the world auto industry*. Boston: Harvard Business School Press.

Cohen, W., and Levinthal, D. 1989. Innovation and learning: The two faces of R&D. *Economic Journal*, 99: 569-596.

Cohen, W., and Levinthal, D. 1990. Absorptive capacity: a new perspective on learning and innovation. *Administrative Science Quarterly*, 35: 128-152.

Cohen, W., and Levinthal, D. 1994. Fortune favors the prepared firm. *Management Science*, 40: 227-251.

Cohen, W.M., and Klepper, S. 1992. The anatomy of industry R&D intensity distributions. *American Economic Review*, 82: 773-799.

Cusumano, M.A., Mylonadis, M., and Rosenbloom, R.S. 1992. Strategic maneuvering and mass market dynamics: the triumph of VHS over Beta. *Business History*, 66: 51-94.

Cyert, R., and March, J. 1963. *A behavioral theory of the firm*. Englewood Cliffs, NJ: Prentice-Hall.

Daft, R., and Weick, K. 1984. Toward a model of organizations and interpretation systems. *Academy of Management Review*, 9: 284-296.

Dierickx, I., and Cool, K. 1989. Asset stock accumulation and sustainability of competitive advantage. *Management Science*, 35: 1504-1511.

Dosi, G. 1990. Finance, innovation and industrial change. *Journal of Economic Behavior and Organizations*, 13: 299-319.

Dosi, G., Teece, D., Rumelt, R., and Winter, S. 1994. "Understanding corporate coherence: theory and evidence." *Journal of Economic Behavior and Organization*, 23: 1-30.

Dutton, J.E., and Dukerich, J.M. 1991. "Keeping an eye on the mirror: image and identity in organizational adaptation." *Academy of Management Journal*, 34: 517-554.

Eldredge, N., and Gould, S.J. 1972. Punctuated equilibria: an alternative to phyletic gradualism. In *Models in Palaeobiology* (ed. T. J. M. Schopf): 82-115. San Francisco: Freeman and Cooper

Foss, N.J., Knudsen, C., and Montgomery, C.A. 1993. Towards a synthesis of evolutionary and resource-based approaches to strategy: some topics for discussion. Unpublished Working Paper.

Ghemawat, P. 1992. A case study in organizational efficiency: competitive position and internal organization. Unpublished Manuscript.

Hambrick, D., and Finkelstein, S. 1987. Managerial discretion: a bridge between polar views of organizational outcomes. In L. L. Cummings and B. M. Staw (Eds.. *New Directions in Organizational Behavior*: 369-406. Greenwich, CT: JAI Press.

Hannan, M.T., and Carroll, G.R. 1992. *Dynamics of organizational populations*. New York: Oxford University Press

Hannan, M., and Freeman, J. 1977. "The population ecology of organizations." *American Journal of Sociology*, 82: 929-964.

Hirsch, P.M. 1975. Organizational effectiveness and the institutional environment. *Administrative Science Quarterly*. 20: 327-344.

Iwai, K. 1984. Schumpeterian dynamics. *Journal of Economic Behavior and Organization* 5: 159-190.

Jensen, M. 1986. Agency costs of free cash flow, corporate finance and takeovers. *American Economic Review* 76: 323-329.

Kauffman, S. 1989. "Adaptation on rugged fitness landscapes." In D. Stein (Ed.), *Lectures in the Sciences of Complexity*. Reading, MA: Addison-Wesley.

Lawrence, P., and Lorsch, J. 1967. *Organization and environment: Managing differentiation and integration*. Boston, MA: Harvard University.

Levinthal, D.A. 1992. Surviving Schumpeterian environments: An evolutionary perspective. *Industrial and Corporate Change* 1: 427-443.

Levinthal, D.A. 1994. Adaptation on rugged landscapes. Unpublished manuscript. Wharton School, University of Pennsylvania.

Levinthal, D.A., and March, J.G. 1993. The myopia of learning. *Strategic Management Journal* 14: 95-112.

Levitt, B., and March, J.G. 1988. Organizational learning. *Annual Review of Sociology* 14: 319-340.

Lippman, S., and Rumelt, R. 1982. "Uncertain imitability: an analysis of interfirm differences in efficiency under competition." *Bell Journal of Economics*, Autumn .

March, J.G., and Simon, H.A. 1958. *Organizations*. New York: John Wiley & Sons.

Marris, R. 1963. A model of the "managerial" enterprise. *Quarterly Journal of Economics* 77: 185-209.

Meyer, M., and Zucker, L. 1989. *Permanently failing organizations*. Newbury Park, CA: Sage Publications.

Milgrom, P., and Roberts, J. 1990. "The economics of modern manufacturing." *American Economic Review* 80: 511-528.

Miner, A. 1994. "Seeking adaptive advantage: Evolutionary theory and management action." In J. Singh and J. Baum (Eds.), *Evolutionary Perspectives on Organizations*. Oxford Press: New York.

Mintzberg, H. 1978. Patterns in strategy formulation. *Management Science* 24: 934-948.

Montgomery, C.A. 1988. Guest editor's introduction to the special issue on research in the content of strategy. *Strategic Management Journal* 9: 3-8.

Montgomery, C.A., and Wernerfelt, B. 1988. Diversification, Ricardian rents and Tobin's q. *Rand Journal of Economics* 19: 623-632.

Nelson, R., and Winter, S. 1982. *An evolutionary theory of economic change*. Cambridge, MA: Harvard University Press.

Peffer, J., and Salancik. G.R. 1978. *The external control of organizations*. New York: Harper & Row.

Peffer, J. 1982. *Organizations and organization theory*. Marshfield, MA: Pitman Books.

Penrose, E. 1959. *The theory of the growth of the firm*. London: Basil Blackwell.

Perrow, C. 1986. *Complex organizations*. New York: Random House.

Porter, M.E. 1980. *Competitive strategy: Techniques for analyzing industries and competitors*. New York: The Free Press.

Porter, M.E. 1981. The contribution of industrial organization to strategic management. *Academy of Management Review* 6: 609-620.

Porter, M.E. 1987. From competitive advantage to corporate strategy. *Harvard Business Review* 65: 43-59.

Porter, M.E. 1990. *The competitive advantage of nations*. New York: The Free Press.

Prahalad, C. K., and Hamel, G. 1990. The core competence of the corporation. *Harvard Business Review*, May-June: 79-91.

Rumelt, R.P. 1974. *Strategy, structure, and economic performance*. Harvard Business School Press: Cambridge, MA.

Rumelt, R.P. 1984. "Towards a strategic theory of the firm." In *Competitive Strategic Management*, ed. R. B. Lamb, pp 566-70. Englewood Cliffs, NJ: Prentice-Hall.

Rumelt, R.P. 1991. "How much does industry matter." *Strategic Management Journal*, 12: 167-185.

Saloner, G. 1991. "Modeling, game theory, and strategic management." *Strategic Management Journal* 12: 119-136.

Schumpeter, J. 1934. *The theory of economic development*. Cambridge, MA: Harvard University Press.

Schumpeter, J. 1954. *Capitalism, socialism, and democracy*. New York: Harper & Row.

Selznick, P. 1957. *Leadership and administration*. Harper & Row: New York.

Senge, P. 1990. *The fifth discipline: the art and practice of learning.* New York: Doubleday.

Shapiro, C. 1989. The theory of business strategy. *Rand Journal of Economics* 20: 125-137.

Staw, B.M. 1981. The escalation of commitment: A review and analysis. *Academy of Management Review* 6: 577-587.

Stinchcombe, A. 1965. "Social structure and organizations." In J March (Ed.), *Handbook of Organizations.* Chicago, IL: Rand McNally.

Sutton, J. 1991. *Sunk costs and market structure.* Cambridge, MA: MIT Press.

Teece, D.J. 1980. Economies of scope and the scope of the enterprise. *Journal of Economic Behavior and Organization* 1: 223-247.

Teece, D.J. 1986. "Profiting from technological innovation: implications for integration, collaboration, licensing and public policy." *Research Policy* 15: 285-305.

Teece, D., Pisano, G. and Shuen, A. 1990. Firm capabilities, resources, and the concept of strategy. Consortium on Competitiveness and Cooperation Working Paper No. 90-8, University of California at Berkeley.

Tushman, M.L., and Anderson, P. 1986. "Technological discontinuities and organizational environments." *Administrative Science Quarterly*, 31 439-465.

Tushman, M., and Romanelli, E. 1985. "Organizational evolution: a metamorphosis model of convergence and reorientation." In L. Cummings and B. Staw (Eds.), *Research in Organizational Behavior* 7: 171-222.

von Hippel, E. 1988. *The sources of innovation.* New York: Oxford University Press.

Waterman, R., Peters, T., and Phillips, J. 1980. "Structure is not organization." *Business Horizons* 23: 14-26.

Wernerfelt, B. 1984. A resource based view of the firm. *Strategic Management Journal* 5: 171-180.

Wernerfelt, B., and Montgomery, C. 1986. What is an attractive industry? *Management Science* 32: 1223-1230.

Winter, S.G. 1984. Schumpeterian competition in alternative technological regimes. *Journal of Economic Behavior and Organization* 5: 287-320.

Winter, S.G. 1987. Knowledge and competence as strategic assets. In *The Competitive Challenge* (Ed.) David J. Teece. Cambridge, MA: Ballinger.

Winter, S.G. 1994. In J. Singh and J. Baum (Eds.), *Evolutionary Perspectives on Organizations.* New York: Oxford Press.

Womack, J.P., Jones, D.T., and Roos, D. 1990. *The machine that changed the world.* HarperCollins: New York.

3

COMPETITIVE ADVANTAGE
AND INDUSTRY CAPABILITIES

Nicolai J. Foss[1]
Institute of Industrial Economics and Strategy
Copenhagen Business School

Bo Eriksen
Department of Management
Odense University

Introduction

Recently, numerous strategy scholars have revitalized the concern with the resources and capabilities side of firms. This trend often referred to as the "resource-based perspective" (RBP), has led to a much improved understanding of firms' diversification strategies (Montgomery and Wernerfelt 19881; Montgomery and Hariharan 1991) and of the underlying conditions for sustained competitive advantage (Barney 1991; Peteraf 1993). Furthermore, the perhaps more dynamic issue of resource-accumulation processes has been treated in some detail (Dierickx and Cool 1989). In terms of the SWOT framework—the overall idea that strategy is a matter of obtaining fit between the Strengths of the firm and the Opportunities of the environment, while simultaneously safeguarding the

[1]The authors wish to thank Cynthia Montgomery, Raffi Amit, Jim Brander, Richard Langlois, and participants at the Conference on Integrating Resource-based and Evolutionary Perspectives on Strategy in Snekkersten, Denmark, August 1993, for helpful comments. The usual disclaimers apply.

Weaknesses of the firm from the Threats of that environment—the RBP may be said to have investigated and added further analytical content to the "Strength-Weaknesses" part.

However, we believe that the other part of the SWOT framework, the "Threats" and "Opportunities" of the environment, has been largely, though consciously, neglected in the RBP. This may reflect the position that analysis of firms' external environment (such as the Porter (1980) framework) alone cannot be a sufficient condition for the sustained competitive advantage of these firms (Barney 1986a, 1991), although it may help them realize normal returns. But it may also reflect the conviction that the RBP has nothing original to say on the environment, and that the environment is satisfactorily approached in the industry analysis framework of, for example, Michael Porter (1980). In this understanding, the RBP and the industry analysis framework are complements.

Like a few recent writers (Amit and Schoemaker 1993), we disagree with the position that the RBP has nothing or close to nothing original to say on the environment. On the contrary, we believe that it is possible to arrive at a resource-based analysis of the environment that is conceptually distinct from the industry analysis framework. In this paper, we try to supply some of the preliminaries of such a resource-based analysis. In order to do this, we also use concepts from evolutionary economics (Alchian 1950; Nelson and Winter 1982) and refer specifically to the process of technological change as one of creation of variety and selection over this variety (Dosi 1982). Much of our analysis is centered around the notion of "industry capabilities." Because of the centrality of this concept for the present paper, let us here provide some of the intuition behind this and related concepts.

Firms are never completely self-contained in the sense that they typically rely on resources and capabilities that are external to them (Richardson 1972). How much they will rely on internal and external procurement, respectively, is determined by a mixture of capabilities considerations and transaction costs (see Chapter 4, Richard Langlois). To the extent that firms rely on external procurement, they may be said to rely on the capabilities and resources of other firms. Furthermore, firms often rely on non-proprietary capabilities that accrue, for example, to "clusters" in specific nations/regions (cf., Porter 1990) or to certain industries, thereby contributing to the competitive advantage of "incumbents." In other words, some *non-traded interdependencies* among geographically bounded firms may be beneficial to these firms. Examples of locations of such beneficial and hard-to-imitate non-proprietary capabilities would seem to include

44

California's Silicon Valley, the Italian textile and ceramics industries, London's City and perhaps also the Keiretsu system of Japan.

Firms confront a large *external resources and capabilities space*. In this paper we introduce and analyze industry capabilities as a subset of this space. We define industry capabilities as non-proprietary capabilities that are shared among a group of firms, and may yield rents,[2] even in the absence of explicit coordination. A partial list of examples may include, standards, knowledge-sharing in R&D networks, and shared behavioral norms.

Such industry capabilities are a subset of a broader category of economic goods, which Lester Telser (1987) has called "semi-private goods," i.e., goods that are intermediate between public and private goods. Although such semi-private goods are not proprietary to specific individuals (firms), they may be proprietary to coalitions of individuals (firms). Drawing on recent resource-based research, we identify the underlying conditions that may make this possible. Furthermore, we also suggest that a number of concepts and insights from the resource-based literature may be meaningfully applied to the analysis of industry capabilities.

For example, industry capabilities may imply *causal ambiguity*, in the sense that it is hard for non-incumbents to understand the causal links between industry capabilities and the competitive successes of incumbents. This causal ambiguity may therefore sustain the rent-yielding potential of industry capabilities. Causal ambiguity may be an important factor in highly vertically and horizontally disintegrated industries where detailed knowledge of the workings of the network of intra-industry interactions may be necessary for successful entry into the industry.

Also, knowledge of industry capabilities may provide focal points for firms' investments. The extent to which there is causal ambiguity about industry capabilities may thus co-determine the degree of success entering firms have in positioning themselves in resource- and capability-space. The extent to which industry capabilities are common knowledge is directly related to the ease of entry into the industry.

---

[2]Dierickx and Cool (1989: 1504) also noticed that firms may derive competitive advantage from non-proprietary factors. Even if accounting statements could deal with intangibles, industry capabilities would not appear as assets on incumbents' balance sheets. So it is not double-counting to say that, in a sense, industry capabilities belong to both the industry and the firms composing the industry.

Another reason why the presence of industry capabilities may impede entry is the extent to which complementary assets are needed to take advantage of them. For example, it may be necessary to acquire a bundle of physical and intangible assets (such as plant, machinery, licensed technology, etc.) in order to gain access to industry capabilities. In this sense, industry capabilities may augment competitive advantages derived from investments in physical and intangible assets.

In Section 2, we detail the notion of industry capabilities, clarify our terminology and provide some empirical examples and taxonomic categories. Section 3 takes a more analytical stance. Based on the conclusions reached in Section 3, Section 4 provides a taxonomy of industry capabilities. Section 5 analyzes how firms may benefit from the presence of industry capabilities, and implications for positioning in resource- and capability-space. Section 6 concludes the paper.

What Are Industry Capabilities?

In this section, we approach industry capabilities in three different ways: we clarify terminology, provide some illustrations and examples, and suggest some taxonomic distinctions. Our aim is to suggest the importance and empirical validity of industry capabilities.

Terminology

Consistent with earlier contributions to the resource-based approach (such as Dierickx and Cool 1989; Teece, Pisano and Shuen 1991; Amit and Schoemaker 1993), we wish to distinguish between *resources* and *capabilities*. One pertinent distinction is that resources can be both tangible (physical capital) and intangible (human capital), while capabilities are always intangible. Furthermore, capabilities emerge from the interaction between multiple agents, and exist in a sense independent of individual agents. They broadly correspond to notions such as "routines" (Nelson and Winter 1982) or "competencies." The economic distinction we adopt between resources and capabilities is that resources are always tradeable, while capabilities are non-tradeable. Capabilities are generally non-contractible because of language limitations or non-verifiability in courts of law.[3] However, non-tradeable capabilities are built up from tradeable resources. Again, we believe this usage is consistent with earlier contributions (Dierickx and Cool 1989; Amit and Schoemaker 1993), and maintain it throughout this paper.

Hitherto, all resource-based analysis has been moving on a strict firm level. For example, the possibility that firms may develop valuable assets in dyadic relationships, assets that may benefit both of the collaborating parties, has not been investigated, in spite of its prominence in much recent literature on, for example, networks and innovation. Furthermore, the industry level has seldom been factored into the analysis.

However, intuitively it is quite meaningful to think of, for example, industry resources. These could be resources acquired only or mostly by incumbents on industry-specific factor markets.[4] General examples of industry resources could be the services provided by industry trade associations or industry lobbyists. A specific example of an industry resource could be the Danish Meat Research Institute, which is a collaborative research venture between the Danish slaughter houses. The houses have all outsourced their R&D and surveillance activities to this research institute, and may all acquire R&D services and market information from it. The existence of the DMRI has allowed the slaughter houses to make substantial savings on overhead, has strongly increased diffusion of new technology, and is generally considered to have a substantial impact on the competitiveness of the houses on the international scene.

While the notion of industry resources may be relatively unproblematic, the notion of *industry capabilities* needs clarification. We conceive of industry capabilities in a way that is quite close to the way that

---

[3]Even though it may be possible to specify the desired effort from an employee, e.g.,. the quality of the work effort, it may not be possible to verify this effort in a court of law. In general, the employer will often be more concerned about the capabilities of the employee, but cannot contract on them. Capabilities can only be accessed by acquiring (or renting) resources, such as human capital. This problem is well known in principal-agent literature and is believed to lead to inefficiencies. In terms of collective capabilities, trade becomes even more complicated, since all the underlying resources must be acquired or rented before a buyer can gain access to the resultant capabilities.

[4]We believe these resources are identical to at least a subset of what Amit and Schoemaker (1993) call "strategic industry factors." Our work extends Amit and Schoemaker by adding the notion of untraded industry capabilities that do not appear on the firm's balance sheet which industry resources would.

the literature has conceived of firm capabilities. Firm capabilities are thought of as emerging in a historical process from the interaction inside the firm of multiple resource-owners. Analogously, industry capabilities emerge in a historical process from the interaction of multiple firms within industries.[5] But although there is an analogy, there are also subtle differences that needs to be clarified. For example, why are industry capabilities non-tradeable? To what extent are industry capabilities also present on the firm level? How do they interact with firm and industry resources? Who captures their rents? Before we turn to more fundamental analysis of the concept of industry capabilities, we will refer to empirical examples to support our assertion that industry capabilities represent a real phenomenon.

Industry capabilities: some examples

Although we believe that the terminology is our own, the return of "industry capabilities" has surfaced before, most significantly in discussions of the competitive advantage of nations (Porter 1990) and industrial districts (Pyke and Sengenberger 1992; Saxonian 1991).[6] But industries that are not usually found under these headings also manifest industry capabilities. Consider the following examples:

---

[5]It may also assist intuition to think of the neo-institutional analysis (e.g.,. Sugden 1986) of the emergence of norms as emerging from iterated prisoners' dilemma or coordination games, and providing positive externalities to agents in the societies that practice the relevant norms.

[6]Theoretical work on industry capabilities goes back, however, to Marshall's treatment of the industrial district and its "external economies" (Marshall 1925: 271-272). What we call "internal capabilities" and "industry capabilities" corresponds to what Marshall calls "internal economies" and "external economies," respectively. Another pertinent reference is Langlois (1992), whose concept of "external capabilities" seems to correspond to our "industry capabilities." However, Langlois primarily addresses how economic organization is influenced by internal and external capabilities. Allen (1983) provides numerous historical examples of industry capabilities, mostly in the context of technological change and under the heading of "collective invention." The notions of "technological paradigm" (Dosi 1982) and "technological regimes" (Nelson and Winter 1982) from evolutionary economics incorporate an understanding of technological change as taking place within structured but non-traded interdependencies. For example, firms that produce within a technological paradigm benefit from the presence of the technological externalities represented by sharing heuristics, agreeing on the overall design of the produced artifact, etc.

A. Industrial districts. Due to the surprising economic success of production activities that are geographically strongly bounded, such as in Silicon Valley in California, Route 128 in Massachusetts, the textile and ceramics districts of the Emilia-Romagna region, Italy, the textile district of the Herning region, Denmark etc., the concept of industrial districts has recently attracted attention from scholars from a broad spectrum of disciplines, including economic geography and innovation studies. Strategic management scholars have shown less interest.

In an introductory essay, Pyke and Sengenberger (1992: 4) see the main characteristics of the industrial district as "....the existence of strong networks of (mainly) small firms which, through specialization and subcontracting, divide amongst themselves the labor required for the manufacture of particular goods: specialization induces efficiency...[and]...specialization combined with subcontracting promotes collective capability." Furthermore, industrial districts promote trust and cooperation (partly through easing monitoring), exhibits a "pervasiveness of entrepreneurial dynamism" and "flexibility" (p. 5).

Here is how Saxonian (1991: 410) describes a prime example of a modern industrial district:

> Silicon Valley today is far more than an agglomeration of individual technology firms. Its networks of independent yet autonomous producers are increasingly organized to grow and innovate reciprocally. These networks promote new product development by encouraging specialization. They spur the diffusion of new technologies by facilitating information exchange and joint problem solving between firms.

An example of an important company operating in this district is Sun Microsystems, which has outsourced everything except the design of hardware and software for workstations, the manufacturing of prototypes, testing, and final assembly. This reduces overhead and insures that the company's workstations use state-of-the art technology (Saxonian 1991: 425). The guiding principle for this company, as well as for other Silicon Valley companies, is to specialize around those dynamic capabilities (cf., Teece, Pisano, and Shuen 1991) that ease flexibility and therefore the ability to rapidly alter the product mix.

Several observations on the literature on industrial districts are in order. First, much of the literature on industrial districts has been largely atheoretical and mostly written from an industrial policy perspective. As a result, theoretical terms remain insufficiently explained and developed. Nevertheless, the literature *does* point to the presence of industry capabilities.

Trivially, the literature shows that firms in industrial districts rely to a larger extent on capabilities that are external relative to themselves, namely on the capabilities of other firms. This is simply a consequence of a higher degree of vertical (and horizontal) disintegration. However, to the extent that firms may acquire resources from well-organized factor markets and reliable suppliers, this is largely a matter of what we have been calling industry *resources*, not capabilities.[7]

Increasing vertical and horizontal disintegration of an industry need not imply the presence of industry capabilities, i.e., non-traded interdependencies. It may be merely a natural response to increasing returns to scale: as demand increases, it becomes more profitable to specialize, and factor markets will emerge to replace vertically integrated production (see Stigler 1951). Geroski and Vlassopoulos (1991) report an interesting case of industry evolution in the U.K. frozen foods industry. The original entrant, Birds Eye was a vertically integrated producer, but as demand for frozen foods increased, separate factor markets emerged for cold storage and transportation, etc. These developments rendered Birds Eye's structure inefficient, and had serious implications for the competitiveness of the firm.

But consider, then, the idea that specialization/vertical disintegration combined with subcontracting promotes a "collective capability." In the Silicon Valley case, this collective capability consists in an ability to rapidly spawn new unanticipated products related to computer systems; in the Third Italy clothing case, it is, for example, a matter of rapidly turning out new designs. Although such capabilities are surely results of the interaction of individual firms, it is not a matter of simply "adding" their capabilities.[8] Rather, it is something that emerges from the interaction between incumbent firms, and emerges in an often unplanned

---

[7]Of course, one could argue that the very presence of well-organized factor markets is a positive externality, since the market institution as such is a non-traded (public) good to firms. For such an argument, see Loasby (1993).

[8]Rather, some kind of sub-additivity is present at the industry level. The way in which an industrial district may yield pecuniary externalities through specialization is conceptually not far away from the economies of scope phenomenon, arising from sub-additivity of cost functions.

—"spontaneous"—way, although rational design may play some role.[9] This "something" is an example of what we call an industry capability.

Similarly, consider the insight that the geographical boundedness of industrial districts promotes the development of trust-relations. Because of the physical proximity and the resulting easy transfer of information, monitoring and enforcement of contractual stipulations is relatively easy, and behavioral norms are easily established and enforced. In this setting, trust may flourish. The resulting low level of transaction and information costs support the vertically disintegrated structure, characterizing the industrial districts. Since this in turn supports beneficial specialization and coordination, the presence of trust relations may be seen as an industry capability.

As we later make more explicit, it is because of the "collective" and "emergent" character of such industry capabilities that they can most efficiently be utilized by incumbents, and it is also these characteristics that underlie their non-tradeability. Intuitively, industry capabilities cannot be separated from the firms that created (perhaps unintentionally) and now maintain them. As a result, they may be very hard to transfer over industry boundaries. Furthermore, it is not possible to trade an industry capability. Also, industry capabilities may require investment in co-specialized resources and capabilities on the firm level before entrants can access them. It may further be extremely difficult for non-incumbents to value the contribution that industry capabilities may give to competitive advantage. An additional complication may be that some industry capabilities, like firm capabilities, may rely on hard-to-transfer tacit knowledge. To the extent that non-incumbents want access to industry capabilities, they will establish themselves in the industry, illustrating the point about the necessity of acquiring complementary resources and capabilities. As Teece (1992: 100) suggests, this access motive seems to be what lies behind Japanese investments in Silicon Valley, although it may prove costly to access these industry capabilities. A further question is whether the value added created by the presence of such industry capabilities can be appropriated by some firms but not others.

B. Porter on the competitive advantage of nations. The basic idea of the literature on industrial districts, that firms may benefit collectively

---

[9]Public intervention has played a major role in the development of Italy's industrial districts. So-called "science parks" are also explicit attempt to "plan external economies."

from being geographically concentrated, is also a prominent idea in Michael Porter's *The Competitive Advantage of Nations* (1990), which in terms of attention paid to resources and capabilities is much closer to basic RBP thinking than his 1980 contribution was. In this contribution, Porter attempts to account for the phenomenon that country of origin seems to strongly condition success in international competition.

One of the reasons has to do with the presence of so-called "related and supporting industries" in the home country. These are particularly important in connection with firms' resource-accumulation processes, since close interaction between users and producers of technical equipment eases the flow of information, and therefore eases the process of upgrading technological knowledge. Porter (1990: 103) even argues that "Competitive advantage emerges from close working relationships between world class suppliers and the industry." If such cooperative user-producer relations are sufficiently prevalent, "...the pace of innovation within the entire national industry is accelerated" (ibid.).

Clearly, Porter is talking both about industry *resources* and *capabilities* in our terminology. For example, he mentions the fact that Danish breweries and producers of dairy products benefit from the presence of local producers of specialized industrial enzymes is a matter of industry resources. However, the fact that there is virtually no close interaction between users and producers of industrial enzymes, and that (uncompensated) knowledge spill-overs are insignificant between producers and between producers and users, implies that technological industry capabilities are virtually non-existing. Almost all of the relevant factors are, as Porter (1990: 135) says, "transferable," that is to say, tradeable on factor markets. So their value-creating potential is at least to some extent registered via the price system.

However, for individual firms, many of the benefits of being part of so-called "clusters" (firm agglomerations) have to do with influences that are not directly registered in the price system, that is, with externalities. And in numerous contexts, Porter mentions several examples of externalities that are close in meaning to industry capabilities, although they in Porter's analysis cut *across* industries.[10] Actually, externalities abound in all of the corners of Porter's diamond (factor conditions, demand conditions, related and supporting industries, and firm strategy, structure

---

[10]To the extent that the capability terminology is applicable to Porter's analysis, perhaps we should talk about "cluster capabilities" (clusters are Porter's units of analysis).

and rivalry), and the combined interaction of the relevant factors create additional externalities. Since these influence firms' asset-accumulation processes, and are in turn influenced by firms' action, the resulting picture of the resource and capability creation ("upgrading of factors") in a cluster is one of extreme complexity. In order to reduce this complexity, we focus in our next example on a specific industry.

C. The U.S. PC industry. The development of the U.S. PC industry provides illustrations of both industry resources and industry capabilities. In the late 1970s the fledgling PC industry was characterized by many competing technological standards, and sales growth was low. However, when IBM chose the MS-DOS operating system for its PC in the early 1980s, a de facto technological standard emerged. In our terminology, MS-DOS is clearly an industry resource, because of its tradeability. However, the MS-DOS standard to some extent steered the evolution of industry capabilities. For example, hardware developers have an incentive to use compatible technologies, and software developers an incentive to create programs that can communicate with other brands. In other words, the standard made possible a number of network-externalities (Farrell and Saloner 1986), which made technological progress faster. This non-traded interdependence constitutes an industry capability.

The early history of the PC industry also exemplifies the presence of important industry capabilities (cf., Langlois 1990). The size, rapid development and uncertainty that characterized the early industry meant that no single firm could develop the necessary capabilities as fast as the decentralized network of firms that together constituted the emerging industry. For example, IBM was forced to vertically disintegrate to a very significant extent in order to build the original PC, since it could not create the necessary capabilities as fast and efficient as the market—meaning other firms—could.

In other words, the decentralized network of the PC industry substituted for the large firm, since it learned faster and more efficiently. The superior learning and innovation capabilities of the industry as a whole were essentially the result of the strong diversity of designs, approaches and products: many different "conjectures" could be "tested" with rapid feedback, and faster learning was the result. Clearly, this superior learning capability is, in our terminology, an industry capability.

Industry Capabilities and Competitive Advantage

There are a number of important questions raised by the PC case in the previous paragraph. Our main concern is whether individual firms can appropriate rents from the presence of industry capabilities. The ability to do so is contingent on two assumptions: one, that industry capabilities augment individual firms' competitive advantages, and two, that there is a limit to the number of firms who can gain access to industry capabilities.

We have suggested that industry capabilities may allow "incumbents" to benefit from their presence. We have also suggested that the presence of industry capabilities may underlie (among other factors) the presence of entry barriers. In this section, we subject these assertions to a more careful analysis. Briefly, we argue that some of the analytical categories developed within the RBP for analyzing the resources and capabilities of the individual firm may also be applied to the analysis of industry capabilities.

Conditions for competitive advantage

Recent resource-based research has clarified how resources and capabilities on the firm level may contribute to firm-level competitive success (Barney 1991; Peteraf 1993). May a similar analysis be applicable to industry capabilities? Since industry capabilities are shared among incumbents, they cannot improve the competitive position of an incumbent firm vis-à-vis other incumbents. However, industry capabilities may strengthen firms' positions vis-à-vis firms from other geographically bounded industries. This is clearly related to the train of thought that underlies Porter's recent work, in which he argues firms may derive competitive advantage from belonging to certain "clusters" (Porter 1990).

Generally, strategically important resources and capabilities allow the firm to exploit opportunities and/or neutralize threats in its environment. Applied to industry capabilities, this implies that industry capabilities may improve the efficiency of the bundle of resources and capabilities under the firm's control. Increased efficiency arises from complementarity between industry capabilities and firm resources and capabilities. For example, the asset accumulation processes of individual Silicon Valley firms are eased by the presence of technological industry capabilities. A firm such as Sun Microsystems draws heavily upon external resources and capabilities, and these help the firm to be at the forefront of the technological evolution in high end workstations.

This example brings the issue of co-specialized resources and capabilities into focus. In order to take advantage of industry capabilities, an entrant must accumulate a bundle of resources and capabilities that are complementary to the industry capabilities (e.g., plant and machinery, skilled labor, technological knowledge, etc.). Thus the industry capabilities and firm-specific resources may augment each other as *resource-position barriers*. The more important each is as an entry barrier, the stronger the effect is on the other.

Valuable resources and capabilities that are possessed by a large number of firms cannot, as a general rule, give rise to sustained competitive advantage. The same logic applies to industry capabilities. In order for industry capabilities to generate rents, they must possess some attribute that limits access to them. We have already touched upon the complementarity issue, but other factors may be important. These factors include causal ambiguity, which may arise because of social or technological complexity, or the time it takes to gain access to industry capabilities.

Social complexity of industry capabilities is illustrated by the Northern Italy ceramic tile industry. Firms in this region are closely linked by family and other social ties, and it may be difficult for entrants to recognize these ties and thus it is difficult for them to gain access to the industry capabilities. Technological complexity may be another source of causal ambiguity about industry capabilities. For example, in highly disintegrated industries it may not be easy for an entrant to know who produces what, or whom to call when you need to get something fixed. Lack of factor market transparency may thus make access to industry capabilities difficult.

In some cases, industry capabilities may be difficult to access because it takes time to learn how to do so, or because entrants face time compression diseconomies in accumulating complementary resources and capabilities. Similarly, if incumbents exhibit asset mass efficiencies in accumulating such complementary assets, entry may be impeded as the complementary assets required to take advantage of industry capabilities are continuously upgraded. These are similar to the mechanisms identified by Dierickx and Cool (1989).

A Taxonomy of Industry Capabilities

As can be inferred from the above examples, industry capabilities come in a variety of forms, although they share certain characteristics (such as their "social" aspect and their non-tradeability). One possible taxonomic distinction could be between *behavioral* industry capabilities and *technological* industry capabilities (cf., David 1987). Norms and trust relations, for example, would clearly be in the category of behavioral industry capabilities, whereas standardized methods for solving certain classes of technological problems (cf., Dosi 1982) would fall in the category of technological industry capabilities.

Another possible distinction could relate to whether (and to what extent) industry capabilities were intentionally designed, as opposed to having emerged in an unplanned manner. A similar distinction can be found in game theory, which distinguishes between cooperative and non-cooperative games. We shall use these synonymously. For example, the development of stable behavioral norms would normally be a matter of gradual, unplanned evolution, while certain industry standards imposed by dominant firms would fall in the design category. Juxtaposing the two distinctions may produce the following taxonomy in Table 1 of industry capabilities and their "institutional" embodiments.

	TECHNOLOGICAL	BEHAVIORAL
COOPERATIVE (PLANNED)	R&D cooperation, know-how sharing, joint ventures, R&D consortia.	Industry and trade associations, cartels.
NON-COOPERATIVE (NON-PLANNED)	Nash equilibria in technology choice games with externalities. "Collective capability" in terms of innovation.	Rules of conduct emerging from repeated PD games. Norms emerging from repeated coordination games.

Table 1 Industry Capabilities and Their Institutional Embodiment

An important question is the ease with which each type of industry capability can be accessed, and what strategies are appropriate for doing so.

Gaining access to cooperative-technological industry capabilities is mostly dependent upon the nature of complementary assets that are required in order to take advantage of them. In formal cooperation such as joint ventures, the cooperating firms have the possibility of deciding which complementary assets are relevant. If these are controlled by separate firms, then it may be even more difficult for entering firms to gain access to industry capabilities.

Cooperative-behavioral industry capabilities often require some sort of "membership" of a coalition of firms. The most striking example of this is the case where incumbents form a cartel that bars entry outright. An example of a less obtrusive case may be when incumbents decide cooperatively on "best business practice" issues, e.g., warranty policies.

Non-cooperative-technological industry capabilities also require investment in complementary assets, but the main problem here does not seem to be in gaining access to them, but in trying to second-guess the incumbents' future moves. Because incumbents share some history (they have played the game in previous periods), whereas the entrant is a newcomer by definition, incumbents may be better able to read one another's signals ie. (the entrant faces more causal ambiguity).

Non-cooperative-behavioral industry capabilities appear to be the most fragile of the four types of industry capabilities. Behavioral equilibria seem less stable than technological, since technological requires certain lock-in because of their complementarity to other resources and capabilities. Further, entry may actually destroy industry capabilities, as some norms are sensitive to the number of actors in the game. For example, in a paper on social capital (which is related to our concept of industry capabilities in spirit), Routledge and von Amsberg (1994) show that, under some circumstances, increases in the number of players may actually lead to the destruction of social capital.

Taxonomic distinctions may not be extremely interesting in themselves. The challenge is to identify in theoretical terms the mechanisms that "produced" the distinctions. And as the above taxonomic distinctions loosely indicate, different industry capabilities may not be given to explanation in the same theoretical terms. For example, in terms of basic game theory, very different games may underlie the emergence of industry capabilities. For example, to the extent that the industry capability of spontaneously developed industry norms is under consideration, it may be best understood in the context of the theory of iterated prisoners dilemma games. Other industry capabilities, such as those emerging from technological standards, may however best be understood in the context of iterated coordination games. In the following, we try to follow up on this and present a less intuitive analysis of industry capabilities and how they interact with resources and firm capabilities.

Analyzing Industry Resources and Capabilities

The issue of gaining access to industry capabilities points to a broader, and perhaps more general issue: where should managers position their firms in resource- and capability-space, given the presence of industry capabilities?

Positioning in the resource and capability space

As asserted earlier, managers face a large external *capability and resource space*. This space includes resources, ranging from those that are completely generic (applicable to any industry; for example, general management skills) to those that are industry-specific, and capabilities (which also may be more or less specialized). In this context managers are here thought of as the persons responsible for choosing subsets of this space to employ in production. This involves acquiring resources on factor markets, evaluating how such resources may contribute to building up internal capabilities, and also evaluating how the firm best utilizes industry capabilities.[11]

The manager confronts a number of *static* and *dynamic* considerations. In a static setting, managers must consider what kind of competition may emerge, in terms of competition for resources (Barney 1986) and competition in terms of asset-accumulation (Dierickx and Cool 1989). Much of the resource-based literature embraces this interpretation of the choice of attractive resource and capability positions (e.g., Barney 1986, 1991): in order to achieve sustainable competitive advantage, managers should maximize the differences in resource and capability positions. However, this line of reasoning ignores many important issues which are often raised in a more dynamic context.

For example, the evolutionary economics literature on technological development (Dosi 1982) argues that technological development is often associated with a number of benefits, for example, benefits of standardization, which strictly dispersed resource and capability

---

[11]The last problem may be a matter of positioning the firm *geographically*, as when a Japanese manager of an computer firm considers setting up a foreign subsidiary in Silicon Valley. Not "belonging" to a geographically bounded industry may exclude one from access to industry capabilities.

positions would seem to preclude.[12]   In other words, some measure of coordination of asset-accumulation processes often takes place, to the benefit of participating firms.

On the other hand, it is variety (in terms of resources and capabilities) that drives the evolutionary process (Alchian 1950). As we saw in the U.S. PC industry case, it was the extreme variety that initially existed in this industry that boosted its technological progressiveness. Although such variety may not have served the interests of individual firms (at least in the short run), it did benefit the industry as a whole. Variety yielded industry capabilities.[13]   In other words, not only does firms' positioning in resource and capability space influence the individual firm's competitive advantage; it also determines the prevalence of industry capabilities. Which factors determine positioning?

One pertinent distinction that influences positioning is the basic one between homogenous and heterogenous resources and capabilities and the implications of these dimensions in terms of rent-yielding potential. Resources and capabilities can in themselves be thought of as multidimensional, i.e., they differ in a number of attributes. If the attributes of the resources and capabilities employed by two firms resemble each other closely, we may speak of (locally) homogenous resources and capabilities (although they may differ substantially from those employed by other firms).

To the extent that industry resources are prevalent, that is, incumbent firms all rely on some resources specialized to the industry, there is homogeneity in terms of resources. Furthermore, to the extent that the

---

[12]We have in mind here, for example, the literature on "technological paradigms" initiated by Dosi (1982). When firms compete within such paradigms, they are producing relatively similar products with resources and capabilities that have a number of characteristics in common. For example, heuristics for technological problem solving are relatively standardized. This yields a number of beneficial behavioral and technological untraded interdependencies (ibid.).

[13]The recent study by Miles, Snow and Sharfman (1993) would seem to suggest that this holds for many industries. Examining 12 American industries, they argued that "....industry variety and performance are positively related, suggesting that interfirm benefits are most feasible in industries characterized by diversity among firms' competitive strategies" (p. 163).

capabilities firms accumulate from resources resemble each other, there is homogeneity in terms of these capabilities.[14]

According to standard resource-based thinking (Dierickx and Cool 1989), managers should maintain heterogeneity of capabilities in order to keep competitive imitation at bay. However, there may be benefits of coordinating asset-accumulation processes either explicitly (public intervention, interfirm arrangements) or implicitly (by making independent but interdependent choices of accumulation of resources and capabilities).

Costs and benefits of homogeneity and heterogeneity

We can think about resource and capability positions as locations in a multidimensional Euclidian space. When managers choose the subset of resources and capabilities they wish to acquire and accumulate, they essentially make a decision about the point in n-space where they wish to locate relative to other firms. The distance between points in n-space can be thought of as the difference between firms' resources and capabilities.[15]

What managers must weigh are the relative costs and benefits of positioning near other firms against the costs and benefits of positioning far away from other firms. In other words, should the firm pursue a heterogenous or homogenous asset-accumulation strategy?

If one interprets, for example, the contributions of Barney (1986, 1991) and Dierickx and Cool (1989) in a game theoretic context, they basically say that pursuing a heterogenous asset accumulation strategy is always a dominant strategy. This is because competition in acquiring homogenous resources (Barney) and developing homogenous capabilities (Dierickx and Cool) will quickly drive their rents down. Ignored in this picture is the fact that there may be benefits of accumulating capabilities that are not completely heterogenous.

---

[14]In terms of theories of technological change, this would be the case in the "paradigmatic" phase of technological developments, whereas the "pre-paradigmatic" phase would be characterized by much greater variety (Dosi 1982).

[15]If we imagine two firms that use one resource with multiple attributes, each firm's choice of attributes represents a point in n-space. The difference between those two points is reflected in the multivariate distance between those two points. This reasoning is analogous to Mahalanobi's distance, which is a standardized multivariate measurement used in various multivariate statistics, e.g., in discriminant analysis, where Mahalanobi's distance is used to measure the differences in means between two (or more) groups with multiple attributes.

Cohen and Levinthal (1989) presented reasoning that supports this conclusion. On standard economic reasoning, firms confront decreasing incentives in the production of new knowledge (R&D), as knowledge spillovers increase (Mansfield 1985). In terms of the RBP, the "homogenizing" force of spillovers implies that firms are unable to capture rents of technological capabilities. But as Cohen and Levinthal pointed out, there may be an offsetting incentive associated with spillovers, since R&D also increases what they call "absorptive capacity," viz. a firm's ability to absorb knowledge from the outside. This implies that "...with an endogenous absorptive capacity, a higher spillover rate provides a positive incentive to conduct R&D by increasing the pool of available knowledge" (1989: 576). What Cohen and Levinthal here discuss is an industry capability—namely accelerated technological development—that benefits incumbents (through easing their accumulation processes), but arises precisely to the extent that the accumulation of (technological) capabilities is not completely heterogenous over firms.[16]

In other words, there are positive as well as negative effects of positioning close and far away in resource and capability space. Table 2 summarizes these effects.

Coordinating investments

There are numerous complications to the above assertions. For example, how do managers decide on which capabilities/assets to accumulate, knowing that other managers confront similar decisions (cf., Richardson 1960)? The most likely outcome is that there may be multiple Nash equilibria in terms of asset investments, and a need to play mixed strategies. However, major "commitment intensive" (Ghemawat 1991) decisions, such as choosing a program for asset investments, are usually one-shot decisions, so the advice to play a mixed strategy is not very useful for a manager (for example, investing in technology A vs. B with 50% probability....).

---

[16]It is essentially also such positive technological externalities that have been highligted in much of the recent literature on industrial districts, under the rubric of, for example, "reciprocity in technological development."

	CLOSE	FAR AWAY
POSITIVE EFFECTS	Increased knowledge spill-over. Inter-firm learning and faster learning. Benefits of standardization. Faster asset accumulation.	Factor market competition may decrease. Competition in terms of accumulation of capabilities may decrease. Greater variety in terms of resources and capabilities may yield faster learning, faster asset accumulation.
NEGATIVE EFFECTS	Increased factor market competition. Increased competition in terms of scarce accumulation of capabilities. Smaller variety in terms of resource and capabilities may yield slower learning, slower asset accumulation.	Little knowledge spill-over. Little interfirm learning. Few benefits of standardization. Slower asset accumulation.

Table 2 Costs and Benefits from Localization in Resource and Capability Space

In spite of the weaknesses of mixed strategy Nash equilibria, we may derive some normative implications from a basic game theoretical perspective. The underlying game being played is a coordination game concerning choices of position in the resource and capability space, given assumptions about the relative benefits of location either close or far away from each other in this space. Thus, the overarching question is, How is such coordination achieved?

A. The first and perhaps most obvious way of achieving coordination is through explicit coordination of investments through public intervention or interfirm agreements. Such coordination has a certain negative ring to it when viewed through traditional anti-trust lenses; however, explicit coordination may yield welfare increases in some cases

(Richardson 1960), such as avoiding investments in duplicative R&D.[17] Furthermore, as Richardson (1972) clarified, coordination in the form of interfirm arrangements (not hierarchical direction) is often necessary when firms need access to the services of "dissimilar" but "complementary" resources and capabilities owned by other firms.

B. Another way of achieving coordination of investments is by signaling intentions, which may be beneficial in providing managers with focal points in resource and capability space. For example, MS-DOS may be seen as one important focal point for investments in the PC industry. Relatedly, a first-mover may become a Stackelberg leader, and maximize his choice of technology, in effect forcing competitors to adopt what may be an undesired technology for them.

C. Finally, coordination of asset investments may come about in a spontaneous way. For example, Giovanni Dosi (1982) argues that "technological paradigms" are established in a largely spontaneous way. Such paradigms contain an "exemplar" (a product, such as a "typical" car) and a set of (problem-solving) "heuristics" that help steer technological evolution. The exemplar and the heuristics act as spontaneously established focal points for managers in resource and capability space.

Summing up

We have conceptualized firms as confronting a large space of resources and capabilities, and have discussed some considerations that managers face when deciding on subsets of this space. Among other things, we argued that it is not necessarily the case that it is in the best interest of firms to maximize the multivariate distance in resource and capability space relative to other firms. This is essentially because there may be net benefits of positioning close to other firms. Economically, these benefits are positive externalities in production and are largely what we have been calling industry capabilities. On the other hand, industry variety may also promote

---

[17]In fact, such possible welfare increases has been the motive force behind recent public intervention in the American semiconductor industry, such as Sematech (Austin, Texas) (*The Economist* April 2, 1994). Sematech is a joint government-industry research consortium dedicated to research in semiconductor technology, and helping both chip manufacturers and the suppliers of chip manufacturing equipment. In particular, formalized R&D cooperation both provides industry resources and eases the diffusion of valuable knowledge within the industry, thus creating industry capabilities in our parlance.

the development of industry capabilities, since variety may imply faster learning.

Obviously, managers may choose to maximize the distance on some attributes of their firms' resource and capability portfolio while minimizing the difference on others. For example this can be done by sharing some technological know-how with competitors while keeping other know-how proprietary. Such sharing is often done in the case of technological innovations in the consumer electronics industry. SONY and Philips licensed their CD technology away, and CD's achieved rapid market penetration. Simultaneously, the same firms invest in their brand names, try to produce unique designs, etc., in order to distinguish themselves from other firms on these attributes.

Positioning close in resource and capability may yield industry capabilities, as may positioning far away. However, the industry capabilities yielded in the two cases are not identical, as is suggested by evolutionary theories of technological evolution (Dosi 1982). In case of "pre-paradigmatic" technological evolution—as in the early U.S. PC industry—the relevant industry capability is the ability to quickly learn from turning out a number of competing products. No individual firm could possess this capability; it is one that is possessed by network of competing firms as a whole. "Paradigmatic" evolution is characterized by much less variety and experimentation, but may still yield industry capabilities, such as strong network externalities. Typically, firms under paradigmatic technological evolution are positioned much closer in resource and capability space than are firms under pre-paradigmatic evolution. The asset accumulation trajectories of individual firms are constrained by the technological paradigm.[18]

Conclusions

Previously, we pointed out that under some circumstances industry capabilities can be important as entry or resource-position barriers. Also, different types of industry capabilities demanded different types of entry

---

[18]In James March's (1991) terminology, firms engage in much less "exploration" of new ways of doing things to the benefit of more "exploitation" of existing ways of doing things. As March also explains this may, however, imply the possibility of being "trapped in suboptimal stable equilibria" (p.1), for example, being surprised by innovative entrants.

strategies. Further, creation of industry capabilities can be analyzed as a coordination problem in a multivariate resource- and capability space.

Industry capabilities as resource-position barriers

Birger Wernerfelt (1984) coined the concept of "resource-position barriers"—the barriers that hinder the equalization of returns over firms—and suggested that although these barriers are broader than entry barriers, the former type underlies the latter type. Consistent with this view, Harold Demsetz (1982) has long argued that entry barriers are either based on property rights or are purely informational. In evolutionary economics, Sidney Winter (1984) has argued that entry may be impeded by the industry specific technology containing "numerous esoteric elements" (p. 297).

We believe our analysis of industry capabilities is consistent with these points of view. For example, industry capabilities may because of their social complexity and possible tacitness contain "numerous esoteric elements." In other words, would-be entrants may confront causal ambiguity because they do not understand precisely how industry capabilities benefit incumbents, or because they do not understand which resources should be acquired in order to benefit from industry capabilities. In other words, the relevant barriers are essentially informational. To the extent that this may help incumbents preserve their superior levels of rent, industry capabilities resemble resource-position barriers.

For example, because of their social and tacit nature, behavioral industry capabilities may be particularly difficult to access for non-incumbents. Conceptually, if industry capabilities are important, while other resources and capabilities are not, then industry capabilities may in fact be the only thing incumbents earn rent from. For example, the small firms in the ceramic tile industry in Northern Italy are tightly interwoven by family, social, friendship, and other ties (Pyke and Sengenberger 1992). These ties are an industry capability.

It may not be difficult for entrants to learn everything about the technology of such small firms, and each firm may not have firm-specific resources and capabilities that will sustain a competitive advantage. In other words, it is relatively easy to identify, acquire and accumulate firm-specific resources and capabilities in this industry. The social networks are a different matter, however. Such relationships may indeed be the most important barrier to entry/resource-position barrier to the ceramic tile industry (see Russo 1985).

However, we should also recognize the possibility that industry capabilities may attract rather than impede entry. Montgomery and Hariharan (1991) essentially argued that entry barriers should be thought of as resource-position barriers. Examining large firms with extant capabilities in R&D and marketing, they argued that empirically these firms chose industries with *high* entry-barriers. This is because the underlying resources and capabilities resembled the resource and capability profiles of these firms. Although Montgomery and Hariharan argue strictly on the firm level, their paper suggests the possibility that entry may happen because firms want access to rent-yielding industry capabilities, and that their resource and capability profiles allow them to obtain this access. As already suggested, this motive may be behind Japanese investments in Silicon Valley (Teece 1992).

Appropriating rent from industry capabilities

We have argued that industry capabilities may conform to the conditions for competitive advantage as presented in recent resource-based research; in other words, they may yield rents. However, since industry capabilities are non-traded and non-proprietary and their services are externalities/external economies to individual firms the problem is, who appropriates the rent from industry capabilities?

Although industry capabilities are non-traded and non-proprietary to individual firms they are still capital assets to incumbents. This narrows the search for those who are able to appropriate rents from industry capabilities to the resource-owners of firms and to suppliers and customers. Important considerations are to what extent co-specialized assets impede entrants' access to industry capabilities, and to what extent the entrant faces a transparent industry. In the case where the industry is not transparent, i.e., there is causal ambiguity, industry capabilities may be difficult to access.

Rents from industry capabilities may be appropriated by shareholders, owners of human capital (employees), suppliers, customers etc. in different proportions depending on such factors as specificity to the firm of the supplied service (since this co-determines bargaining power). This is not conceptually different from resource-based analysis of who may reap rents from firm resources and capabilities (e.g., Peteraf 1993).

However, it considerably complicates the matter here that firms that share in industry capabilities may be—and typically will be—on competitive terms with each other. In other words, product market competition will co-determine who will get the rents from industry capabilities. Conceptually consumers may in the limit obtain all the benefits in the form of low product prices. The upshot is that who will appropriate rents from industry capabilities cannot be determined on an *a priori* basis.

Coordination of investments

In this paper, we have made a number of conceptual points that all relate to the RBP. On an overall level, we have suggested a resource-based analysis of firms' environments. The concepts of industry resources and capabilities signify this. Generally, we conceive of strategy as a matter of choosing a position or asset accumulation path in the relevant resource and capability space. This space includes non-proprietary assets that may nevertheless benefit firms in an industry. These assets are industry capabilities.

Furthermore, we have suggested that the normative resource-based conclusion that managers should maximize the multivariate distance to other firms' resources and capabilities does not necessarily hold water when examined in the context of industry capabilities. There may be numerous benefits associated with (intentional or non-intentional) coordination of accumulation strategies. Rapid imitation and consequently diffusion of knowledge that benefits all "incumbents" (Cohen and Levinthal 1989) may be one such benefit. However, against this speaks the point implied by basic evolutionary economics that learning and technological development may also progress through selection forces (rather than imitation), that is, the market sorting among a number of competing designs, strategies etc., and their underlying bundles of resources and capabilities.

Clearly, the existence of industry capabilities poses a coordination problem for managers. That is to say, they must position their firms in resource- and capability-space according to a cost and benefit calculation of localizing close to or far away from other firms. Under certain circumstances, coordination through explicit means (such as public intervention), signalling, and leadership may yield advantages. There are limitations to how much explicit coordination is desirable or possible. Some industry capabilities are impossible to plan or "order" (such as widespread trust-relations). In other cases, planning for industry capabilities may suppress variety. Finally, leaving the market to coordinate through, for example, signals and strategic moves may yield the best result for the society and industries.

References

Alchian, A.A. 1950. "Uncertainty, evolution, and economic theory." In idem. 1977. *Economic Forces at Work*. Indianapolis: Liberty Press.

Allen, R.C. 1983. "Collective invention." *Journal of Economic Behavior and Organization* 4: 1-24.

Barney, J.B. 1986. "Strategic factor markets: expectations, luck and business strategy." *Management Science* 32: 1231-1241.

Barney, J.B. 1991. "Firm resources and sustained competitive advantage." *Journal of Management* 17: 99-120.

Cohen, W.M., and Levinthal, D.A. 1989. "Innovation and learning: the two faces of R&D." *Economic Journal* 99: 569-596.

David, P.A. 1987. "Some new standards for the economics of standardization in the information age." In Dasgupta, P. and P. Stoneman (eds.) 1987. *Economic Policy and Technological Performance*. Cambridge: Cambridge University Press.

Dosi, G. 1982. "Technological paradigms and technological trajectories." *Research Policy* 11: 147-162.

Demsetz, H. 1982. "Barriers to entry." *American Economic Review* 72: 47-57.

Dierickx, I., and Cool, K. 1989. "Asset stock accumulation and sustainability of competitive advantage." *Management Science* 35: 1504-1511.

Farrell, J., and Saloner. G. 1985. "Standardization, compatibility, and innovation." *Rand Journal of Economics* 16: 70-83.

Geroski, P., and Vlassopoulos. 1991. "The rise and fall of a market leader: frozen foods in the UK." *Strategic Management Journal* 12: 467-478.

Ghemawat, P. 1991. *Commitment: the dynamics of strategy*. New York: The Free Press.

Langlois, R.N. 1990. "External economies and economic progress: The case of the microcomputer industry." Mimeo, Department of Economics, University of Connecticut.

Langlois, R.N. 1992. "Transaction cost economics in real time." *Industrial and Corporate Change* 1: 99-127.

Loasby, B. 1993. "Understanding markets." Mimeo, Department of Economics, University of Stirling.

Mansfield, E. 1985. "How rapidly does new industrial technology leak out?" *Journal of Industrial Economics* 34: 217-223.

March, J. 1991. "Exploration and exploitation in organizational learning." *Organization Science* 2: 1-19.

Marshall, A. 1925. *Principles of economics*. 8th ed. London: Macmillan.

Montgomery, C. A., and Hariharan, S. 1991. "Diversified expansion by large established firms." *Journal of Economic Behavior and Organization* 15: 71-89.

Montgomery, C.A., and Wernerfelt, B. 1988. "Diversification, Ricardian rents, and Tobin's q." *RAND Journal of Economics* 19: 623-632.

Nelson, R.R., and Winter, S.G. 1982. *An evolutionary theory of economic change.* Cambridge: Belknap Press.

Porter, M.E. 1980. *Competitive strategy.* New York: Free Press.

Porter, M.E. 1990. *The competitive advantage of nations.* New York: Free Press.

Pyke, F., and Sengenberger, W. (eds.). 1992. *Industrial districts and local economic regeneration.* Geneva: International Institute for Labor Studies.

Richardson, G.B. 1960. *Information and investment.* Oxford: Oxford University Press.

Richardson, G.B. 1972. "The organisation of industry." *Economic Journal* 82: 883-896.

Routledge, B., and von Amsberg, J. 1994. "Endogenous social capital." Mimeo, University of British Columbia.

Russo, M. 1985. "Technical change and the industrial district: the role of interfirm relations in the growth and transformation of ceramic tile production in Italy." *Research Policy* 14: 329-343.

Saxonian, A. 1991. "The origins and dynamics of production networks in Silicon Valley." *Research Policy* 20: 423-437.

Stigler, G. 1951. "The division of labor is limited by the extent of the market." *Journal of Political Economy* 59: 185-193.

Sugden, R. 1986. *The economics of rights, cooperation, and welfare.* Oxford: Basil Blackwell.

Teece, D.J. 1992. "Foreign investment and technological development in silicon valley." *California Management Review* 34 (2): 88-106.

Teece, D.J., Pisano, G., and Shuen, A. 1991. "Firm capabilities, resources, and the concept of strategy." Mimeo, University of California, Berkeley.

Wernerfelt, B. 1984. "A Resource-Based View of the Firm." *Strategic Management Journal* 5: 171-180.

Winter, S.G. 1984. "Schumpeterian competition in alternative technological regimes." *Journal of Economic Behavior and Organization* 5: 287-320.

4

CAPABILITIES AND COHERENCE IN FIRMS AND MARKETS

Richard N. Langlois[1]
Department of Economics
The University of Connecticut

This volume seeks to open a dialogue between the evolutionary approach to economics and the resource-based approach to strategy. Despite their differences in intellectual origin and explanatory purpose, these two intellectual strands intertwine for a considerable distance. Rather than attempt a detailed comparison, however, this chapter tries to illuminate the overlap by examining one particular issue of common interest: the nature of "coherence" in economic organization. As Foss, Knudsen, and Montgomery noted in their introductory chapter, coherence has to do with whatever it is "that fundamentally distinguishes the viable firm as a historical *entity*, rather than just an arbitrary collection of businesses held together by the thin glue of transaction-cost minimization" (p. 13).

Indeed, evolutionary economics and resource-based thinking in strategy raise common issues that reanimate an old and fundamental debate in the economics of organization: What exactly *is* a firm, anyway? And what is it that makes a firm different from a market? As I will suggest

[1]This paper benefited from the discussion at the Conference on Evolutionary and Resource-based Approaches to Strategy, August 27-29, 1993, Scanticon Conference Center, Denmark. The author would also like to thank Dominique Foray, Pierre Garrouste, Paul Hallwood, Steven Klepper, Brian Loasby, Claude Ménard, Lanse Minkler, Cynthia Montgomery, Paul Robertson, Richard Rumelt, Louis Putterman, and Art Wright for helpful comments and discussions.

below, much of transaction-cost economics has reached the conclusion that the distinction between firm and market is little more than semantics. By offering concepts like routines and capabilities, by contrast, evolutionary and resource-based theories appear to supply to the concept of the firm some solid cement in place of the mucilage of transaction-cost economics.

It is one line of argument in this chapter that, although notions of routines and capabilities do offer a theory of coherence, they do not *ipso facto* solve the problem of defining firm and market. Both the evolutionary and the resource-based approaches concentrate far too exclusively on the capabilities and routines of the firm, and they neglect the large extent to which *markets* also possess capabilities, embody routines, and learn over time.

Moreover, by adopting the perspective of transaction-cost economics, this chapter will try to shed some light on the differences between evolutionary economics and resource-based work in strategy. The two approaches imply different, but arguably complementary, theories of vertical integration, that is, theories of why some activities are organized within the boundaries of the firm and some organized across markets. And both of these theories are at variance with those dominant in the present-day theory of transaction cost economics.

Strategic Factors: Contestable and Non-Contestable

The firm exists, Coase argued, because there is a cost to using the price system. And "a firm will tend to expand until the costs of organizing an extra transaction within the firm become equal to the costs of carrying out the same transaction by means of an exchange in the open market or the costs of organizing in another firm" (Coase 1937: 395). Inspired by Coase, a school of transaction-cost economics sprang up in which peculiarities in the process of exchange—that is to say, the costs of contracting—explain the firm. Costs of production figure in very little, and the process of production even less (Winter 1988).

More recently, however, an alternative approach has begun to coalesce in which production figures prominently and contracting costs take a back seat. Inspired by Edith Penrose's (1959) theory of the growth of firms, some economists and business strategists have come to stress the importance of the distinctive productive and organizational knowledge that firms possess.[2]   In an early and important, albeit strangely neglected, contribution, G. B. Richardson (1972) coined the term *capabilities* to refer to the distinctive knowledge and abilities a firm possesses.   Those capabilities determine which activities a particular firm can undertake effectively. To the extent that a firm undertakes more than one activity, it will tend to stick to activities that are *similar*, that is, activities that draw on more-or-less the same capabilities. The chain of production, however, requires a sequence of activities that are *complementary* but not necessarily similar. For example, a firm producing ink may have capabilities similar to those needed for producing clothing dyes but not at all similar to those needed for activities—like paper-making, printing, or manuscript acquisition—that are complementary to ink in the chain of book production.

None of this denies the importance of transaction costs in determining the boundaries of the firm. In fact, in articles that parallel Richardson quite closely, David Teece (1980, 1982) has argued that production-cost concerns alone do not determine whether complementary activities will take place under joint ownership and control, even when there are technological indivisibilities or so-called economies of scope in the production function. And, indeed, Richardson points out that even dissimilar activities may require joint ownership and control when they are closely complementary—an implicit argument from transaction costs. Nonetheless, Richardson believes that, in a world of complementary activities requiring dissimilar capabilities, we will tend to see a pattern of (what nowadays would be called) strategic alliances among firms each of which is fundamentally limited in its scope. As Brian Loasby (1991: 81) rightly observes, this has the effect of standing on its head the principal presumption of transaction-cost theorists: that such contractual relationships among firms must generate the hazard of opportunism and thus lead to vertical integration. Richardson's vision is one in which the difficulties of managing dissimilar activities outweigh contractual hazards on the whole and militate in favor of widespread disintegration.[3]

---

[2]The approach I'm describing here might best be called the dynamic capabilities approach (Teece, Pisano, and Shuen 1992), which borrows from both evolutionary thinking in economics and resource-based thinking in strategy. For a more detailed discussion of schools of thought, see the chapter by Foss, Knudsen, and Montgomery in this volume.

[3]A number of writers have made the argument that distinctive productive competences tend to outweigh transaction-cost consideration in the explanation of integration. For example, Paul Hallwood (1994) has made this case in the context of the multinational. And Bruce Kogut and Udo Zander (1992: 394) argue more generally that:

How does this "capabilities" approach fit with the Coasean dictum that firms exist because of the costs of using the price system? True to its neoclassical roots, transaction-cost economics starts from the unarticulated presumption that all factors of production are readily available on "the market." By contrast, it is a theme in the capabilities literature that some activities can be undertaken *only* within the firm. This might occur where the firm's capabilities to engage in a specific set of activities are distinctive (that is, not possessed by others) and *inimitable*.[4] For example, Mahoney and Pandian (1992) distinguish between "contestable synergy" and "idiosyncratic synergy."[5] When factors or resources—terms I will use interchangeably to refer to the outputs of activities that are part of the production process—are contestable, there is "a combination of resources that create value but are competitively available" (Mahoney and Pandian 1992: 368). Idiosyncratic synergy, on the other hand, occurs when the outcome is specific to the particular resources that are being combined and substitutes are not available. Although I will follow Mahoney and Pandian in the use of the term "contestable" here, I must also confess some unease at borrowing so fundamentally neoclassical a term; and when I use it I will have in mind simply the idea that resources are available for purchase from other firms.[6]

"Opportunism is not a necessary condition to explain why technology is transferred within the firm instead of the market. Rather, the issue becomes why and when are the costs of transfer of technology lower inside the firm than alternatives in the market, independent of contractual hazards. The relevant comparison, in this sense, are the efficiencies of other firms. ... [T]he most important variable is the indicator of differential firm capabilities, that is whether the firm or supplier has the lower production costs. Transaction-cost considerations matter but are subsidiary to whether a firm or other suppliers are more efficient in the production of the component."

[4]Dierickx and Cool (1989), for example, argue that the firm possesses certain critical or strategic asset stocks that are nontradable, nonimitable, and nonsubstitutable. The last of these presumably means that a rival firm cannot produce the same output using an alternative set of capabilities.

[5]Mahoney and Pandian actually refer to "idiosyncratic bilateral synergy," which they define as "the enhanced value that is idiosyncratic to the combined resources of the acquiring and target firms" (1992, p. 368). As I am interested in the broader context of the boundaries of the firm—which may involve any number of activities sharing idiosyncratic synergy—I will simply talk about contestable and non-contestable activities.

[6]In the neoclassical theory of contestable markets, products need not be actually available for purchase but may be *potentially* available. Nonetheless, as this potential

74

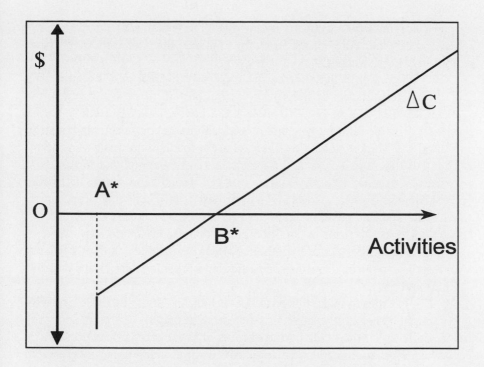

Figure 1

Consider now Figure 1. On the X-axis we can array activities or stages of production in order of increasing cost of internal production. ΔC graphs the normalized per-unit cost premium the firm must pay for the output of a particular activity if it integrates into that activity, measured relative to the per-unit cost it would incur by obtaining the output on contract from a distinct firm. Whenever this premium is negative, there is a cost advantage to internal organization. And, as Coase suggested, the firm will acquire additional activities until the premium is zero, in this case at B*. Activities in the range OB* are within the boundaries of the firm; the rest are left to the market. If, because of idiosyncratic synergy and lack of imitability, the outputs of certain activities are not separately available in the market (over some specified "run"), then the cost advantage to

---

availability is instantaneous (or, rather, timeless), this is as good as saying that products are actually available.

internal organization is effectively infinite. These activities constitute what we can call the "core" of the firm. In Figure 1, the core consists of those activities in the range OA.*

Although it may not be the only way to look at the matter, this Coasean formulation is helpful in a number of respects. Notice, for example, that "the market" is always the benchmark. But what is "the market"? Is the relevant benchmark an ideal market or an actually existing market? "Market failure" is everywhere a loaded and misleading term. But there is nonetheless a difference between saying that firms exist because a specific actually existing market "failed" and saying that firms exist because markets always (or at their best)[7] "fail," i.e., that firms can do what markets can never do. My argument here is that the explanation for the existence of firms is an inherently contingent one: firms arise in response to failures not of hypothetical markets (markets at their best) but in response to the inadequacies of particular market institutions at particular times and places.[8]

In order to make this case, let us look in detail at the reasons why ΔC might be negative; that is, why firms might undertake certain activities internally rather than procure the outputs of those activities externally.

We can consider two logically distinct categories: *contestable factors* and *non-contestable factors*. In the first category, the complementary factors necessary for production are available from other firms (that is, available from "the market") at least as cheaply as they can be produced internally. (By "at least as cheaply" I mean to include only production costs in the traditional sense and to exclude transaction costs and other as-yet-unidentified costs.) The second category encompasses the

---

[7]As I will make clearer below, my ideal of a market at its best is not the neoclassical picture of atomistic, timeless, anonymous, spot-contract exchange. Rather, what I have in mind is the existence of a dense network of "external economies" in Marshall's sense. Indeed, as Brian Loasby (1993b) points out, the neoclassical discussion of perfect markets is not about markets—which are institutions—at all, but is about exchange. "To confuse exchange and markets is a category mistake. An exchange is an event—or, if one wishes to include all preliminaries, it is a process: it is something that happens. A market is a setting within which exchanges take place—a setting which 'refers to a group or groups of people, some of whom desire to obtain certain things, and some of whom are in a position to supply what the others want'" (Marshall 1919: 182).

[8]Obviously, firms are also in reality imperfect institutions. But I am *not* arguing that really existing firms are never superior to hypothetical markets. I am saying that hypothetical firms (firms at their best) are never superior to hypothetical markets (markets at their best).

76

situation in which the necessary complementary resources are not available as cheaply elsewhere. This obviously includes (a) the case in which the resources are in fact available on the market but the firm is able to produce more cheaply internally and (b) the case in which the resources are simply unavailable elsewhere.

Contestable Resources

If all resources are contestable, production costs do not explain the extent of the firm: the market can always do at least as well as the firm. Thus, there must be other reasons for the existence of the firm. (See Figure 2.)

Category 1: Contestable Factors					
Transaction Costs		Strategic Appropriation		Selection Mechanism	
Contracting costs	Contractual hazards	Equity positions	Creating inimitability	"Mistaken" integration	Firm as strategic reserve

Figure 2

Here, of course, we find the traditional bailiwick of transaction-cost economics. Although Williamson (1985), for example, is clear that he seeks to explain organizational forms as minimizing the sum of production costs and transaction costs,[9] his analytical interest lies unmistakably with the case in which production-cost differences are not crucial.[10]

---

[9]On the functionalist character of this kind of explanation, see Langlois (1984, 1986). I will touch on this issue presently in a slightly different guise.

[10]A point with which Williamson (1988: 361) himself, agrees.

Transaction costs

There are a number of ways to decorticate the transaction-cost onion. For present purposes I will list only contracting costs and contractual hazards. The former are principal among the possibilities Coase had in mind: a firm-like organization might be superior if it is costly to renegotiate contracts in a market on an ongoing basis. The standard parable is that of the secretary. It would be costly to consummate a separate piece-rate contract each time one wanted a letter typed or a phone answered. It is thus a better idea to hire the secretary under an employment contract, which delimits possible tasks only in broad outline and allows the employer to specify more precisely as needed.[11] The second category is that of contractual hazards, which arise because of "opportunism." Following Alchian and Woodward (1988), we can split these hazards further into cases of opportunism caused by asset specificity and instances of opportunism driven by moral hazard. The first case arises when one or both parties have invested in assets highly specific to a particular transaction; in view of these specific assets, one party may try to "hold up" the other in an attempt redistribute the rents of production in his or her favor. The possibility of such opportunism *ex post* is a cost of contracting *ex ante*. Moral Hazard arises whenever there is enough "plasticity"[12] in a transacting relationship to allow one party to attempt to pursue his or her own interests at the expense of the other party. This too is obviously an *ex ante* cost of contracting.

Indeed, phrased this way, the two kinds of opportunism are not very different. Carl Dahlman (1979) long ago pointed out that all transaction costs are fundamentally information costs. Opportunism and moral hazard both produce costs because and to the extent that the writers of contracts do not have the information (or knowledge) necessary to specify all possible contingencies in advance or to determine whether all

---

[11]This example is in many ways more subtle and interesting than the contractual-hazards view of transaction costs. The costs of contracting here are in many ways a response to uncertainty—one cannot predict ahead of time which tasks will be required at any particular time, which calls for a form of organization that is adaptable. (For an excellent development of this idea of task uncertainty, see Stinchcombe (1990), chapter 2.) In this sense, Coase's conception of the nature of the firm is not far from the idea of the firm as a strategic reserve against uncertainty or, indeed, the Knightian theory of the firm (both of which I develop below).

[12]A term from Alchian and Woodward (1988).

parties are in fact adhering to the terms of the contract. Therefore, as I have argued elsewhere (Langlois 1992b), all traditional transaction costs (whether Coasean costs of contracting or costs that arise from contractual hazards) are essentially short-run phenomena. They occur only in the true Marshallian short run, which is the time before major uncertainties have resolved themselves and before production has settled into routine. In a (hypothetical) long-run world in which change has ceased,[13] routine (or, rather, *routines* in the sense of Nelson and Winter (1982)) attenuate any problem of writing repeated contracts; plasticity vanishes; and various external social institutions arise to mitigate any residual tendency to opportunism or moral hazard.

The relevant point here is that, if a short-run of change and uncertainty accounts for the kinds of transaction costs that preoccupy the literature, then perhaps we ought to look not at transaction costs *per se* but at their source: change and uncertainty. Change and uncertainty offer us explanations for the existence of firms that arguably go beyond traditional transaction-cost explanations.

Strategic appropriation

As Figure 2 suggests, another class of explanations for vertical integration focuses on problems of appropriability. David Teece (1986), for example, has suggested that one might want to internalize certain complementary activities in order to profit from the appreciation of assets associated with those activities. Of course, appropriation of this sort may require nothing more than an equity interest (Hirshleifer 1971; Casson 1982: 206-8). At least in principle, an investor at the turn of the twentieth century needed only go short on buggy whips and go long on automobile parts in order to profit from a perception that automobiles would come rapidly to replace buggies.[14] Suppose, on the other hand, that the investor needs to *create* the possibility of appreciation by innovating, that is, by deliberately altering the existing chain of complementary activities in some

---

[13]This concept of the long run is essentially equivalent to Schumpeter's (1934) notion of the circular flow of economic life. For an argument that it is also Marshallian, see Currie and Steedman (1990).

[14]This does not violate the assumption that the firm does not have superior production costs: in the more-or-less neoclassical world of Figure 2, imitation is costless, so other firms could in fact produce just as cheaply. In the terminology of Barney (1991), strategic factor markets are perfectly competitive.

way.[15] If there are no effective patent barriers to imitation, the entrepreneur might be motivated to internalize the activities into an organization like a firm in order to set up, as it were, homemade barriers to imitation.[16] The more general case, of course, is one in which knowledge is not instantly and costlessly transferred; and one might well wonder whether the ubiquity of inherent difficulties in imitation does not call into question the importance of the appropriability argument (the artificial creation of barriers to imitation) as a rationale for internal organization.

Selection mechanism

A key assumption of the Coasean approach to explaining the boundaries of the firm is that the organizational forms we observe reflect (and therefore may be explained in terms of) the minimizing of production and transaction costs. This is a somewhat problematical assumption.[17] If we transport out of the neoclassical world into a more evolutionary space, we might well wonder whether selection pressure is always strong enough to weed out inefficient forms right away.[18] John Jewkes (1930) long ago suggested, for example, that vertical integration may be prevalent during periods of rapid growth because the excess demand during such periods permitted the existence of highly integrated structures that would otherwise have been revealed to be inefficient. In a boom period, the personal peculiarities of particular entrepreneurs may be vital, especially when one or more of the leading firms is controlled by an empire builder who instinctively favors integration. And even Williamson (1985: 119) allows of the possibility of "mistaken" integration, citing as an example the empire Henry Ford built on the Rouge.

---

[15]And, in fact, General Motors, unlike Ford, started out as little more than a holding company. But, as I will suggest below, even Billy Durant, GM's founder, had to coordinate production in order to reap the benefits he sought.

[16]Aren't I forgetting other kinds of "barriers to entry" that might lead to integration? Demsetz (1982) has effectively demonstrated that the only sensible meaning of a barrier to entry is a property right—like a legal monopoly, a patent, or even a simple title to assets, which includes the right to prevent or limit access in order to create inimitability. It is significant that Rumelt (1987: 145) uses the term "quasi-rights" to refer to the various "lags, information asymmetries, and frictions" that slow imitation.

[17]Again, see Langlois (1984, 1986) for a more detailed development.

[18]See Levinthal (1992) for a discussion of many of the issues involved.

Brian Loasby (1991: 32) puts an intriguing twist on this argument. Like the institution of money, an institution like a firm can function as a "strategic reserve" against an unknown future.[19] Even when one can purchase resources as or more cheaply on the market, one may prefer to produce internally in order to maintain within the organization a set of capabilities that could not otherwise be as easily redeployed in the face of changed circumstances.[20] Thus, rather than being "mistaken," integration that looks inefficient (that is, high cost) from the perspective of a moment in time may actually be more efficient than nonintegration over the longer haul. I will return to these ideas below. Notice, however, that this argument reinforces the point I made above: organizational forms may arise because of uncertainty and the lack of knowledge about the future—in a sense more general than is implied in standard transaction-cost arguments.[21]

Non-Contestable Factors

Consider now the second—and arguably more important—category: situations in which strategic resources are not contestable, that is, situations in which the outputs of some activities are not available on the market at production costs less than or equal to those of internal organization. As Figure 3 suggests, there are two alternatives. Either the outputs are inherently unavailable on the market or they are unavailable temporarily. In the first case, the possessor of the required capabilities can never be imitated: even a market at its best can never do what the firm can do. In the second case, the firm's distinctive capabilities give it access for a time to certain strategic factors that the market—other firms—cannot match; eventually, however, those capabilities diffuse into the market so that, *ceteris paribus*, the firm loses its production-cost

---

[19]This argument goes back, in spirit at least, to Loasby (1976). See also Loasby (1993a, 1994).

[20]Williamson (1991: 292-293) does mention the idea that firms may possess greater adaptability than does contracting. But he does not make this in any way a central organizing principle in his work.

[21]Obviously a thorough analysis of this idea would require modeling of how various institutional forms survive under various regimes of institutional change. This is an intriguing research agenda for the future.

advantage.[22] In the second case, then, firms are superior not to markets at their best but to actually existing markets, which may ultimately get better.

Category II: Non-contestable Factors			
Inherently non-contractible		**Temporarily non-contractible**	
Judgement	Entrepreneurship	Schumpeterian integration	Penrosean growth

Figure 3

If one is to make the argument that firms exist because they are inherently superior to markets, one has to specify why even markets at their best cannot do whatever it is one thinks firms do better. The answer must be that some factor is inherently non-contractible: because of its very nature, the factor can never be sold on the market, and therefore its production must necessarily be undertaken internally. We can imagine a number of activities whose outputs are perhaps inherently *costly* to exchange through markets. The results of research and development is an oft-cited example (Caves, Crookell, and Killing 1983). But costly is not impossible.

Judgment and entrepreneurship

Two candidates for inherently non-contractible activities are judgment and entrepreneurship.[23] These are closely related, and may even be two words for the same thing. By "judgment" I have in mind a function that Frank Knight (1921) saw as central to explaining the existence of

---

[22]Actually, the firm's own capabilities do not have to diffuse. All that is required is that others in the economy learn to produce the same outputs at equal or lower cost. Those outsiders may in fact learn to produce the same results using entirely different kinds of capabilities.

[23]To the extent that one wishes to view the production of certain kinds of knowledge, including perhaps some kinds of R&D, as inherently non-contractible, it is arguably because that production actually partakes of judgment or entrepreneurship.

firms. Knight's theory is much controverted and misunderstood; but what I view as a correct reading would go something like this (Langlois and Cosgel 1993). Because of the non-mechanical nature of economic life, novel possibilities are always emerging, and these cannot be easily categorized in an intersubjective way as repeatable instances. To deal with this ("Knightian") uncertainty, one must rely on judgment, that is, on an ability to process complex and incomplete information usefully in an intuitive way.[24] Such judgment will be one of the skills in which people specialize, yielding the usual Smithian economies.[25] Moreover, some will specialize in the judgment of other people's judgment, which leads to the hierarchical relationship we know as a firm. Notice that this idea is related to, if perhaps a bit more general than, Coase's idea of task uncertainty. It is also obviously related to the idea of the firm as a strategic reserve against the future.

In precisely what sense, however, is judgment non-contractible? If one specialty in a world of novel possibilities is to judge the judgment of others, why cannot the judgment of others, once judged, be hired on contract? More precisely, why cannot one hire judgment through a type of contract other than the employment contract, which, in some eyes, defines the firm? The answer must be that, because one can judge the judgment of another only at an abstract level—that is, because one by definition cannot predict in detail how the hired judgment will be exercised[26]—the buyer of judgment cannot write a fully specified contract with the seller of judgment.

The result of this non-contractibility (or imperfect contractibility) need not always be a firm. In many cases, contracting parties of various sorts are able to function with ongoing open-ended contracts (Ben-Porath 1980). Nonetheless, a number of writers have argued, in a rather Knightian spirit, that in the end the exercise of judgment must be linked to another activity, which we can call responsibility or control. The recent literature on incomplete contracts (Grossman and Hart 1986; Hart 1988, 1989; Moore 1992) distinguishes between two types of rights one might possess under

---

[24]On this point see Eliasson (1990: 282-283. Also see Schumpeter's (1934) famous discussion of the intuitive character of entrepreneurship.

[25]See also Casson (1982) for the idea that entrepreneurship consists in specializing in judgment.

[26]See Minkler (1993) for a discussion of the case in which the knowledge of agents differs qualitatively from that of principals, who therefore cannot monitor agents even when information (in the sense of traditional principal-agent models) is costless.

a contract: specific rights and residual rights. Specific rights are those spelled out, as it were, in black and white; residual rights are whatever rights are "left over," that is, rights to decide or to have one's way under circumstances not specified in the contract. The possession of residual rights is the possession of control or responsibility. If the acquisition of another's judgment implies contractual incompleteness, and if contractual incompleteness implies the existence of residual rights, then the individual who exercises judgment in the acquisition of another's judgment must also necessarily undertake the activity of responsibility or control. The exercise of judgment thus logically implies vertical integration.[27]

We might well wonder, of course, whether this kind of integration explains very much about the firms we observe in the world. In the hands of the present-day theorists of incomplete contracts, non-contracibility has strong implications for the boundaries of the firm (and, indeed, the definition of the firm). For these authors, the Knightian function of judgment is necessarily integrated not only with responsibility and control but also with the *ownership of assets*. For example, Grossman and Hart (1986: 694) "virtually define ownership as the power to exercise control." That is, they hold not only that contractual incompleteness implies rights to control but also that rights to control imply ownership of assets. This is not a nonsensical position. Responsibility and the right to control are surely rights that owners possess under at least some meanings of ownership. If we accept the identification of responsibility and control with ownership, then contractual incompleteness has implication for the ownership of assets. Consider two assets that cooperate in production. If unforeseen contingencies call for a reorientation of the productive process and a reworking of the contractual relationship, the two separate owners would

---

[27]The possibility of contractual incompleteness resulting in an ongoing open-ended contract rather than an employer-employee relationship is not a counterexample. Even in open-ended contracts there have to be residual rights. Often those rights are specified de facto or by convention. In the mostly defunct traditional marriage contract, for example, the husband and wife each had spheres of decision-making assigned to them by convention—the wife in areas of internal household management, the husband in areas of external relations. In such a case, we can say that the functions of responsibility and control are partitioned. It is also conceivable, however, that residual rights are so poorly specified that neither party exercises them. Of course, restraint from exercising one's rights of control may in some cases have the external benefit of helping the long-run functioning of the organization. But poorly specified rights of control that can never be exercised arguably lead to inefficiency. The complaint that no one is in charge or no one takes responsibility is a familiar one in organizations, and its implications are well known.

have to agree on a course of action. Because of differences in knowledge and bargaining power, that reorientation could proceed inefficiently—for example, if the owner whose asset contributed relatively little to the joint rents of production were the one with the greater portion of control, that owner might choose a course of action that maximizes his or her return at the expense of the total joint rents. The prediction of incomplete-contracts theory is thus that the owner whose contribution is significantly more important to the joint rents will tend to exercise all the residual rights of control by buying out the other asset owner, possibly hiring him or her as an employee to operate or manage the asset.[28] The extent of asset ownership also serves as a definition of the extent of the firm. Notice, however, that this link between control and ownership of assets depends on the possibility of opportunism, which returns us to the "contractual hazards" box in Figure 2. As I argued in that context, opportunism is not an inherent problem of markets but is a short-run problem, a problem of certain actually existing markets.

In the end, then, can we assert that ownership of assets is inherently inseparable from responsibility, control, or the exercise of judgment? One author who thinks otherwise is Israel Kirzner (1973). In his theory of entrepreneurship, as in Knight's, entrepreneurship arises as a consequence of the possibility of novelty. For Kirzner, entrepreneurship consists in the alertness to or noticing of new and superior means-ends relationships. Rather than merely doing the best one can with given alternatives, entrepreneurship involves discovering new alternatives. Kirzner (1973: 83) agrees with Knight that entrepreneurship is inseparable from responsibility and control. But he also insists, with Schumpeter,[29] that the entrepreneur is never an asset owner. "Purely entrepreneurial decisions are by definition reserved for decision-makers who own nothing at all" (p. 47). Owners are just suppliers of factors. And what they earn is not profit: if they are lenders of capital, they earn interest, and if they are asset owners, they earn quasirents (p. 55). Only entrepreneurs earn profits, the pure return to noticing new alternatives.

---

[28]Yoram Barzel (1987) tells a strikingly similar story from the perspective of moral-hazard theory.

[29]Kirzner's view (1973: 81), Schumpeter's notion of the entrepreneur as someone who "carries out new combinations" (Schumpeter 1934: 66) is a special case of Kirzner's own more general and abstract conception.

Louis Putterman (1988) has raised some of the same issues, albeit in different language. He points out that, in much of the literature, there is an implicit or explicit assertion that "the party that *controls* the firm, or chooses its production program, is also the party that has contractual rights to dispose of the residual income of the firm" (p. 247, emphasis original). In this interpretation, control means "choosing the production program," which is arguably an entrepreneurial function. And the entrepreneurial control function is linked not to ownership of assets but to ownership of the bundle of residual rights. It is this bundle of rights that gets bought and sold as the commodity called the firm.

Do responsibility and control imply ownership? And if so, ownership of what? This is an intriguing question, but one best left for another place. The important question here is this: can we say that the function of judgment (or entrepreneurship), made necessary by a world of novel possibilities, logically implies a firm-like organization? To put it another way: does the necessity of judgment imply an area in which firms are inherently superior to markets, even "markets at their best"? Consider Massimo Egidi's assertion "that organizations perform a more complex function than the market; i.e., they take on the function of designing the division of labor and the function of coordinating the tasks so divided, while the market limits itself to coordinating the activities of its agents within a structure of the division of labor that has already been established" (Egidi 1992: 148). But does one need "an organization" to accomplish this more complex function? Can an entrepreneur effect change in the existing division of labor simply by persuading other independent economic agents to change their production plans and enter into a new pattern of contracts?[30] I believe that history shows the answer to be yes. As I suggest below, we can sometimes explain vertical integration precisely by the inability of the entrepreneur cheaply to inform and persuade owners of complementary assets to cooperate in innovative production. But that inability has to do not with any hyothetical failing of markets but rather with the suitability to the innovation of the particular market institutions in place at the time in question.

---

[30]Consider, for example, the case of Steven Jobs and Stephen Wozniak redesigning the division of labor at Apple Computer in the late 1970s. In the beginning, they had very few employees, preferring instead to subcontract almost all functions, including assembly. Only as the developing industry matured did Apple integrate significantly: that is, the company was *more* integrated once the new division of labor was in place than while they were redesigning it (Langlois 1992a).

The relevance of all this to the dialogue between evolutionary economics and the resource-based approach becomes clearer when we consider what I call Schumpeterian Integration and Penrosian Growth (Figure 3). In these areas, where transaction-cost economics normally fears to tread, internal production has a cost advantage because the firm possesses or can generate certain capabilities that other firms cannot immediately imitate or substitute for. These capabilities are the sorts of strategic resources that the resource-based approach to strategy urges firms to seek out (Wernerfelt 1984; Dierickx and Cool 1989; Rumelt 1984, 1987). There are, however, two basic patterns according to which firms might possess hard-to-replicate capabilities superior to those available in the market. These patterns, which I label Schumpeterian integration and Penrosean growth, correspond respectively to demand-side effects and supply-side effects. They also correspond, roughly speaking, to the perspectives of evolutionary economics and resource-based thinking, respectively.

Schumpeterian integration

Schumpeterian integration occurs when an entrepreneur (who may or may not control an existing firm) perceives a profit opportunity for the taking if the existing chain of activities could be reorganized. In order to reap this profit opportunity without integration, the entrepreneur would have to inform and persuade those with the relevant capabilities to reorient their activities into a new chain of complementary activities. This may prove costly.[31] According to Nelson and Winter (1982), production is a matter of carrying out routines. And the downside of routine behavior is that it is refractory to change when change is desirable.[32] As Schumpeter (1934) emphasized, a significant part of the entrepreneurial function involves overcoming the resistance of entrenched convention and vested interests.

---

[31]Morris Adelman (1955) was one of the first writers to associate vertical integration with economic change. In a rapidly growing industry, he argued, suppliers of intermediate goods may not be able to expand quickly enough to meet the needs of the producer of final goods, thus motivating that producer to integrate backwards. He also hinted at such effects as informational difficulties and potential hold-up problems.

[32]And, of course, the upside of routines is also that they are refractory to change—when change is undesirable.

Morris Silver (1984) tells the story, perhaps more usefully, in informational terms. For reasons that have to do—significantly—with limited capabilities, the entrepreneur would like very much to "carry out new combinations" through the market. But it may prove far more costly to inform and persuade those with the necessary capabilities than to do it oneself, that is, to integrate, albeit reluctantly, into the necessary complementary activities. Integration might take place either through the creation of a new organization and new facilities or through the acquisition of existing organization and assets. When he was rebuffed by railcar manufacturers, who refused to invest in facilities to produce the refrigerated cars he needed for an innovative meat-packing scheme, Gustavus Swift (reluctantly) bought himself a car maker (Chandler 1977: 299-302). He was then able to exercise control and "direct the production program" of the acquired firm. Langlois and Robertson (1989) argue that something similar explains the much-controverted case of General Motors' acquisition of Fisher Body in 1926: Fisher failed to share GM's entrepreneurial vision of the growth of closed-body vehicles, and GM needed control to see its vision through. As Coase (1988: 42-46) also argues about the Fisher Body case, highly specific assets were not the issue.

The extent of integration, then, depends on the costs of informing and persuading outside suppliers, an aspect of what I have called dynamic transaction costs[33] (Langlois 1992b). These costs depend on the nature of the innovation involved;[34] but they also depend on the existing level and configuration of "external" capabilities (Langlois 1992a) in the economy. One would therefore expect less integration in an economy with highly developed capabilities than in a more "primitive" economy.[35] To a significant extent, the rise of the large vertically integrated firm in the United States in the late nineteenth and early twentieth centuries (Chandler 1977) was a response to the inability of the existing decentralized system of capabilities in the economy to respond to the possibilities for systemic

---

[33]Loosely put, dynamic transaction costs—or, more generally, dynamic governance costs—are the costs of not having the capabilities you need when you need them. This is obviously related to what Dierickx and Cool (1989) call "time-compression diseconomies."

[34]In particular, dynamic transaction costs depend on the extent to which innovation is *systemic* or *autonomous*. On these issues see Langlois (1992b) and Langlois and Robertson (1992).

[35]A point not unknown in the literature of economic development. In addition to Silver (1984), see especially Dahmén (1971) and Leff (1978).

reorganization and mass-production attendant on rapid population growth and lower transport and communication costs. That is to say, the superiority of such large integrated enterprises was arguably a historically contingent one.

In a sense, of course, the level of external capabilities in an economy is a relative rather than an absolute matter. In 1908, for example, the Detroit region contained a high level of general-purpose machining and metal-working capabilities.[36] It was indeed these "external economies" that had shaped the development of the early American automobile industry as a regional agglomeration of small firms. Even the major manufacturers were actually assemblers, drawing on a wealth of local parts suppliers and other services, including local bank finance. But even those relatively sophisticated capabilities could become obsolete in the face of a Schumpeterian innovation. Henry Ford's entrepreneurial vision of mass producing an undifferentiated low-cost vehicle led him eventually to the moving assembly line and related techniques, which could make parts more cheaply than could existing outside suppliers. It was this innovation—not transaction costs in any standard sense—that led Ford to integrate vertically. That is, he integrated because his distinctive capabilities gave him a production-cost advantage over those who relied on resources available through contract. If transaction costs were involved, they were the dynamic transaction costs of teaching outside suppliers the Ford techniques—an unfolding body of partly tacit knowledge—and persuading them to use those techniques. Far from trying to appropriate this innovation through secrecy, Ford actively abetted the spread of his ideas, which did eventually diffuse to outside suppliers, making it less necessary for competitors like General Motors to integrate production.[37]

This story of Schumpeterian integration would seem to support Egidi's assertion that the firm can "perform a more complex function than the market" because it is able to "design the division of labor." It is certainly true that designing (or redesigning) the division of labor often

---

[36]This paragraph draws on Langlois and Robertson (1989).

[37]Indeed, if anyone in the industry could be said to have had a pure motive of rent appropriation, it was Billy Durant, the founder of GM. He ran the organization as a holding company, and was forced into (a relatively minimal) coordination function only by the dynamic state of the industry and the lack of sophisticated financial markets. In fact, the first appearance of automotive stock on the New York exchange was the sale of General Motors voting trust certificates in 1911 (Pound 1934: 113).

requires some kind of coherent central vision.[38] Nonetheless, it would be hasty to assume that a firm-like organization has an advantage in, or is even necessary for, implementing such a vision. As I have already hinted, what is necessary to effect an entrepreneurial redesign of the division of labor is responsibility and control. This is clearly a kind of "authority." But it is a mistake, I believe, to identify responsibility and control with the so-called authority relation of a managerial hierarchy. In a bureaucratic hierarchy, especially a complex and long-established one, the holders of nominal power are tightly constrained by rules and routines and have very little actual power to redirect the production program (Crozier 1964). Moreover, responsibility and control often do not require an organization: an entrepreneur can sometimes redirect the division of labor through contract and persuasion.

Indeed, there is a sense in which "the market" can sometimes redesign the division of labor more effectively than existing firms. In the computer industry, for example, a network of small vertically and laterally specialized firms is at the moment redesigning the division of labor to the detriment of the large, vertically integrated firms like IBM, DEC, and Fujitsu (Langlois 1992a; Ferguson and Morris 1993).

Penrosean growth

The main characteristic of what I have called Schumpeterian integration is that it is driven by the demand side, that is, by the entrepreneur's demand for the capabilities necessary to bring about a redesign of the chain of complementary activities. As a consequence, Schumpeterian innovation normally involves integration into dissimilar activities that the entrepreneur would have preferred to leave to others (Silver 1984). By contrast, Edith Penrose's theory of the growth of the firm is essentially supply driven. The firm grows in order to take advantage of excess capacity, notably in managerial and technical capabilities, that arise

---

[38]It is not clear, however, that such a centralized vision is always necessary. Like social institutions more broadly (Langlois 1986), the division of labor in the economy can in many ways be the result of the unintended consequences of the activities many individuals—it can be the result of human action but not of human design. Indeed, one might say that, from the perspective of the economy as a whole, the division of labor is *always* the result of such "spontaneous order" (Hayek 1967). It is the various subsystems of the overall division of labor —sometimes small, sometimes extensive—that are each the result of a coherent entrepreneurial vision.

because resources often come in indivisible bundles (Penrose 1959; Teece 1980, 1982). In this story, integration is a matter of gradual diversification into more-or-less similar activities. Thus, the pattern of activities within a firm is driven by what the firm can do, not by what (an entrepreneur thinks) the market needs.[39]

In an important recent paper, Teece, Rumelt, Dosi, and Winter (1994) have outlined a theory of the boundaries of the firm that builds on the Penrosean approach. The main components of the theory are (1) the regime of learning; (2) the nature of path dependency; and (3) the effectiveness of the selection mechanism. The regime of learning seems to mean the rate at which learning takes place, and includes the extent of exogenous and endogenous technological opportunity. The authors do not spell any of this out in much detail, however, and they do not distinguish between intra-organizational learning and the general rate of diffusion of capabilities in the economy. By path dependency they mean the Penrosean idea that a firm builds on what it already knows. History matters because a firm does not have a neoclassical menu of technological alternatives: what it chooses to do (or know) in the future depends on what it chose to do (what it knew) in the past. Apparently, path dependency can vary, presumably according to the contours of technological (and perhaps other kinds) of knowledge. If technologies are generic and converging,[40] firms can skip relatively easily across wide distances in the production space. But if path dependencies are "tight" or "high," the firm is rigidly constrained to stay close to its past. The selection mechanism also matters, for reasons akin to those I discussed under a similar heading above. If the selection mechanism is loose, firms may without penalty roam far from what they had done in the past, and indeed far from their "core competencies." (Conglomerates, they seem to think, are manifestations of a loose selection environment.) If, however, the selection mechanism is tight, "the boundaries of the corporation are likely to be drawn 'close in' to core competencies" (Teece *et al.* 1992: 26).

---

[39]It is often forgotten, however, that Penrose devotes the third chapter of *The Theory of the Growth of the Firm* to the role of entrepreneurship and the extent to which the size of the firm is limited by "'productive opportunity,' which comprises all of the productive possibilities that its 'entrepreneurs' see and can take advantage of" (Penrose 1959, p. 31). Nonetheless, the main thrust of the book—and the aspect that has mst influenced the resource-based approach—concerns the supply side of firm growth.

[40]In the sense of Rosenberg (1976).

Notice that Schumpeterian innovation is missing from this schema. In the case of Schumpeterian integration, an organization can be integrated into dissimilar activities even when the selection mechanism is tight and path dependencies are high.[41] Of course, one might expect an organization that integrated for Schumpeterian reasons to divest itself eventually of the most dissimilar activities, especially if the selection mechanism is indeed tight. But this is to say no more than that integration motivated by transaction costs—even dynamic transaction costs—is a short-run phenomenon. By contrast, the patterns of integration Teece and his coauthors discuss are relatively longer-run (if not necessarily long-run) phenomena. In the economics of organization as in traditional price theory, supply-side explanations are of a longer-run nature than demand-side explanations (Langlois 1992b).

Learning in Firm and Market

Adding Schumpeterian integration to the story of Penrosean growth through diversification suggests the possibility of path dependency in a sense somewhat different from that of Teece and his coauthors. The pattern of organization we observe at any time may depend not only on what firms knew in the past but on how they were organized in the past[42] (Langlois 1984, 1988). The importance of this kind of path dependency may depend

---

[41]In part, this may depend on one's understanding of "the selection mechanism." Teece *et al.* (1992: 25) lay great stress on the internal cash position of the firm as a buffer against selection. In this sense, a Schumpeterian innovation can provide a buffer against selection because, by creating value and satisfying wants in a superior way, it generates the cash necessary for integration into dissimilar activities. In a deeper sense, however, it is not so much that the selection mechanism is loose as that the innovation is a superior adaptation to the existing environment, which may have been a rigorous and demanding one from the point of view of the prior economic structures. It is probably true that Henry Ford's excesses in the 1920s—which went beyond the highly integrated River Rouge plant to iron and coal mining; lumbering; limestone; silica sand; Brazilian rubber; and railroad and shipping—were probably "mistaken integration" permitted by the cash he had amassed. But his early pattern of integration—which also went far beyond his starting competences and which was supported by retained earnings—was a successful innovation that *created* the cash flow in the first place.

[42]These two notions are obviously related, in that the structure of a firm (or, as we will see, of a market) is closely related to what it "knows." In many ways, knowledge *is* structure (Langlois 1983). But Teece *et al.* focus on the historical dependence of a firm's capabilities on its past capabilities.

92

on the extent of selection pressure, which is to say, competition. If competitive pressures are strong enough, the past may not matter, and observed levels of integration may depend only on factors in operation at the moment of observation. In general, however, the organizational past may matter.

Henry Ford's early acquisition of the J. R. Keim Mills affords one example (Langlois and Robertson 1989). Keim was a supplier to Ford; but, because largely of labor unrest, Keim threatened to become a bottleneck to Ford production. So, for what were ordinary reasons of "hold up" costs, Ford bought Keim and eventually moved its equipment from New York State to Highland Park. Once the equipment was in the Ford plant, Ford engineers noticed ways to improve the technology and integrate it better into the rest of Ford's internal production system. This had the effect on the margin of biasing technological change in a systemic direction and further reinforcing Ford's trend toward vertical integration. An opposite example may be the microcomputer (Langlois 1992a). Here IBM's decision to modularize the PC and outsource its construction had the (largely unintended) effect of reinforcing the autonomous character of innovation and setting the American industry on a market-based organizational trajectory (Langlois and Robertson 1992). This stands in contrast to the ecologically protected Japanese industry, which developed competing incompatible proprietary platforms (Cottrell 1994). In this case, however, selection pressure may be exerting itself and forcing the Japanese belatedly in the direction of the American organizational structure.

Indeed, we can unpack the idea of the "selection mechanism" a bit by thinking of it in terms of the relative rates of intra-organizational and market learning. A firm experiencing tight selection keeps "close in" to core competencies because markets—other firms—can acquire slightly dissimilar capabilities faster and more easily than the firm. Obviously, this ability of markets to learn quickly depends on the existing level and pattern of "external" capabilities. Like firms, markets must have the "absorptive capacity" (Cohen and Levinthal 1990) to learn, which means they must already possess capabilities similar to those needed for the innovation in question. The capabilities of the Detroit region in 1908 were highly developed but unable to absorb the moving assembly line, at least as fast as Ford could develop it internally. But the international network of electronics suppliers and software developers in the 1980s was far better able to absorb the innovation of the microcomputer than were the internal capabilities of IBM, DEC, and other large firms (Langlois 1992a).

What, then, are "markets"? They are not, nor should they be, the neoclassical ideal of fully informed, atomistic, price-mediated spot contracting. Rather, markets are bodies of productive capabilities. As Brian Loasby (1990: 120) notes, Marshall understood that both firms and markets "are structures for promoting the growth of knowledge, and both require conscious organization." That is to say, markets as well as firms use non-price information, and both involve institution building. Ken-ichi Imai puts it this way.

> Needless to say, a market is a place where information is translated into prices and where the adjustment of economic activity takes place. We also receive nonprice information in the market, and this information, too, plays an important role in the adjustment process. The entrepreneur is the one who implements such nonprice adjustments, and he is able to bring about such an adjustment because he has formed a new context in the market. For instance, it is sometimes difficult to predict trends in future demand, and this in turn makes investment decisions difficult.... If one is able to persuade the suppliers of hardware and software to reach some sort of commitment prior to going to the market, then one has created a context in the market that is separate from prices. If, as a result, one can supply good quality items at relatively low prices in the future and the undertaking succeeds, then it may appear as if prices had determined the situation. In actuality, however, the *ex ante* coordination was performed by an entrepreneur creating a new context, and the price adjustment, assuming such entrepreneurial activity as a prerequisite, appears only as its result (Imai 1990: 188).

This is not the neoclassical picture of a market. In this picture, however, markets, like firms, are institutional structures. Markets thus come in many configurations; they develop over time; and they can learn. As a historical matter, moreover, firms do not always, or perhaps even typically, supersede markets, as is virtually taken for granted in the transaction-cost literature. As I hinted above, firms—especially those that arise out of Schumpeterian integration—can form as a response to a lack of (the right kind of) market; and markets then *supersede firms*.

Teece *et al.* (1994) discuss the issue of *corporate* coherence. They seek to determine why firms "hang together," why their production draws on a relatively restricted set of capabilities. This is an important question, especially coming from a perspective of corporate strategy, where the appropriate focus is on firms and their survival. Economic theory—in its neoclassical as well as its evolutionary guise—is concerned, however, with the aggregate or market level. This implies a focus at the level of population, which is normally interpreted to mean the population of firms. But there is an even more fundamental unit of analysis: capabilities themselves. These can sometimes survive and reconfigure themselves even when the corporation that created them ceases to exist. Teece and his coauthors devote a good deal of attention to an issue that has attracted much attention of late: the "hollow corporation." This is a corporation that relies on arm's-length contract for almost all the activities it comprises, including fundamental technological activities like manufacturing.[43] The authors sensibly assert that, by relying on competitively available strategic resources, such a corporation is unlikely to survive long, since even its "core competencies" can be easily imitated. I would like to go a step further and suggest an even more abstractly organized form: *the non-corporation.* Without any central corporate governance at all, the Lancashire cotton textile industry of the nineteenth century performed all the functions that the Boston Associates in the United States performed within their Waltham and Lowell mills—and did so with greater success (Temin 1988). And the American microcomputer industry performs in a similarly headless fashion the functions that IBM, DEC, NEC and others have tried and failed to perform within a corporate structure. Perhaps these are variants of what Teece *et al.* call *network firms.* But perhaps another term for a network firm is a market.

---

[43]Teece *et al.* refer to such a firm as merely a "nexus of contracts." This is a meaning of the term different from that found in the transaction-cost literature. In authors like Cheung (1983), the term is taken to mean that all firms—even those with inimitable technological core competencies—are only nexuses of contracts. The contracts involved may be employment contracts or other long-term arrangements. But they are still just contracts.

References

Adelman, M. 1955. "Concept and statistical measurement of vertical integration." In *Business Concentration and Price Policy*. Princeton: Princeton University Press: 318-320.

Alchian, A., and Woodward, S. 1988. "The firm is dead; long live the firm: a review of Oiver E. Williamson's *The Economic Institutions of Capitalism*." *Journal of Economic Literature* 26(1): 65-79 (March).

Barney, J.B. 1991. "Firm resources and sustained competitive advantage." *Journal of Management* 17: 99-120.

Ben-Porath, Y. 1980. "The F-Connection: families, friends, and firms in the organization of exchange." *Population and Development Review* 6(1): 1-30.

Casson, M. 1982. *The entrepreneur: an economic theory*. Totowa, N.J.: Barnes and Noble Books.

Caves, R., Crookell, H., and Killing, P.J. 1983. "The imperfect market for technology licenses. *Oxford Bulletin of Economic Statistics* 45(3): 249-267.

Chandler, A.D., Jr. 1977. *The visible hand: the managerial revolution in American business*. Cambridge: The Belknap Press of Harvard University Press.

Cheung, S.N.S. 1983. "The contractual nature of the firm." *Journal of Law and Economics* 26: 386-405 (April).

Coase, R.H. 1937. "The nature of the firm. *Economica* (N.S.) 4: 386-405 (November).

Coase, R.H. 1988. "The nature of the firm: influence." *Journal of Law, Economics, and Organization* 4(1): 33-47 (Spring).

Cohen, W.M., and Levinthal, D.A. 1990. "Absorptive capacity: a new perspective on learning and innovation." *Administrative Science Quarterly* 35: 128-152.

Cottrell, T. 1994. "Fragmented standards and the development of Japan's microcomputer software industry." *Research Policy* 23(2): 143-174 (March).

Crozier, M. 1964. *The bureaucratic phenomenon*. Chicago: University of Chicago Press.

Currie, M., and Steedman, I. 1990. *Wrestling with time: problems in economic theory*. Ann Arbor: University of Michigan Press.

Dahlman, C. 1979. "The problem of externality." *Journal of Law and Economics* 22: 141-162.

Dahmén, E. 1971. *Entrepreneurial activity and the development of Swedish industry, 1919-1939*. Homewood, Ill.: Richard D. Irwin.

Demsetz, Harold. 1982. "Barriers to entry." *American Economic Review* 72(1): 47-57.

Dierickx, I., and Cool, K 1989. "Asset stock accumulation and sustainability of competitive advantage." *Management Science* 35(12): 1504-1511.

Egidi, M. 1992. "Organizational learning, problem solving, and the division of labor." In Herbert Simon *et al.*, eds., *Economics, Bounded Rationality, and the Cognitive Revolution.* Cheltenham: Edward Elgar.

Eliasson, G. 1990. "The firm as a competent team." *Journal of Economic Behavior and Organization* 13: 275-298.

Ferguson, C.H., and Morris, C.R. 1993. *Computer wars: how the west can win in a post-IBM world.* New York: Times Books.

Grossman, S., and Hart, O. 1986. "The costs and benefits of ownership: a theory of vertical integration." *Journal of Political Economy* 94: 691-719.

Hallwood, C.P. 1994. "An observation on the theory of the multinational firm." *Journal of Institutional and Theoretical Economics*, in press.

Hart, O.D. 1988. "Incomplete contracts and the theory of the firm." *Journal of Law, Economics, and Organization* 4(1): 119-140 (Spring).

Hart, O.D. 1989. "An economist's perspective on the theory of the firm." *Columbia Law Review* 89(7): 1757-1774.

Hayek, F.A. 1967. *Studies in philosophy, politics, and economics.* Chicago: University of Chicago Press.

Hirshleifer, J. 1971. "The private and social value of information and the reward to inventive activity." *American Economic Review* 61: 561-574.

Imai, K. 1990. Patterns of innovation and entrepreneurship in Japan." In Arnold Heertje and Mark Perlman, eds., *Evolving Technology and Market Structure.* Ann Arbor: University of Michigan Press: 187-201.

Jewkes, J. 1930. "Factors in industrial integration." *Quarterly Journal of Economics* 44: 633-635.

Kirzner, I. 1973. *Competition and entrepreneurship.* Chicago: University of Chicago Press.

Knight, F.H. 1921. *Risk, uncertainty, and profit.* Boston: Houghton Mifflin.

Kogut, B., and Zander, U. 1992. "Knowledge and the firm: combinative capabilities and the replication of technology." *Organizational Science* 3(3): 383-97 (August).

Langlois, R.N. 1983. "Systems theory, knowledge, and the social sciences." In Fritz Machlup and Úna Mansfield, eds., *The Study of Information: Interdisciplinary Messages.* New York: John Wiley: 581-600.

Langlois, R.N. 1984. "Internal organization in a dynamic context: some theoretical considerations." In M. Jussawalla and H. Ebenfield, eds., *Communication and Information Economics: New Perspectives.* Amsterdam: North-Holland: 23-49.

Langlois, R.N. 1986. "Rationality, institutions, and explanation." In R.N. Langlois, ed., *Economics as a Process: Essays in the New Institutional Economics.* New York: Cambridge University Press: 225-55.

Langlois, R.N. 1988. "Economic change and the boundaries of the firm." *Journal of Institutional and Theoretical Economics* 144(4): 635-657, reprinted in Bo Carlsson, ed., *Industrial Dynamics: Technological, Organizational, and Structural Changes in Industries and Firms.* Dordrecht: Kluwer Academic Publishers, 1989: 85-107.

Langlois, R.N. 1992a. "External economies and economic progress: the case of the microcomputer industry." *Business History Review* 66(1): 1-52 (Spring).

Langlois, R.N. 1992b. "Transaction-cost economics in real time." *Industrial and Corporate Change* 1(1): 99-127.

Langlois, R.N., and Cosgel, M.M.. 1993. "Frank Knight on risk, uncertainty, and the firm: a new interpretation." *Economic Inquiry* 31: 456-465 (July).

Langlois, R.N, and Robertson, P.L. 1989. "Explaining vertical integration: lessons from the American automobile industry." *Journal of Economic History* 49(2): 361-375 (June).

Langlois, R.N., and Robertson, P.L. 1992. "Networks and innovation in a modular system: lessons from the microcomputer and stereo component industries." *Research Policy* 21(4): 297-313.

Leff, N. 1978. "Industrial organization and entrepreneurship in the developing countries: the economic groups." *Economic Development and Cultural Change* 26(4): 661-675 (July).

Levinthal, D. 1992. "Surviving schumpeterian environments: an evolutionary perspective." *Industrial and Corporate Change* 1(3): 427-443.

Loasby, B.J. 1976. *Choice, complexity, and ignorance.* Cambridge: Cambridge University Press.

Loasby, B.J. 1989. "Knowledge and Organization: Marshall's Theory of Economic Progress and Coordination." In Loasby, *The Mind and Method of the Economist.* Cheltenham: Edward Elgar.

Loasby, B.J. 1990. "Firms, markets, and the principle of continuity." In J. K. Whitaker, ed., *Centenary Essays on Alfred Marshall.* Cambridge: Cambridge University Press.

Loasby, B.J. 1991. *Equilibrium and evolution: an exploration of connecting principles in economics.* Manchester: Manchester University Press.

Loasby, B.J. 1993a "The organisation of industry." Manuscript.

Loasby, B.J. 1993b. "Understanding markets." Manuscript.

Loasby, B.J. 1994. "Organisational capabilities and interfirm relations" *Metroeconomica,* forthcoming.

Mahoney, J.T., and Pandian, J.R. 1992. "The resource-based view within the conversation of strategic management." *Strategic Management Journal* 13(5): 363-380 (June).

Marshall, Alfred. 1919. *Industry and trade.* London: Macmillan.

Minkler, A.P. 1993. "Knowledge and internal organization." *Journal of Economic Behavior and Organization* 21: 17-30.

Moore, J. 1992. "The firm as a collection of assets." *European Economic Review* 36: 493-507.

Penrose, E.T. 1959. *The theory of the growth of the firm.* Oxford: Basil Blackwell.

Pound, A. 1934. *The turning wheel: the story of general motors through twenty-five years, 1908-1933.* Garden City: Doubleday, Doran.

Putterman, L. 1988. "The firm as association versus the firm as commodity: efficiency, rights, and ownership." *Economics and Philosophy* 4(2): 243-66 (October).

Richardson, G.B. 1972. "The organisation of industry." *Economic Journal* 82: 883-96.

Rosenberg, N. 1976. *Perspectives on technology.* New York: Cambridge University Press.

Rumelt, R.P. 1984. "Towards a strategic theory of the firm." In Robert Boyden Lamb, (ed.), *Competitive Strategic Management.* Englewood Cliffs: Prentice-Hall.

Rumelt, R.P. 1987. "Theory, strategy, and entrepreneurship." In David J. Teece, (ed.), *The Competitive Challenge: Strategies for Industrial Innovation and Renewal.* Cambridge: Ballinger.

Schumpeter, J.A. 1934: *The theory of economic development.* Cambridge: Harvard University Press.

Silver, M. 1984. *Enterprise and the scope of the firm.* London: Martin Robertson.

Stinchcombe, A.L. 1990. *Information and organizations.* Berkeley: University of California Press.

Teece, D.J. 1980. "Economies of scope and the scope of the enterprise." *Journal of Economic Behavior and Organization* 1(3): 223-247.

Teece, D.J. 1982. "Towards an economic theory of the multiproduct firm." *Journal of Economic Behavior and Organization* 3(1): 39-63.

Teece, D.J. 1986. "Profiting from technological innovation: implications for integration, collaboration, licensing, and public policy." *Research Policy* 15: 285-305.

Teece, D.J., Rumelt, R.P., Dosi, G., and Winter, S.G. 1994. "Understanding Corporate Coherence: Theory and Evidence." *Journal of Economic Behavior and Organization* 23: 1-30.

Temin, P. 1988. "Product quality and vertical integration in the early cotton textile industry." *Journal of Economic History* 48: 891-907 (December).

Wernerfelt, B. 1984. "A resource-based view of the firm." *Strategic Management Journal* 5: 171-180.

Williamson, O.E. 1985. *The economic institutions of capitalism.* New York: The Free Press.

Williamson, O.E. 1988. "Technology and transaction cost economics: a reply." *Journal of Economic Behavior and Organization* 10: 355-363.

Williamson, O.E. 1991. "Comparative economic organization: the analysis of discrete structural alternatives." *Administrative Science Quarterly* 36: 269-296.

Winter, S.G. 1988. "On coase, competence, and the corporation." *Journal of Law, Economics, and Organization* 4(1): 163-180 (Spring).

5

INERTIA AND TRANSFORMATION

Richard P. Rumelt[1]
INSEAD

In this article I argue that strategy scholars have incorrectly borrowed from economists the assumption of organizational plasticity. Particularly in large firms, inertia, rather than plasticity, is the norm. Unfortunately, there can be no simple theory of inertia as its causes are multiple and varied. After sketching out the shapes of the most important sources of inertia, I turn to the problem of overcoming inertia—the question of organizational transformation. Starting with a simple model of organizational capabilities as existing on two levels (unit-based and rooted in coordination among units), I draw some preliminary conclusions about the shape of organizational transformation. In particular, I focus on the interplay between incentive intensity and coordinative capacity and argue that most transformations move through a sequence of phases in which coordinative capacity is first dramatically reduced and then rebuilt along new lines.

Introduction

Roughly fifteen years ago the field of business and corporate strategy began to incorporate economic reasoning into its research program.

[1]Financial support from INSEAD's Corporate Renewal Initiative (CORE) is gratefully acknowledged. My understanding of the issues surrounding corporate transformation has benefitted from discussions with Sumantra Ghoshal, Chris Bartlett, and John Stopford.

The first step was the adoption of traditional industrial organization economics, with its emphasis on barriers to entry and collusive reductions in rivalry (Porter 1980). Subsequently, strategy researchers developed what is now called the resource-based view of the firm.[2] This theory sees firms as collections of resources and sees performance differences as largely reflecting differences in resource quality. Whereas traditional industrial organization saw high profits as stemming from collusive reductions in competition or strategies of entry deterrence, the resource-based view sees high profits as the rents accruing to specialized and difficult-to-replicate or non-imitable resources.

Thus, today strategy researchers work with a complex amalgam of economic and quasi-economic reasoning. We envision the firm as striving to maximize value, but also see it as working with factors of production that are far from mobile, as dealing with ambiguous production functions, and as possessing or controlling collections of tacit knowledge and externally held attributions (reputation) that evolve over time in response to investment, activity and imitation.

It is useful to note that this new view has not been developed by "applying" economics to strategy. Rather, it has been accomplished by carefully identifying the assumptions within received economic models that prevented or ruled out strategic phenomena, and by then analyzing the situations created by altered assumptions. In particular, a central dogma of neoclassical microtheory, especially that part associated with traditional industrial organization, was the basic homogeneity of firms within industries (but for scale). Differences in performance were thus attributed to differences in scale or its collective equivalent, concentration. By contrast, the resource-based view has as its central dogma the heterogeneity of firms induced by heterogeneous resources.

The power behind this research stream has, in large measure, come from the clarity and strength of the theory (neoclassical microeconomics) which it attacks. In fact, the neoclassical model maintained such a grip on the minds of economists that they often spoke of its failures as "market failures," as if it were somehow the responsibility of reality to live up to theory rather than the theorist's responsibility to describe reality.

---

[2]Early contributions were made by Lippman and Rumelt (1982), Teece (1982), Wernerfelt (1984), Rumelt (1984), Porter (1985) (who made the "activity" the central element of his revised view), and Barney (1986). Reviews of the topic are provided by Conner (1991) and Grant (1991).

One problem with this research strategy is that the foil, neoclassical microtheory, has died. Game theory now provides the basis for reasoning in industrial organization economics; agency theory provides explanations for non-optimal firm behavior, and transaction-cost economics describes the limits of markets in carrying out coordination and exchange. One might argue that this is fine—the resource-based view together with revived microtheory is the strategic theory of the firm. However, I believe that despite the flowering of this rich new microtheory, we have dealt with only one part of the story. There are a number of erroneous assumptions that most economically-oriented strategy researchers continue to borrow from economics. At this moment those that are clearest are plasticity, rationality of collective action, and homogeneity of beliefs. I believe that the most important of these is plasticity—the assumption that firms readily respond to exogenous shocks and changes in competitive conditions. The centerpiece of microeconomics is the deduction of the total economy's autonomous responsiveness (mediated by self-interest) to changes in prices, technology, taxes, etc. Yet the truth is that firms change only with difficulty. Changing strategy and the structural forms and administrative procedures that undergird strategy is difficult, costly, risky, and time consuming.

I shall call this lack of plasticity *inertia*. Inertia is the strong persistence of existing form and function. If the form is efficient, inertia is costless and arguably beneficial. However, if the firm's form or practices are inefficient, inertia is a problem. Indeed, the most direct evidence of inertia is the persistence of inefficient forms and practices.[3]

A widely cited example of organizational inertia is General Motors. Once the world leader in automobile production efficiency, General Motors was eclipsed in this regard by leading Japanese manufacturers during the 1970s. Senior management understood the nature of the productivity gap by 1979, yet, despite a joint venture with Toyota in which world-class methods were used, the company has been unable to change its overall productivity in any substantial way. In fact, many GM plants became less productive during the 1980s, while Chrysler and Ford made broad and significant gains. Clearly, the basic problem facing the senior management

---

[3]One research stream in economics labels persistent inefficiency in the use of inputs as "X-inefficiency," in contrast to the more commonly understood problem of allocative inefficiency. For a survey of this literature as well as empirical estimates of the amount of X- inefficiency see Frantz (1988)].

of General Motors is not product-market strategy, but organizational change. Their challenge is not really competition, but their company's own inertia.

The fact of organizational inertia is not simply an "implementation" problem. If firms lack plasticity then the formulation of product-market and corporate strategy is itself fundamentally altered:

• Good product-market strategy must take into account a firm's inertia and not create new inertia without sufficient reason.

• The important strategy problem facing a firm may well be internal inertia rather than product-market conditions.

• Leaving inertia out of an analysis underestimates, perhaps drastically, the payoff to strategic change and innovation. Modern economic analysis of strategy presumes alert responsive competitors who will compete away a firm's profits unless there are the protections afforded by property rights, reputation, tacit know-how, or other strategic resources and isolating mechanisms. But if competitors are subject to inertia, this analysis is incorrect. Some of the great strategic success stories are due as much to the (temporary) inertia of competitors as to the cleverness of the innovator (e.g., Timex, Federal Express).

A basic question motivating much of the research into the resource-based point of view was "Why are firms different?" The question I suggest requires equal attention is "What are the sources of organizational inertia?" Or, "Why is change so difficult?"

Inertia and Evolution

The inertia of firms is a dominant theme in two fields loosely coupled with strategy: organizational ecology and evolutionary economics. Main-line organizational ecology assumes that firms are immutable (once born) and that populations of firms change over time through processes of birth, selection, and death. In evolutionary economics there is the additional theme that firms change, though not always adaptively, as occasional innovation and trial-and-error processes affect their work-routines and policies.

Within organization ecology, Hannan and Freeman (1984) define inertia as change that is slow relative to the environment, so that a firm that is considered flexible in one setting might still have too much inertia to compete in a still faster-changing industry. Hannan and Freeman argue that much inertia is the unavoidable consequence of specialized investment in physical assets and social structures. In particular, they argue that these specialized investments meet the organizations need for reliability and accountability—the need to repeatedly produce the same type of product or process and the need to justify and explain process and choice to outsiders. They identify reproducibility with institutionalization, which gives "an organization a taken-for-granted character such that members do not continually question organizational purposes, authority, relations, etc." (1984:154). Hannan and Freeman follow other sociologists in arguing that organizations have "cores" which are very difficult to change relative to more peripheral elements. The four core elements they identify are: stated goals, the form of authority, the basic technology, and the marketing strategy.

Within evolutionary economics the explanation for inertia is rooted in bounded rationality, routines, and tacitness. Nelson and Winter (1982) argue that the skills and capabilities of organizations are bound up in their routines for accomplishing tasks. These routines, and the fact that they are routine, constitute the skill set and the memory of the firm. Within this framework, inertia is the natural state of affairs—firms can only do what they have routines for doing. Lacking a routine for a new task, the new task does not really get done.

These perspectives are both helpful in understanding inertia. However, neither attempts to be comprehensive or analytic. In the next sections I begin to build a framework that attempts to encompass a broader managerial view of inertia and begins to allow analysis of the constellation of inertial forces at work in different situations.

The Five Frictions

With a nod to Michael Porter, I have organized the main sources of inertia into five groups, called the five frictions:

• Distorted Perception

• Dulled Motivation

• Failed Creative Response

• Political Deadlocks

• Action Disconnects

In many cases, the components of these frictions are well known or easily comprehended. In other cases the issues are novel or subtle. I shall pass swiftly over many the straightforward issues in order to concentrate on those that are novel or complex.

Distorted perception

Change begins with perception. If perception is distorted, then change may be impeded. The fundamental sources of perceptual distortion inducing organizational inertia are: myopia, hubris and denial, and grooved thinking.

Myopia. A firm suffering from myopia is unable to look into the future with clarity. Various individuals within the firm may be aware of the future consequences of current action or inaction, but the organization, taken as a whole, acts as if only the short-term matters.

The simplest source of myopia is turnover. If a manager expects to move to another firm in the near future, the weight placed on future profits is diminished. Suppose, for example, that the natural annual discount rate is r, that a manager believes the chance of leaving in any given month is constant (i.e., an exponential departure time) and believes the expected time to departure to be τ years. Then the manager's effective discount rate[4] for decision-making is $r+1/\tau$. Thus, the 20 percent annual turnover in managers experienced during the halcyon years of Silicon Valley may have increased the effective discount rates used in decision-making from a normal 15 percent to 35 percent.

---

[4]This analysis assumes no ex-post settling up. That is, when leaving the firm the manager escapes the future negative consequences of myopic decisions.

106

Myopia is to be expected in a firm that has employed high-intensity short-term controls. In such a case individuals bias their allocations of attention and effort toward problems that effect current performance. Less obvious is the fact that myopia is characteristic of a firm which is "forgetful." That is, when individuals do not expect the organization to remember the connections between current actions and future results. In forgetful firms, characterized by mergers, reorganizations, frequent personnel changes, etc., individuals have no realistic expectation that future results will be attributed to their current actions or decisions.

When managers are myopic, the subtle consequence is that senior management will also behave myopically, expressing a rational disbelief in the claims of future threat or opportunity expressed by lower level managers. Thus the expectation of myopia in others leads, in turn, to further myopic behavior.

A final source may be the failure of planning systems to counteract normal human myopia. Empirical evidence suggests that people's time-discount functions are steeper-than-exponential, leading to time-inconsistent behavior.[5] Well-functioning organizational systems, it may be argued, help counteract short-term impulsiveness. And, by contrast, poorly functioning planning and review systems fail in this regard, fostering organizational myopia.

Hubris and denial. A serious source of perceptual distortion is denial—the rejection of information that is contrary to what is desired or what is believed to be true. Denial may stem from hubris—overweening pride in past accomplishments—or it may derive from fear. In his work on barriers to organizational learning, Argyris (1990) has argued that a virtually universal organizational response to information or analysis which threaten a loss of face is *defensive behavior*: denial of the validity of the data, cover-up of the situation, and cover-up of the cover-up. For example, for years the senior management of General Motors refused to admit that Japanese firms had higher absolute levels of productivity, denying the existence of the problem. In part, management could not believe that another company knew more about producing cars than did GM (hubris), and in part it was less embarrassing to believe other theories about the rising tide of imports.

Hubris is also explainable as *superstitious learning*—learning based on associating past success with factors that were coincidental with it but

---

[5]See Postrel and Rumelt (1992) for a full discussion.

bear no causal relationship to the success. Skinner (1948) showed that when pigeons receive random reinforcements (feedings), they become conditioned to repeat some behavior that is accidentally correlated with the stimulus. Similarly, managers in highly uncertain environments (e.g., the entertainment industry) may cling steadfastly to policies that were only accidentally correlated with some past success.

A related syndrome is information filtering—the selective rejection of information that is unpopular, unpleasant, or contrary to doctrine. During the Vietnam war, for example, U.S. commanders defined the conflict as a war of attrition which was being won over time and systematically withheld from Washington information which contradicted their vision (Sheehan 1988).

Grooved thinking. Janus (1972) has described as "groupthink" the restricted thinking that groups impose, punishing or rejecting ideas and information that deviate too much from orthodoxy. A somewhat different perspective is provided by Margolis (1993) who views patterns of thinking as mental habits whose structure and function are the same as physical habits. Finally, a third type of grooved thinking comes from the use of the "wrong" metaphor. Just as policy makers may struggle to decide whether the situation in Bosnia is "another Kuwait" or "another Vietnam," a metaphor, once accepted, acts as a powerful restriction on future thought.

Dulled motivation

Even if perception is accurate, organizations may resist change because the need is not felt with sufficient sharpness. The lack of sufficient motivation may be rational, or it may reflect agency or psychological problems. The most important motivational dampers are: direct costs of change, cannibalization costs, and cross-subsidy comforts.

Direct costs of change. It is likely that change temporarily increases the risk of organizational failure (mortality), disrupts operations, and involves a great deal of expensive effort. Even more importantly, change may imply the abandonment of costly sunk specific investments. If these considerations apply to the firm as a whole, they are rational impediments to change. Applied to individuals or groups, they point to agency problems.

Note that an impediment to change may be rational. When Timex created the disposable watch, there were no imitators for ten years. Some of the inertia was surely wasteful, but some may have been rational. Were a quality Swiss manufacturer to produce disposable watches it would risk damage to its reputation. Similarly, whereas firms making new investments may be able to justify an expensive new technology, a firm with adequate though less efficient capacity may not be able to economically justify switching to the newer technology.

Cannibalization costs. When a new product's success eats into the sales and profits of an older product, the older product is said to have been cannibalized. Cannibalization problems may be rational or simply reflect sub-group interests. Rational cannibalization problems occur under conditions of buyer loyalty (or switching costs). Loyal buyers will stay with a firm's old product despite competitors' introductions of new versions, but will switch to the new version when offered by the firm they favor.

This asymmetry in buyer response, when coupled with the fact of lower profits on the newer products, can induce a firm to exploit its buyers' loyalties by withholding introduction of the new product. For example, when interest rates rose sharply in the late 1970s, many banks and S&Ls began to offer new money-market accounts and other innovative services. However, those institutions with the largest volume of savings account deposits (paying 5 percent interest when market rates were 17 percent) were least likely to market the new products. They did, of course, lose some customers to other banks. But they also reasoned that they would lose even more savings account customers were they to market the new products heavily themselves—the new products would cannibalize the very high profits being earned on the old products.

Cross subsidy comforts. The motivation to change is inhibited when a problem business is subsidized by rents from another business. The subsidy may be direct, in the form of management's toleration of losses in a business that is compensated for by gains elsewhere. Or, it may be indirect, obtained through artificial transfer prices or through bundling businesses together so that separate measures are not obtained.

Failed creative response

If perception is acute and motivation sharp, change may still be blocked by other forces. In particular, it may be difficult for the organization to choose a direction out of its difficulties. The impediment may be in the analysis of the situation or in choice itself. The major categories of friction in this area are: speed and complexity, reactive mind-set, and inadequate strategic vision.

Speed and complexity. In the 1970s John Boyd, a captain in the U.S. Air Force, concluded a study of why U.S. aviators had been so successful in air combat in Korea.[6] He found that although the MiG-15 was faster, quicker in the turn, and could climb faster than the U.S. F-86, the critical factor was that the F-86 provided better visibility and faster control. Thus the U.S. pilot could remain a step ahead, maintaining the initiative. Most importantly, Boyd found that once the MiG pilot found himself outmaneuvered, he froze or panicked.

Analysis is blocked or frozen when things happen too fast. If a competitor can go around the "Boyd loop" of observation, orientation, decision, and action faster than an opponent, the opponent may not simply struggle along, he may freeze-up or collapse. The "Boyd loop" phenomena is one form of what is known to everyone as "having the initiative" in a game.

When the decision situation is very complex, there may also be a similar blockage. For example, U.S. firms all dropped out of the liquid crystal flat-screen technology race when Japanese firms jumped too far ahead. The pace of events overtook their resource allocation systems and the complexity of the judgments to be made exacerbated the situation.

Reactive mind-set. Change is inhibited when people adhere to the view that their problems are natural and inevitable. The most common reactive mind-sets are that the industry is "mature" that the problems are industry problems and not the fault of the firm. These points of view have great validity behind them—the weight of expert advice and analysis. They are also self-fulfilling. If all competitors define their market as mature they will surely be correct.

Senior management may also be stuck in a reactive mind-set if they possess too little detailed understanding of the business to take a proactive creative stance. Entrepreneurial creativity requires a closeness to issues of commerce, technology, and/or buyer behavior that may be lacking in a senior management group that came to power in a different era or who have backgrounds unconnected to current business issues.

Inadequate strategic vision. Even when analysis and choice have not been blocked, the direction chosen and especially its articulation may be so flawed that change is blocked. Vision (direction) also may be inadequate because it is hypocritical. Hypocritical vision is dishonest, claiming values and goals that are known to be false. Announcing "We are a community ..." is a lie for a firm that is about to lay off one-third of its

---

[6]See Fallows (1981) and Smith (1985). Thompson (1992) provides a business-oriented interpretation.

workforce.   Managers know when goals of "quality" or of being "ecologically sound" are hypocritical and cannot help but treat the rest of the vision with cynicism.

Vision can be inadequate because it is unresponsive to the clear challenges facing the firm.   An unresponsive vision can hardly inspire commitment and change.   Finally, vision can be ineffective because there is no trust in senior management's commitment to the vision.   If people believe that this "vision" is simply today's plan, only to be replaced by another tomorrow, there will be no willing followers.   If managers are to commit their energy, careers, time, and attention to a program of change, there must be trust that the direction chosen will not be lightly altered.   Here we touch the central paradox that change may require the promise of future inertia.

Political deadlocks

Politics, especially organizational politics, is frequently seen as somehow tainted or improper.   But politics is simply about influence on decisions and is absent only in absolute dictatorships.   The three main sources of disagreement among men are differences in personal interest, differences in belief, and differences in fundamental values.   These are also the underlying themes of the three types of political deadlocks: departmental politics, incommensurable beliefs, and vested values.

Departmental politics.   This is one of the most obvious sources of inertia and little more need be said.   Managers rarely act to unseat themselves or to terminate their own departments.   Yet change inevitably involves winners and losers;   some people and departments will gain resources and prestige and others will be lessened.   Change will be fought by those who will clearly lose thereby and departmental wrangling over who will win and lose can slow change to a crawl.

Incommensurable beliefs.   More interesting than the politics of self interest is the problem that arises when different individuals or groups hold sincere but differing beliefs about the nature of the problem or its solution. Figure 1 illustrates the classic Condorcet paradox.   Here three managers face three alternatives (downsize, merge, and R&D), and each ranks the three differently.   The problem here is that the group's preferences are intransitive.   If any of the three alternatives is taken to be the status quo, there is always an alternative preferred to it by a 2-to-1 majority.   Here "R&D" beats "downsize," "merge" beats "R&D," and "downsize" beats "merge."   There is no stable resting place among the cyclic preference mix.

111

	Manager		
	John	**Jan**	**Jon**
Downsize	1	2	3
Merge	2	3	1
R&D	3	1	2

Figure 1 Condorcet Preferences

This sort of problem in aggregating individual preferences led Arrow (1963) to his *Impossibility Theorem* and has inspired a stream of related work. It all points to the fact that traditional concepts of "public interest" or the "organization's goals" are empty of rigorous meaning unless there is uniformity of opinion.

What happens when these managers are asked to reach a "consensus?" Modern political theory establishes that here (and in general) there is no "rational" outcome, and that any of the outcomes can be obtained by manipulation of the agenda.[7] My belief is that there are four basic patterns that can emerge. First, a leader may simply impose a decision, eliminating the illusion of group choice. Secondly, the choice process may cycle for some time without generating an outcome. Thirdly, the managers may recognize the "irrationality" of the situation and withdraw from participation (essentially colluding to avoid choice). Finally, other considerations or "games" may change the relative influence the managers have, resolving the paradox.

When managers disagree, there is no "rational" way to combine their beliefs. If speed is mportant, leadership may have to abandon group decision processes. When process is important, and beliefs differ, inertia may well be the outcome.

Vested values. The third source of political deadlock is the presence of vested values. Unlike the cases of differing interests or beliefs, here individuals and departments are taken to have strong emotional or

---

[7]The McKelvey (1976) *Chaos Theorem* established that absent a clearly dominant policy, a group using majority-rule voting can be led to *any* outcome by a sufficiently clever manipulation of the agenda.

value attachments to products, policies, or ways of doing things. These vested values and interests can easily be the greatest impediments to change.

For many years a central concept in the strategy field was the experience curve—the idea that the cost of doing something falls as cumulative experience (production) increases. By analogy, I suggest that there is a vested value "curve": the more one does a task the more one sees value in that activity. I am careful not to say one "likes" the activity, for that is another issue.[8]

The psychology of vested value is dissonance reduction—the repetition of something difficult makes sense if it is valued. If one has been rewarded for doing the task, it will not only be valued, but liked as well.

Vested values lie at the heart of institutions. The defenders of vested values are usually the informal leadership network—the defenders of the society and of its norms. The paradox of change is that these same people, perhaps the best and the brightest, easily become the source of inertia. The problem of vested values is not with simple foot dragging, but with the organizational equivalent of patriotism.

Action disconnects

The fifth source of friction concerns those forces which prevent action. Even if perception has been sound, analysis and choice have proceeded, and the problems of politics overcome, there may still be no change. The basic reasons for action blockades and disconnects are: leadership inaction, embedded routines, collective action problems, and capabilities gaps.

Leadership inaction. For change to begin, the leadership must articulate a vision for change, must alter incentives, must take direct action where possible, and must shift power. If it fails to do these things, change will be inhibited. The need for direct action is particularly worth emphasizing. The concept of leadership comes from the military notion of being "in front," of providing courage and energy by example. In business, the analog is for the senior management group to lead by example. If a new emphasis on service is the centerpiece of the strategy, and the marketing manager keeps on an old friend, the head of market research, despite a wide

---

[8]Many Marines value boot camp without liking it.

reputation for providing bad service to the product groups, there has been a failure of leadership by example.

Leadership may also fail to act because of its attachment to the status quo. In business, radical change in strategy or structure rarely happens without a change in leadership. Leaders may inaugurate change, but that change itself then becomes the new status quo.

Leadership is committed to the status quo for several reasons. The first is simple ego-involvement. If the current leaders were the architects of the status quo, then they will feel a special attachment to it as well as having a deep appreciation for its (original) functionality. The second reason is that the status quo is known whereas new structures and strategies are not. As Burke pointed out in his critique of the French revolution, new and as yet untried systems generally have terrible and as yet unimagined flaws. The third and most subtle reason is that leadership, by its nature, involves commitment. The leadership of an organization must be the guarantor of explicit contracts, both internal and external. In particular, organizational members give energy and their own commitment to broad goals only to the extent that they perceive that the leadership itself has made a strong commitment to a particular set of priorities and ways of doing things. Major change requires a leader to repudiate prior commitments, thus lessening his or her ability to lead in the future. Hence, entrenched leadership is normally a source of inertia.

Embedded routines. The life functions of a business are its processes—its ways of doing things. Complex processes possess great inertia. The knowledge of how certain steps are performed may be tacit, no one may have a complete understanding of the process, and changing one aspect of a process may have significant unanticipated consequences on other parts of the organization. Finally, the various routines that make up the process take on the force of habit. From a purely economics perspective, organizational change only requires a change in incentives. However, the habitual patterns of work have an inertial force that can be much stronger than any practical incentives.

Process inertia arises not only through the attraction of the habitual, but also because change may mean doing things for which the organization has no process experience. If change simply requires substituting one known process for another, things are relatively straightforward. But taking the organization beyond its repertoire of routines is difficult. In general, one cannot ask an organization to do something which has not been reduced to a routine. If novel routines are required, then macro-routines for creating novelty, with all their slowness and cost, are required.

114

Collective action problems. Action can be blocked by a variety of collective action problems. The simplest is the first mover problem: if senior management has called for new initiatives, does it pay to be a first-mover? In many situations the incentives are clearly in favor of waiting to see how the first mover does. In such cases, the equilibrium is for no one to move at all. There are also analogous problems of free-riders that inhibit change even when first-movers have led the way.

The more complex collective action problem is that best described as *cultural.*[9] A dysfunctional culture may block change and itself be virtually impervious to alteration. Consider, for example, the simple question of cooperation (coordination) versus competition among departments. As a step towards a model, suppose that individuals in an organization meet in pairs and must each decide whether to cooperate (**C**) or compete (**X**). Each individual has information that the other does not and each controls some resources that the other does not. Cooperation means trying to act for the good of the company as a whole. In particular, it means making claims on the other person's resources that are justified by one's private information and accepting the other person's claims on one's own resources as valid. Competition means trying to act (covertly) for the good of the local unit. Concessions from the other are sought that will benefit one's own unit.

To make the game more concrete, example payoffs are shown in Figure 2. The net payoffs to each player are symmetric and are simply weighted averages of the local and corporate payoffs. Figure 3 shows that if enough weight is placed on corporate payoffs, the equilibrium in the simple single-meeting game is **C**. If local payoffs dominate, the equilibrium is **X**. At intermediate levels of weighting, there are two pure-strategy equilibria: **C** and **X**. That is, there are two possible cultures and theory has little more to say about which will exist.

---

[9]For a good discussion of the fundamental concept, see Ouchi and Wilkins (1985). For a technical view of the behavioral preconditions to social exchange, see Elster (1989).

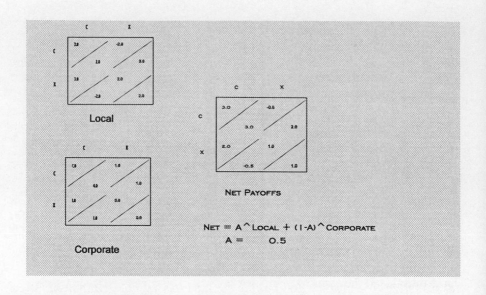

Figure 2 Payoffs in Cooperate vs. Compete Game

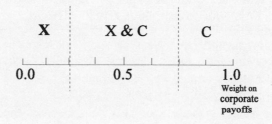

Figure 3 Equilibria vs. Payoff Weighting

Suppose a firm had, over time, developed a culture having equilibrium **X**. How might management move it to **C**?[10] If a charismatic leader were able to convince the group that it was truly at **C**, then the equilibrium would indeed change.[11] Another strategy is to break off a small unit of the organization and focus resources and attention on changing its culture. Then, the old organization can be slowly recombined with the new culture in such a way as to preserve the new rather than overwhelm it with the old. A third strategy would be to merge with a firm having culture **C** and hope that the combination tilts in the right direction.

Because culture depends on mutual expectations, it is not easily changed. A culture that resists change or that does not fit the direction the firm needs to take can be an insurmountable source of inertia.

Capabilities gaps. The final action blockade is simply a gap or disconnect between the tasks that need to be performed and the competencies and capabilities within the firm. Prahalad and Hamel (1990) have introduced the term "stretch" for the sense of tension between reality and aspiration, and have argued that healthy organizations are in a constant state of stretch. But too great a gap is discouraging and is more likely to inhibit than induce change.

The Process of Transformation

Transformation is the process of engendering a fundamental change in an organization with the goal of achieving to a dramatic improvement in performance. The fundamental change may involve strategic redirection, but always includes structural change and a dramatic alteration in the behavior of individuals. Transformation always involves overcoming large amounts of organizational inertia.

In certain exceptional cases inertia is greatly reduced by the existence of an already proven major invention or strategic innovation. Because the new business provides the motivation and the resources for change it takes the sting out of having to abandon old ways for new. Nourished by a steady stream of entrepreneurial rent, new structures and roles can flourish and develop as energy and attention are naturally drawn from mature or declining areas to the new richer terrain. Thus, for example,

---

[10]Assume incentives are not sufficient and complete monitoring is not feasible.

[11]In this case one should play **C** if one believes that at least 60 percent of the others are playing **C**.

Intel's shift away from being a "memory chip" company was greatly facilitated by the fact that its microprocessor business was profitable and growing rapidly. Top management had only to coordinate the reallocation of resources from the old to the new business (Burgelman 1991).

Absent an innovation in hand, transformation contexts can be usefully divided into those in which operating efficiency is primary and those in which the adroit utilization or reallocation of resources is primary. Figure 4 is a guide to these contexts. The horizontal axis (capability) measures the relative efficiency of the firm at performing its tasks. The vertical axis (fit) measures the adequacy of those tasks in meeting product-market demands. The ideal firm is both capable and fit (adapted).

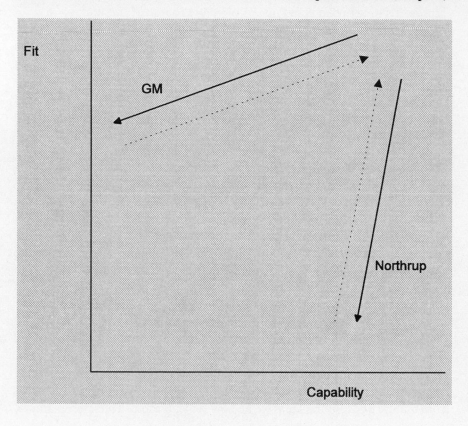

Figure 4 Change Contests

Corresponding to these two change contexts are two transformation tasks: recovery and renewal. Put simply, *recovery* is the process of regaining lost (relative) efficiency whereas *renewal* is the process of developing new skills and resources or of discovering new uses for extinct skills and resources.

Recovery is regaining efficiencies and skills that the firm used to have or would now possess if it had followed the evolution of the industry leaders. Firms requiring recovery have been literally frozen in time by organizational inertia, failing to increase their efficiency as fast as the leaders. In some cases efficiency will have suffered an absolute decline. The rents financing such significant inefficiencies are the fruits of past strategic victories. A product patent may generate the rents that permit a company to live with sloppy manufacturing methods while close competitors are forced to improve their methods to survive in their unprotected markets. Or a company may enjoy a strong enough reputation with buyers, or be protected by large buyer switching costs, that it can survive years of declining efficiency, quality, and innovation.

The recent problems at General Motors, one could argue, stem from a decline in relative capability. The basic strategy of the firm, its overall product line, its distribution system, its essential product-technology, are not the problem. Thus, GM is a case of decline in capability rather than fit and the problems of inertia it faces are those associated with developing and learning new or improved capabilities. Its transformation challenge is therefore one of recovery.

By contrast, IBM remains a capable manufacturer of main-frame computers. Its recent problems arise from the growing lack of fit between its capabilities and the environment. Market demands are less for main-frames and more for very inexpensive PCs networked into work-groups.[12] IBM's fit with this new world is poor. Thus, the inertial problems IBM faces are quite different from those facing GM. Its management must deal with moving resources away from activities that are clearly being done well (on a technical basis) and which are valued for having been the wellsprings of the firm's past success. The transformation challenge faced by IBM is primarily one of renewal.

---

[12]Another firm clearly in this position is Northrop, the maker of the Stealth Bomber. Its capabilities at its historic mission are superb, but the mission appears to be obsolete.

In order to discuss the specifics of transformation it is necessary to have a view as to the structure of a firm's competencies. The general viewpoint adopted here is that competencies are hierarchical in structure and exist in *layers*, the existence of a higher layer being dependent upon competent execution of lower layers.

An analogy to human skills may be helpful. Consider the performance of a helicopter pilot. The most fundamental skills (layer 1) are visual (sharpness, field of view, depth perception, etc.), basic motor coordination, and kinesthetic sense. Given layer 1 skills, the beginning pilot can learn specific tasks—taking off, landing, level flight, hovering, turning, and so on—that qualify as layer 2 skills. Given layer 2 skills, the pilot begins to integrate them into a fully coordinated competence at flying, where lower-level routines are called on unconsciously as needed and smoothly integrated. A layer 3 competent pilot will still need to work to accomplish layer 4—flying in close formation with other helicopters.[13] Clearly, layer 3 skills must be considerable and automatically available if layer 4 is to be attained. And the hierarchy continues—formation flying in bad weather, under combat conditions, etc.

Returning to the firm, one could obviously define skills in layer 1 as being basic manufacturing operations, selling activities, etc. Layer 2 might then be defined as the coordination of these skills into a coherent business. Layer 3 would then be the coordination among related businesses and layer 4 the adaptation of this pattern to local conditions throughout the world.

Whatever the complexity of reality in particular situations, the basic arguments I wish to advance can be made with a simple two-layer model. The model has the following characteristics:

1.   Work performed by departments varies along four dimensions: task, method, waste, and routinization.

   a. Task is the production process being done—making plastic cups versus making paper cups. Major changes in strategy normally imply redesigned portfolios of tasks.

---

[13]In Vietnam U.S. pilots flew formations so tight that the rotors overlapped.

b. Method is the efficiency of the practices used to accomplish the task. A department's methods may be woefully inefficient or they may be state-of-the-art.

c. Waste is the level of inefficiency, *given* the task and method. It represents the degree to which people work honestly and diligently and the degree to which supervision facilitates and encourages good work.

d. Routinization is the degree to which the work has been practiced and can be smoothly performed. Note that poor methods and waste can nevertheless be accompanied by smoothly functioning routine.

2. Coordination skills (level 2) can only be developed when level 1 skills are routinized.

3. Coordination skills are specialized to the tasks and methods used by individual departments.

4. Individual departmental performance is measurable with much less error than individual contributions to coordinative activity. Level 1 department performance can be measured, compared across departments, benchmarked with comparable departments in other firms, and subjected to causal analyses. The overall effectiveness of Level 2 coordination can be measured (with error), but it is extremely difficult to assess the contributions of individual departments to the whole.

5. Coordination is costly to departments. It is work and it results in some degree of *de*specialization.

With regard to element 5, it is worth emphasizing that coordination is not costly just because it is work, but also because it interferes with routine. The most fundamental economic proposition about organization is the existence of gains to specialization. If there are gains to specialization, it means that it is most efficient for a department to concentrate on one task rather than spread its efforts among two or more tasks. So, to the extent that there are gains to specialization, there must be concomitant costs to coordination due to the despecialization it requires.[14]

Element 4 is a reminder that coordination is team production and that it is notoriously difficult to measure the individual contributions to team output. If monitoring of individual contributions is weak or inaccurate, then items 4 and 5 taken together create an incentive for free-riding by departments—rather than work at coordination they may simply stick to their knitting. To make more precise the idea that departmental work and coordinative work compete for a department manager's time and energy, the following conjecture is offered:

Conjecture 1   *Increases (decreases) in departmental incentive intensity reduce (increase) coordinative activity.*

Appendix A provides a demonstration of this conjecture in a simple setting.

The negative relationship between incentive intensity and coordinative activity is illustrated in **Figure 5**. As the requirement for coordination rises, the intensity of department incentives must be reduced. Conversely, reductions in the requirement for coordination permit increases in local department incentives. As the requirements for coordination drop below some critical level, say C_0, organizational governance is replaced by market governance and arm's-length transactions take place. Of course, the idea of a sharp dividing line is a gross simplification—some market relationships exist with fairly large levels of coordination, aided by bilateral dependence and repeated experience, and some interorganizational relationships have the sharp incentives and impersonality ordinarily ascribed to market transactions.

---

[14]For example, coordinating manufacturing to customer needs may mean interrupting production runs, using more set-ups, and increasing the variety of materials that must be carried in inventory. Of course it still may be optimal to bear these costs due to the extra value obtained through coordination.

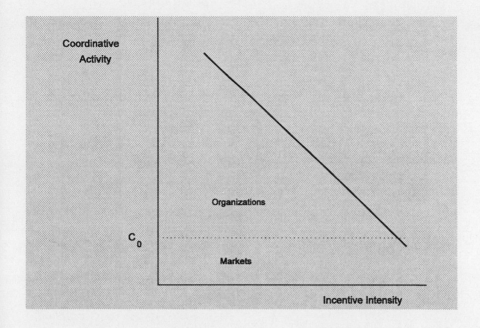

Figure 5 Coordinate Activity versus Incentive Activity

Transaction cost economics focuses on the costs of reducing opportunism in bilateral exchange, where the specificity of the parties is induced by asset specificity. Such an analysis would see coordination as requiring investment in tangible or intangible capital specific to the other party and, therefore, as benefiting from non-market governance mechanisms. The argument advanced here does not rest on assumptions about asset specificity. Rather, if coordination is a team effort that is supplemental to basic department operations, then incentive intensity must be reduced below "marketplace" levels in order to divert effort away from department performance per se and towards coordinative activities.[15]

Note particularly that it is common for transaction cost analysts to see the reduction in incentive intensity accompanying internalization as an unavoidable cost to internalization. That is, with a full market interface between a buyer A and a supplier B, the supplier A has high powered

---

[15]Williamson (1985, Ch. 6) provides a good comparative view of the costs and benefits of both high and low-powered incentives both in firms and in markets.

incentives to produce efficiently. However, when A and B are departments within a single firm, incentives are unavoidably dulled. As Kreps (1990: 756) notes,

> If A buys out B's assets and employs B, then A is unable to match such strong incentives in the employment contract she gives to B. She has a difficult time monitoring the effort B expends, and she has an especially difficult time seeing how B expends whatever effort he does expend.

What is different in the analysis presented here is that it has firms existing to provide an escape from the high-powered incentives of the marketplace. Within the firm, where incentive intensity can be reduced by design, it is possible to generate more and richer coordinative activity than can be accomplished in markets. Thus, in contrast to transaction-cost theory, it is the gains to greater coordination that rationalize the firm.

Key inertias

The description of the five frictions was intended to explore the range and depth of forces at work. Now, in order to facilitate reasoning within a simple model, it is useful to make some simplifying assumptions. Accordingly, I make the reasonable assumption that resistance to change is embodied in the following five inertias:

- Cross-subsidy comforts from bundled businesses
- Departmental politics rooted in self-interest
- Embedded processes that link departments
- Cultural inertia
- Vested values in current methods and products

Observation 1 *Fragmentation and increased incentive intensity act to reduce each of the first four sources of inertia.*

Fragmentation means cutting the company into smaller departments, reducing interdependencies, measuring each department's performance and tying managerial pay and career potential to results. Fragmentation eliminates cross-subsidy comforts. It breaks political coalitions, asserts the center's legitimate authority over behavior, and

124

compels attention to performance rather than discussion. It reduces the inertia of embedded (coordinative) processes by reducing their importance or by literally tearing them out. Fragmentation breaks the larger culture into smaller cultures, and cooperative behavior is more likely to emerge in smaller groups. Vested values are not strongly affected by fragmentation because it acts on behavior and attention rather than values or beliefs. Finally, fragmentation helps reveal the loci of department competencies, triggering key decisions on readjustments in the portfolio of departments and redesign of the overall strategy.

Of course, fragmentation can be very costly: it drastically reduces the amount of coordination within the firm. This, in turn, may sharply reduce the company's ability to design products, service customers, and perform other complex coordinative tasks. Furthermore, fragmentation may have little to do with the direction in which management would like to take the firm. Observation 1 does not claim that fragmentation is always a desirable direction. It merely notes that without fragmentation the journey may never begin.

Observation 2 *Transformation always involves an initial reduction in the amount of coordination among departments.*

If the transformation task is renewal, new departmental tasks must be defined and new methods discovered. Elements 2 and 3 of the competence model imply that changes in departmental methods imply replacing the present coordinative regime with a new one. That is, because coordination is specialized to task and method, new coordinative skills need be developed. This, in turn, implies that coordination will first be reduced, as the old system is scrapped and departments drive to adopt new methods.

If the transformation task is recovery, the need is to identify and remedy poor methods and waste. The practical approach to this issue involves some fragmentation, clearer measures, and increased incentive intensity. The focus on department performance will produce a reduction in coordinative activity (Conjecture 1). This leads directly to the following point:

Observation 3 *The cost of fragmentation is reduced by the necessity for reductions in coordination.*

The cost of using fragmentation to cut inertia is the consequent loss of coordination. But Observation 2 assures us that coordination will be reduced anyway. Consequently, fragmentation becomes an even more attractive method for starting a transformation.

Observation 4 *The initial stages of transformation will be accompanied by increased incentive intensity.*

This simply follows from Observation 3 and the necessity to motivate departmental action during the first stages of either renewal or recovery.

Transformation cannot, however, consist simply of fragmentation and increased incentive intensity. Business effectiveness also requires the close and subtle coordination among departments. But our model suggests that there is a necessary sequence of action in transformation. From the competence model (elements 2 and 3) we know that layer 2 cannot be built or developed until layer 1 is smoothly operating. Hence:

Observation 5 *Rebuilding coordination among the departments must await task redefinition, the adjustment of methods, the elimination of waste, and the routinization of new work standards.*

Coupling Observation 5 with Conjecture 1 leads to the final deduction about sequence:

Observation 6 *Rebuilding coordination among the departments requires a reduction in incentive intensity.*

Transformation profiles

According to the analysis just completed, the most direct way of reducing organizational inertia is to exploit the reduction in organizational cohesiveness that accompanies the first phases of transformation. In addition, the analysis points to a predictable sequence of events in organizational transformation. In the first phase, not directly discussed, managers within the firm become aware of the need for change and begin to formulate views as to appropriate new directions. In the second phase, top management imposes structural fragmentation and increased incentive intensity. These moves have the effect of reducing coordinative activity, breaking some of the inertias that have impeded action, and focusing departmental attention on improving methods and eliminating waste. Once departmental performance has been improved, attention turns to rebuilding coordinative activity. To accomplish this, the incentive intensity must be reduced, else departments will have little reason to invest in difficult-to-measure coordinative efforts. As coordination increases, best practices and other fruits of the central phase can be spread throughout the firm.

This sequence has a resemblance to that observed by Baden-Fuller and Stopford (1994). The middle two stages of their *crescendo* model are *simplify* and *build*, where the first involves removing outdated and unnecessary products, activities, and systems and the second is the construction, perhaps through trial and error, of new strengths, activities, and systems. However, the distinction emphasized here is between sub-units with measurable outputs versus coordinative activities whereas their distinction is between the "backbone" elements of the business and the complex structure of less critical "weeds" that have grown up over time.

As the rebuilding of coordination requires the reduction in incentive intensity, it sets the stage for future problems. The benefits of increased coordination among departments should be clear, but it should also be clear that reduced incentive intensity invites another round of internal decay. Absent strong local performance incentives, waste can develop, poor methods can persist, and other inefficiencies appear. As we come to better understand this cycle of decay and renewal, we may someday know how to transform organizations without also planting the seeds of future decay.

Conclusions

If firms are not easily changed, there are important implications for strategy. The overwhelming evidence is that organizations possess considerable inertia, yet strategy content models, including the resource-based view of the firm, tend to sidestep this issue. A complete strategic theory of the firm must deal squarely with the issue of inertia.

Whereas the resource-based theory of the firm has had the advantage of using as a foil a corresponding model of the firm, there is no clear simple model of management or organizational process. Hence the study of inertia and transformation is complex and requires looking into a variety of disciplines.

In this article I have offered a number of ideas and conjectures garnered from economics, organizational sociology, cognitive psychology, political science, and general common sense. They have led to the elucidation of the five key frictions that impede change, a hierarchical view of the architecture of organizational competence, and a set of predictions about the time sequence of transformation phases.

Appendix A

Incentive intensity and coordination

In the discussion of competence architecture and transformation sequences, Conjecture 1 was offered, positing a negative relationship between incentive intensity (the strength of departmental performance incentives) and inter-department coordination. Looking closely at such an issue requires a dip into some agency theory. To accomplish this a modified version of Milgrom and Holmstrom's (1990) linear model will be analyzed. The modification is the introduction of multiple agents and payments based on team production.

A linear agency formulation

Milgrom and Holmstrom (1990) build a principle-agent model in which the agent makes a choice of how much effort (or time) to spend on a number of tasks. The simplifications they introduce to permit analysis are linear wage rules, constant absolute risk aversion of the agent, independent normally distributed errors in measurement, and signals whose expected values are linear in the agent's effort. The model here is based upon theirs but adds the element of team production.

The agent's effort is divided between two tasks, with effort t_1 spent on the first and t_2 on the second. There are η agents and the principal observes each of their type-1 efforts individually with additive error ε_1 which is normally distributed with zero mean and variance σ_1^2. However, the principal can only observe the total type-2 effort τ put forward by all agents, again with additive error ε_2 distributed normally with mean zero and variance σ_1^2. All errors are independent. The agent's wage is

$$w = \alpha_1(t_1 + \varepsilon_1) + \alpha_2(\tau + \varepsilon_2)/n + \beta \tag{1}$$

128

Thus α_1 is the payment rate for local effort and α_2 is the payment rate for the *average* collective effort. The agent has constant absolute risk aversion r (that is, a utility function of the form $u(w) = -e^{rw}$). The agent's personal cost of effort is $C(t_1,t_2)$, which is convex. With these specifications, the agent's certainty equivalent is

$$CE = \alpha_1 t_1 + \alpha_2 \tau/n - (r/2)[\alpha_1^2 \sigma_1^2 + \alpha_2^2 \sigma_2^2] - C + \beta \tag{2}$$

In solving the agent's maximization problem the question arises as to the value of $d\tau/dt_2$. If the agents are purely non-cooperative, then $d\tau/dt_2 = 1$, whereas fully cooperative behavior would imply $d\tau/dt_2 - n$. Assume that each agent possesses some *zeal* and increases his or her output by the fraction λ of the *average increase in output per agent that can be attributed to others*. Then

$$\frac{d\tau}{dt_2} = 1 + \lambda \frac{n-1}{n} \frac{d\tau}{dt_2}$$

so that

$$\frac{d\tau}{dt_2} = \frac{n}{\lambda + n(1 - \lambda)} \tag{3}$$

For simplicity define $k = \lambda + \eta(1-\lambda)$. When $\lambda = 0$ we have the non-cooperative solution ($k = \eta$) and when $\lambda = 1$ we have the fully cooperative solution ($k = 1$).

Let $C_1 = \partial C/\partial t_i$. Then the agent's maximization problem is solved (as long as $t_i > 0$) by setting

$$C_1 = \alpha_1 \tag{4}$$

and

$$kC_2 = \alpha_2 .$$ (5)

Define $C_{ij} = \partial^2 C / \partial t_i \partial t_j$ and take partial derivatives of (4) and (5) to give

$$\partial \alpha_1 / \partial t_i = C_{1i}$$

and

$$\partial \alpha_2 / \partial t_i = kC_{2i} .$$

Using the Inverse Function Theorem we have

$$\begin{pmatrix} \partial t_1/\partial \alpha_1 & \partial t_1/\partial \alpha_2 \\ \partial t_2/\partial \alpha_1 & \partial t_2/\partial \alpha_2 \end{pmatrix} = \begin{pmatrix} C_{22} & -C_{12}/k \\ -C_{12} & C_{11}/k \end{pmatrix} / [C_{11}C22 - C_{12}^2] .$$ (6)

The expected state of affairs is for $C_{ij} > 0$. That is, more effort on some task should make additional effort on it or some other task even more costly. In addition, we expect $\partial t_1/\partial \alpha_1 > 0$ and $\partial t_2/\partial \alpha_2 > 0$ because a larger incentive placed on task i should call forth more effort on task i. Consequently, the denominator of the right-hand matrix must be positive in a well-behaved specification. The sought-after result is thus immediate: $\partial t_2/\partial \alpha_1 < 0$. Increased local incentive intensity (α_1) reduces effort devoted towards coordination (t_2). It can also be observed that this connection does not depend upon the level of cooperation (k).

References

Argyris, C. 1990. *Overcoming organizational defenses: facilitating organizational learning*. Needham, MA: Allyn & Bacon.

Arrow, K.J. 1963. *Social choice and individual values*. New Haven, CT: Yale University Press (1st ed. 1951).

Baden-Fuller, C. and Stopford, J.M. 1994. *Rejuvenating the mature business*. Boston: Harvard Business School Press.

Barney, J.B. 1986. "Strategic factor markets: expectations, luck, and business strategy." *Management Science* 32: 1231-1241.

Burgelman, R.A. 1991. "Intraorganizational ecology of strategy and organizational adaptation: theory and field research," *Organizational Science* 2: 239-62.

Conner, K.R. 1991. "A historical comparison of resource-based theory and five schools of thought within industrial organization economics: do we have a new theory of the firm?" *Journal of Management* 17: 121-54.

Elster, J. 1989. *The cement of society*. Cambridge: Cambridge University Press.

Fallows, J. 1981. *National defense*. New York: Random House.

Frantz, R.S. 1988. *X-efficiency: theory, evidence, and applications*. Boston: Kluwer Academic Publishers.

Grant, R.M. 1991. "The resource-based theory of competitive advantage." *California Management Review* 33: 114-135.

Hannan, M.T. and Freeman, J. "Structural inertia and organizational change." *American Sociological Review* 49: 149-64.

Janus, I. 1972. *Groupthink*. New York: The Free Press.

Kreps, D.M. 1990. *A course in microeconomic theory*. Princeton, N.J.: Princeton University Press.

Kuran, T. 1988. "The tenacious past: theories of personal and collective conservatism." *Journal of Economic Behavior and Organization* 10: 143-71.

Lippman, S.A., and Rumelt, R.P. 1982. "Uncertain imitability: and analysis of interfirm differences in efficiency under competition." *Bell Journal of Economics*. 13: 418-438.

Margolis, H. 1993. *Paradigms and barriers: how habits of mind govern scientific beliefs*. Chicago: University of Chicago Press.

Milgrom, P., and Holmstrom, B. 1990. "Multi-task principal-agent analyses: Incentive contracts, asset ownership and job design." Working paper.

McKelvey, R.D. 1976. "Intransitivities in multidimensional voting models and some implications for agenda control." *Journal of Economic Theory* 16: 472-82.

Nelson, R.R., and Winter, S.G. 1982. *An evolutionary theory of economic change*. Cambridge, Mass.: Harvard University Press.

Ouchi, W.G., and Wilkins, A.L. 1985. "Organizational culture." *Annual Review of Sociology* 11: 457-83.

Porter, M.E. 1980. *Competitive strategies: Techniques for analyzing industries and competitors.* New York: Free Press.

Porter, M.E. 1985. *Competitive advantage: Creating and sustaining superior performance.* New York: Free Press.

Postrel, S., and Rumelt, R.P. 1992. "Incentives, routines, and self-command." *Industrial and Corporate Change* 1: 397-425.

Powell, W.W., and DiMaggio, P.J. (eds.). 1991. *The new institutionalism in organizational analysis.* Chicago: University of Chicago Press.

Prahalad, C.K., and Hamel, G. 1990. "The core competence of the corporation." *Harvard Business Review* 68: 79-91.

Rumelt, R.P. 1984. "Towards a strategic theory of the firm." In R.B. Lamb (ed.), *Competitive strategic management.* Englewood Cliffs, N.J.: Prentice-Hall: 556-570.

Rumelt, R. P. 1991. "How much does industry matter?" *Strategic Management Journal* 12: 167-186.

Sheehan, N. 1988. *A bright and shining lie.* New York: Vantage.

Shesple, K. 1979. "Institutional Arrangements and Equilibrium in Multidimensional Voting Models." *American Journal of Political Science* 23: 27-59.

Skinner, B.F. 1948. "Superstition in the pigeon." *Journal of Experimental Psychology* 38: 168-172.

Smith, D. 1985. "The roots and future of modern-day military reform. *Air University Review* 16: 33-40.

Thompson, F. 1992. "First with the most: the boyd cycle and business strategy." Working Paper, Willamette University, Oregon.

Teece, D.J. 1982. "Towards an economic theory of the multiproduct firm." *Journal of Economic Behavior and Organization*, 3: 39-63.

Teece, D.J., Pisano, G., and Shuen, S. 1990. "Firm capabilities, resources, and the concept of strategy." Working Paper, University of California, Berkeley.

Wernerfelt, B. 1984. "A resource-based view of the firm." *Strategic Management Journal* 5: 171-180.

Williamson, O.E. 1985. *The economic institutions of capitalism: firms, markets, relational contracting.* New York: Free Press.

6

RESOURCE-BASED STRATEGY IN A STOCHASTIC MODEL

Birger Wernerfelt
Sloan School of Management
Massachusetts Institute of Technology

I develop a stochastic dynamic version of the resource-based view of the firm. The theory reduces to an extreme version of the evolutionary approach in one special case and to a deterministic resource-based approach in another. I go on to characterize circumstances under which each special case is more pertinent. The theory implies a natural division of labor between the resource-based and the evolutionary approaches.

1. Introduction

I will here characterize the resource-based approach to strategy in a stochastic environment. It will be argued that this version is free of some of the less appealing properties of deterministic versions. The theory will reduce to an extreme evolutionary approach in an important special case. This relationship allows one to use evolutionary theory in a normative way.

The central model is conceptually simple. By modeling the dynamics of the firm as both controllable and subject to stochastic shocks, I combine the two central forces in the resource-based and the evolutionary approach. Without stochasticity the model reduces to a deterministic system, the dynamics of which are completely determined by the initial conditions. This shares many features with the ideal-typical version of the resource-based approach. If we, conversely, retain stochasticity and eliminate controllability, we end up in an extreme evolutionary model of individual firm dynamics. (It is true that selection constraints impose rationality at the market level in evolutionary models, but this is not true at the firm level.)

Having illustrated how such a formal synthesis could look, the discussion naturally turns to the question of the relative importance of controllable and stochastic factors. A couple of simple examples will be put forth to address this issue. In a monopolistic model, I find that investment intensities vary positively with productivity and negatively with stochasticity. In a simple resource development game between an established firm and a start-up, I find an equilibrium where the established firm takes the "low variance" route using its development efforts to enhance its existing resources, while the start-up will gamble on new, but high-variance, technologies. Consistent with casual observation, this suggests that the stochastic factors are more important for our understanding of volatile resources (such as technical skills) and smaller firms. Conversely, an emphasis on controllable dynamics is more appropriate for more stable resources and larger firms.

In Section 2, I will provide a brief characterization of the resource-based and the evolutionary approaches and some important problems raised by typical applications. With this background, I will suggest how a stochastic version of the resource-based approach may be seen as a synthesis which addresses these problems. The general model is described in Section 3, while Section 4 presents some examples. Finally, Section 5 contains a discussion with links to other streams of work in the strategy area.

2. Background

A rough sketch of the resource-based and the evolutionary approaches will motivate the analysis in Sections 3 and 4. I will highlight their essential and inessential characteristics and note some unappealing features of standard applications.

In its simplest form, the resource-based approach to strategy is derived in a static model. Given an exogenously specified set of interfirm resource differences, one can derive equilibrium strategies as functions of these differences and interpret profits as returns to the resources. The argument has a logical dynamic extension based on the premise that the firm's stock of resources can be changed in ways which depend on its current level. In the ideal-typical version of the resource-based approach, this process is deterministic and controllable (subject to constraints). In such a model, strategies reflect a consumption-investment tradeoff between leveraging and developing resources, and the net present value of profits is a function of initial resource stocks (Wernerfelt 1984).

Most, if not all, applications of the resource-based approach postulate rationality and perfect foresight on the part of firms. I will argue that neither assumption is essential. They are used for purposes of simplification. On the other hand, the assumption of perfect foresight provides a useful ideal-typical point on which to contrast the resource-based and the evolutionary approaches. I would like to highlight three problems with the ideal-typical resource based analyses. First, many inimitable (valuable) resources have this status exactly because they are irreplicable; for example, because their origin is poorly understood (Lippman and Rumelt 1982). So it will often be difficult or impossible to purposively enhance them. Second, the model places considerable weight on initial resource stocks, but is not able to explain these in any satisfactory way. In the limit one ends up regressing to the abilities of the founders of the firm. When coupled with the forward-looking dynamics, this yields the absurd conclusion that the value of the firm is attributable to the genetic material of perhaps long gone founders. A related problem, noted by Foss, Knudsen, and Montgomery (Chapter 1), is that the resource-based approach has relatively little to say about small entrepreneurial firms.

The evolutionary perspective on strategy is derived from Nelson and Winter's work on industry evolution (1982). While the theory initially was conceived to describe industry change, it has been proposed as a framework for firm-level strategic analysis. In the ideal-typical version, the resources (routines) available to firms are exogenously different and change over time in a stochastic and non-controllable fashion. The theory is often coupled with assumptions about bounded rationality, but I will suggest that this is inessential. What is essential, and what constitutes an interesting contrast to the ideal-typical resource based approach, is the insistence that the resources develop stochastically.

The theory has many attractive features in this respect, but some problems crop up in typical (perhaps naive) applications. First, there is a lot of indeterminacy in recommendations and explanations. This is sometimes due to researchers' beliefs that firms cannot specify probability distributions over competitors' actions or technical changes. Alternatively it is due to "weak selection pressures" which allow several strategies to survive, coupled with unwillingness to specify an objective function for the firm (the manager). A second problem, often seen in the "population ecology" literature, is that because of the dominating role given to stochastic factors, the model would seem to leave little room for long-term strategy by the firm or its competitors. I will take the position that evolutionary theory could be formulated in an equilibrium framework, such that this indeterminacy is inessential and planning is possible. It is possible that followers of the evolutionary perspective disagree.

These are clearly simplified interpretations of the resource-based approach and the evolutionary approach, but they will appear below as special cases of a more general model in which the resource-based approach is applied to a stochastic environment.

3. Model

We will look at a two-period model of an industry with n firms and heterogeneous buyers. In period $t = 1, 2$, the vector of resources controlled by firm j is denoted by r_{jt}, while $r_t \equiv (r_{1t}, \cdots, r_{jt}, \cdots, r_{nt})$ is the vector of resources available to the firms in the market. In each period the firm has at its disposal a matrix of control variables: m_{jt} , $t = 1, 2$ describing how r_{jt} is deployed across the activities of the firm. The set of feasible m_{jt}'s is given by the constraint $f_t(m_{jt}, r_{jt}) \geq 0$. This constraint describes the "capacity" limitations on r_j, including irreversibility constraints. These deployment patterns influence contemporaneous profits and m_{j1} may also influence the resources available in period 2. The profits of firm j are given by $\Pi_{jt}(m_t, r_t)$, where $m_t \equiv (m_{1t}, \cdots, m_{jt}, \cdots, m_{nt})$, and resources in period 2 are given by $a_{j2}(m_1, r_1, \theta)$, where θ is a vector of random variables, whose distribution may depend on m_1 and r_1.

To find equilibrium strategies, we define $x_{-jt} \equiv (x_{1t}, \cdots, x_{j-1t}, x_{j+1t}, \cdots, x_{nt})$. We can now characterize equilibrium in period 2, called m_2^*, as

$$m_{j2}^* = \text{argmax } \Pi_{j2}(m_{j2}, m_{-j2}^*, r_2)$$

$$\text{S.T. } f_t(m_{j2}, r_{j2}) \geq 0$$

Assume that this equilibrium exists and is unique. If so, we can describe equilibrium profits in period 2 as a function $\Pi_{j2}^*(r_2)$. Suppose that all firms discount period 2 payoffs by the discount factor δ. Equilibria in period 1 are those m_1^* which solve, for $j = 1, \cdots, n$:

$$\max_{m_{j1}} \Pi_{j1}(m_{j1}, m_{-j1}^{\cdot}, r_1) + \delta E \Pi_{j2}^{\cdot}(r_2[m_{j1}, m_{-j1}^{\cdot}, r_1, \theta])$$

$$\text{S.T. } f_t(m_{j1}, r_{j1}) \geq 0$$

Let us now assume the existence and (for convenience) the uniqueness of this equilibrium.

In the deterministic case, where θ can only take one value, we can drop it and the expectations operator and express $v_j = \Pi_{j1} + \delta\Pi_{j2}$ as a function of r_1. Given the initial resource endowments, firms make period 1 decisions m which are individually optimal given equilibrium play by others and equilibrium play in period 2. This is the case mentioned in Section 2, where all play is explained by initial conditions.

Consider next the "opposite" case, in which r_2 is a function of θ, but not of m_1. Under such circumstances, purposive development of resources is infeasible and strategy is reduced to myopic period-by-period play, much as mentioned in Section 2.

In contrast, the intermediate case where r_2 is a function of a nontrivial θ as well as m_{j1}, is very rich and satisfactory. The firms both exploit their resources and try to develop them. On the other hand the development process is stochastic such that outcomes depend on initial conditions and luck. So the initial state a_1 should be interpreted as a result of "earlier" states $(r_0?)$ and luck. This therefore gives us a consistent model with heterogeneous, yet value-maximizing, firms.

It would be tempting to claim that this is a true synthesis in the sense that the model in the two above-mentioned special cases reduces to exactly the resource-based and the evolutionary approach. If so, one could look at this as "the resource-based approach in a stochastic environment" or "the evolutionary approach with controllable dynamics." Unfortunately, the latter characterization may be objectionable to followers of the evolutionary approach. (Hence the characterization "pure" evolutionary approach used in several places.) The problem is not the lack of a selection criterion, nor is it true that the model is less rich than evolutionary theory because the number of firms is fixed. The number of active firms need not be fixed and this dynamic contains a selection mechanism. In period 1 $n' < n$ firms could have resources such that they prefer to set their m_{j1} at passive (nonproducing) levels. Some of these firms could still experience a change in their r_{j2}, such that they will produce in period 2. Similarly, some of the $n - n'$ firms which were active in period 1 could experience adverse developments causing them to prefer passivity in period 2. It is also not essential that m_1^* and m_2^* be found by the rational argmax operator. The model makes sense with bounded rationality. The critical assumption, which may be objectionable to followers of the evolutionary approach, is that the stochasticity can be probabilistically described *ex ante*. To the extent that followers of the evolutionary approach view it as inherently incompatible with this feature, it is not an exact special case of this model.

Suppose we were interested in making statements about the determinants of the relative importance of stochastic versus deliberate factors in growth. One set of determinants would be those which influence entire industries, and another interesting set of factors are those which determine the degree to which a firm exposes itself to stochasticity. That is, some shocks may go with the industry, but others may be avoidable if the firm, for better or worse, takes a "safe" path. I will now simplify the model to a couple of examples in order to look at these issues.

4. The Relative Importance of Stochastic versus Planned Growth

As an example, suppose that $n = 1$, $r_1 = 1$ and that $1 - m$ is used in current production while m is invested in resource development. The outcome of the development process is

$$r_2 = \alpha(1 - \theta)m + \theta , \quad \alpha > 0$$

where θ is binomial, taking the value 1 with probability ρ and else 0. So ρ is an indicator of the importance of stochasticity in the process. Large values of θ suggest that shocks will render current resources obsolete and create new ones. Similarly, α is an indicator of the productivity of purposive resource development. We finally assume that profits in any given period are an increasing concave power function of resources used for production in that period. Since the game ends in period 2, all of r_2 is used for production and expected profits are

$$(1 - m)^\beta + \delta[(1 - \rho)(\alpha m)^\beta + \rho^\beta], \quad 0 < \beta < 1 .$$

This gives the following first-order condition for m^* :

$$-\beta(1 - m)^{\beta-1} + \delta(1 - \rho)\beta\alpha(\alpha m)^{\beta-1} = 0.$$

By direct differentiation of this, we can use the implicit function theorem to show that

$$\frac{dm_*}{d\alpha} > 0 \quad and$$

$$\frac{dm_*}{d\rho} < 0 \; .$$

So more will be invested in resource development and the resource-based view will be more pertinent if the investment is more productive. Conversely, less will be invested and the evolutionary view will be more pertinent if stochastic factors are more important. At the extremes, if $\rho = 1$, no purposive investments will be made, and if $\rho = 0$ stochasticity plays no role.

Consider next an industry with an established firm e and a startup firm s. There are two resources, skills in the current technology and skills in an alternative technology. If a firm has "normal" skills in the current technology or skills in the alternative technology, it can produce with variable costs 1. If a firm has "extra" skills in the current technology, its variable costs are $\frac{2}{3}$. At the start of period 1, the established firm has skills in the current technology, while it has no skills in the alternative technology. The startup has neither type of skill. During the first period, each firm can invest in one, but only one, technology, in order to increase their resources for the second period. Investments in the alternative technology succeed with probability p in which case they give the investor normal skills in that technology. Investments in the current technology always succeed, giving the established firm "extra" skills and the startup normal skills in the technology. The investment strategies are denoted by a (alternative) or c (current). If any firm succeeds with the alternative technology, only that technology is viable. After investing, the firms play a Cournot game with inverse demand $3 - q_e - q_s$. These assumptions have the following implications for payoffs.

1. *The startup gets 0 unless its project succeeds.* If s plays c and fails, it has no resources and therefore cannot produce.

2. *If only one firm succeeds with* a, *it gets costs 1, giving it monopoly payoffs 1, while the competitor gets 0.* Because the alternative technology renders the current technology obsolete. Our specification is such that normal monopoly rents equal unity.

3. *If both firms fail with* a, e *gets monopoly payoffs 1.* This is because its current costs are 1.

4. *If* e *plays* c *and* s *fails with* a, e*'s payoffs are 49/36.* This should be thought of as *e* perfecting the technology and thus earning "extra" monopoly profits.

5. *If both firms succeed with* a, *duopoly payoffs for each are 4/9.* The sum of the duopoly profits is smaller than the monopoly profits.

6. *If* s *plays* c *and* e *fails with* a, *duopoly payoffs for each are 4/9.* That is, it is possible for *s* to "catch up" to *e*, if the latter does not invest in *c*.

7. *If both play* c, e*'s payoffs are 64/81 , while* s *gets 25/81.* So *e* can "stay ahead" if he wants to. (See Aron and Lazear 1990) for a somewhat similar model.)

Given these assumptions we can find expected profits Π_j from each pair of strategies. If the first argument of Π is the strategy of *e*, we get

$$\Pi_e(a,a) = 1 - p + \frac{4}{9}p^2$$

$$\Pi_s(a,a) = p\left(1 - \frac{5}{9}p\right)$$

$$\Pi_e(a,c) = \frac{4}{9} + p\left(\frac{5}{9}\right)$$

$$\Pi_s(a,c) = (1 - p)\frac{4}{9}$$

$$\Pi_e(c,a) = (1 - p)\frac{49}{36}$$

$$\Pi_s(c,a) = p$$

$$\Pi_e(c,c) = \frac{64}{81}$$

$$\Pi_s(c,c) = \frac{25}{81}$$

I would like to show that *(c, a)* is an equilibrium. For this to be true, we need:

$$\Pi_e(c,a) > \Pi_e(a,a) \quad \text{and} \tag{1}$$

$$\Pi_s(c,a) > \Pi_s(c,c). \tag{2}$$

More generally, the first condition is not strong. To see this, make the reasonable assumption that p is relatively low such that $\Pi_e(a,a)$ is small, and recall that $\Pi_e(c,a)$ is e's "extra" monopoly profits if he improves his position. To interpret the second condition recall that $\Pi_s(c,a)$ is the expected profits from gambling to become a monopolist. On the other hand, $\Pi_s(c,c)$ is the profits from becoming a dominated player in the industry. For the typical startup, these will be very small. For completeness, note that *(a,c)* is not an equilibrium because $\Pi_e(a,c) < \Pi_e(c,c)$.

In this example, (1) and (2) will hold if *.31* • *p* • *.58* such that *(c,a)* is an equilibrium for those values of *p*. If *p* • .31, both will invest in *c*, and if *p* • *.58*, both will invest in *a*. It is never an equilibrium for the established firm to invest in *a* while the start-up invests in *c*.

So under reasonable conditions we have showed the following:

(a) The growth and strategy of the established firm will be influenced relatively more by its initial resources than by stochastic shocks.

(b) The growth and strategy of the startup firm will be influenced relatively more by stochastic shocks than by its initial resources.

Intuitively, the result obtains because the established firm has another (better) investment opportunity than the startup. By the same token, however, the established firm does not invest in the alternative technology because I constrained it to exactly one project. This is clearly an unreasonable assumption, but one which allow me to eliminate the well-known effect, due to Arrow (1962), that the established firm has less to gain and thus invests less. If we change the model such that the established firm may invest in both projects, it may well do so. Overall, however, its growth path is still determined less by stochastic factors than that of the startup. On the other hand, it may also be unreasonable to assume that the firm's investment costs are identical (here zero). If the established firm finds investment more expensive, it may invest less than the startup.

The result is largely consistent with casual observation. A very large number of startups gamble on different technologies and a vanishing fraction make it big. In contrast, established firms have much higher success rates.

If we expand the model by allowing several (*N*) startups, the equilibrium depends on the correlation between the probabilities that individual startups succeed with *a*. In the extreme, if the correlation is zero and *N* is large, someone will almost surely succeed and the established firm has to invest in *a* as well. On the other hand, if either all or none of the startups succeed, the equilibrium is much like *(c, a)* with the exception that the expected payoffs are smaller for the startups if they succeed with a. (See also Winter 1984.)

Coming back to the relationship between the resource-based and the evolutionary approach, it is tempting to interpret the models as suggesting that the resource-based approach applies best to more stable resources and larger firms, while the evolutionary approach is more appropriate for more volatile resources and smaller firms.

5. Conclusion

Some evolutionary theorists may feel that I have used their approach as a straw man or have neglected central parts of it. This is possible, but the argument should be sufficiently transparent that it can be left up to the reader to decide.

I would like to end by making a few comments on the relationship between the resource-based approach and the other approaches rooted in economics.

(1) The traditional structure-conduct-performance view as applied by Porter (1980) explains a firm's success as a function of the industries in which it competes. Empirical work (Schmalensee 1985, Wernerfelt and Montgomery 1988, and Rumelt 1991) certainly supports this. However, the work of Montgomery and Hariharan (1991) suggests that industry participation ultimately can be explained by resource endowments. In this light the resource-based approach is not in conflict with the "industry analysis" approach.

In fact, one can easily illustrate the tradeoff between market attractiveness and resource fit in an example: Consider a duopoly where firm 1 has resources which yield variable costs of ⅔ in market I, and 1 in market II. Conversely, firm 2's variable costs in market I are 1, while they are ⅔ in market II. Inverse demand is $3 - q_1 - q_2$ in both markets, but market II is less attractive because it requires a fixed cost k. If each firm can enter only one market and k is ≈ 0, there are two equilibria: one (1, I, 2, II) where firm 1 enters I, and firm 2 enters II, and another (1, II, 2, I) where they do the reverse. The (1, II, 2, I) equilibrium disappears as $k > 17/81$ and the (1, I, 2, II) equilibrium disappears as $k > 341/324$. In the latter case, the only equilibrium is that where both firms enter I. This example illustrates the following: (i) it is attractive to avoid competition (as in (1, I, 2, II) and (1, II, 2, I)), (ii) the equilibrium where firms follow their resource fit is more robust than that where they do not, and (iii) as a market becomes very unattractive, even firms with superior resource fits will shy away from them.

I hasten to admit that this example is incomplete because entry is exogenously limited. However, it is suggestive of the type of analysis one could pursue.

(2)   The efficiency/transaction cost approach advocated by Williamson (1991) suggests that "strategic" distortions are unimportant and that efficient utilization of resources generally is the optimal strategy. He also suggests (1991: 76) that the resource-based approach is efficiency based. I find myself in some disagreement with this. Relative to the industry analysis approach, it is true that the resource-based approach emphasizes profit maximizing deployment of assets, rather than oligopolistic attempts to limit competition. It is also true that resource-based theories of corporate scope (Montgomery and Wernerfelt 1988) rely heavily on transaction cost arguments. However, the fundamental goal of the firm within the resource-based approach is the extraction of Ricardian rents. So the focus is on profit maximization rather than efficiency.

(3)   The game theory approach discussed by Saloner (1991) is clearly different from the efficiency approach, reducing to it only under certain conditions. If we look at the determinants of firm performance in typical game theory models, we are led to first mover advantages and luck, but only rarely to other asymmetries. In light of the resource-based approach, being the first mover is clearly a resource, but one might be interested in a deeper understanding of the reasons for a firm's first mover advantage. This would then lead to the identification of further resources. There is nothing in the "ideology" of game theorists which prevents them from looking at games with significant heterogeneities. (See e.g., Ericson and Pakes 1989; Hopenhayn 1992.) The fact that they so far have done so only infrequently is probably due to problems identifying compelling types of heterogeneity. If the list of possible heterogeneities is very long, theories about individual members are less interesting. Accordingly, homogeneity is a focal point. Another factor favoring models with homogeneous firms is the value of simplicity. If an outcome can occur without heterogeneity, we have a simpler and cleaner theory. In the future, one could hope that these researchers focus more directly on specific types of heterogeneity, especially types identified by the strategy community. If so, their work will be very valuable for others working with the resource-based approach. As indicated by the example analyzed in (1) above, many very simple models could provide insights.

References

Aron, D. , and Lazear, E.P. 1990. "The introduction of new product." *American Economic Review, Papers and Proceedings* 80, no. 2: 421-26.

Arrow, K.J. 1962. Economic welfare and the allocation of resources for invention." In R. Nelson (ed.), The Rate and Direction of Inventive Activity. Princeton, NJ: Princeton University Press.

Ericson, R., and Pakes. A. 1989. "An alternative theory of firm and industry dynamics." Mimeo, Yale University.

Foss, N.J., Knudsen, C., and Montgomery, C.A. 1995. An exploration of common ground: integrating evolutionary and strategic theories of the firm. In C.A. Montgomery (ed.), *Resources from an evolutionary perspective: towards a synthesis of evolutionary and resource-based approaches to strategy.* Norwell, MA: Kluwer Academic Publishers.

Hopenhayn, H.A. 1992. "Entry, exit, and firm dynamics in long run equilibrium." *Econometrica* 60: 1127-50.

Lippman, S.A., and Rumelt, R.P. 1982. "Uncertain imitability: an analysis of interfirm differences in efficiency under competition." *Bell Journal of Economics* 13: 418-38.

Montgomery, C.A., and Wernerfelt, B. 1988. "Diversification, Ricardian rents, and Tobin's q," *RAND Journal of Economics* 19: 623-32.

Montgomery, C.A., and Hariharan, S. 1991. "Diversified expansion by large established firms." *Journal of Economic Behaviour and Organization* 15: 71-89.

Nelson, R.R., and Winter, S.G. 1982. *An evolutionary theory of economic change.* Cambridge, MA: Belknap Press.

Porter, M.E. 1980. *Competitive strategy.* New York, NY: Free Press.

Rumelt, R.P. 1991. "How much does industry matter?" *Strategic Management Journal* 12: 167-186.

Saloner, G. 1991. "Modeling, game theory, and strategic management." *Strategic Management Journal* 12, special issue: 119-36.

Schmalensee, R. 1985. "Do markets differ much?" *American Economic Review* 75: 341-51.

Wernerfelt, B. 1984. "A resource-based view of the firm." *Strategic Management Journal* 5: 171-80.

Wernerfelt, B. 1989. "From critical resources to corporate strategy." *Journal of General Management* 14, no. 3: 4-12.

Wernerfelt, B., and Montgomery, C.A. 1988. "Tobin's q and the importance of focus in firm performance." *American Economic Review* 78: 246-50.

Williamson, O.E. 1991. "Strategizing, economizing, and economic organization." *Strategic Management Journal* 12, special issue: 75-94.

Winter, S.G. 1984. "Schumpeterian competition in alternative technological regimes." *Journal of Economic Behavior and Organization* 5: 287-320.

7

FOUR Rs OF PROFITABILITY:
RENTS, RESOURCES, ROUTINES, AND REPLICATION

Sidney G. Winter[1]
The Wharton School

This paper seeks to connect related strands of thought in evolutionary economics and the resource-based view of the firm. Although conceived primarily as an approach to the descriptive analysis of the firm and industry, evolutionary economics offers a distinctive view of the firm that is adaptable for the purposes of normative analysis (Winter 1987). The resource-based view, as it has been developed in the strategy literature, seeks to derive normative guidance for business decision making from a deeper understanding of the sources of interfirm profitability differences (Wernerfelt 1984; Rumelt 1984). It interprets these as reflections of differences in streams of rents and quasi-rents accruing to firms, which in turn are attributed to differences in the control and management of strategic resources.

Both approaches place major emphasis on the heterogeneity of the population of business firms and on the sources of that heterogeneity in the idiosyncratic internal features of individual firms (Rumelt 1984; Nelson 1991). Although the focal issues differ somewhat, there are areas of substantial overlap.

---

[1]With the customary caveats, I would like to express my appreciation for the helpful comments on an earlier draft that I received from Connie Helfat, Dan Levinthal and—especially—Cynthia Montgomery.

147

A prominent example of such overlap relates to the nature and sources of productive competence in the individual firm. In evolutionary economics, a business firm is first and foremost an organization that knows how to do something. In the resource-based view of the firm, the scope of the term "resources" is certainly broad enough to include the knowledge underlying the firm's productive competence (Wernerfelt 1984).

The heart of the normative guidance offered by the resource-based view lies in the idea of leveraging the idiosyncratic profit opportunities latent in existing resource endowments. When the resources in question are productive routines, such exploitation often takes the form of replicating the firm's routines in the quest for greater profit through growth, a process that is a central feature of evolutionary economics. These relationships between the two approaches suggest an inviting target for further inquiry, and a "compare and contrast" analysis of this area is the general purpose of this paper.

Agenda

The strategy field has its "5 forces" analysis and its "7-S" framework; this paper has a "4 Rs" theme: rents, resources, routines and replication. Routines are the building blocks of organizational capability. As such, routines clearly qualify as resources, given the expansive use of the term "resources" in the literature of the resource-based view. On the other hand, resources in a narrow sense (e.g., appropriately specialized labor and machinery) are requisites of the performance of most routines, and the knowledge underlying a routine is embodied or embedded to a large extent in its associated human, physical and organizational capital. The first objective here is to further explicate this routines/resources relationship.

The next step is to fit the rents and replication pieces into the profitability picture. An emphasis on replication, and on the types of resources that can be exploited through replication, differentiates the evolutionary approach from the resource-based view. Replication of profitable routines is only one approach to leveraging the profit opportunities latent in an initial resource endowment. Compared, however to the broader idea of "leveraging," it is relatively specific in its content and implications.

The four Rs discussion turns up two sets of issues that deserve closer analysis. Both have to do with appraising the results of the quest for profitability. The first set relates to the problem of conceptualizing and

148

measuring profitability itself, and the second to the problem of appraising the social implications of profit-seeking behavior. Both sets include some difficult analytical and conceptual issues. An exploratory treatment of these matters occupies two sections of the paper. A brief concluding comment looks again at the wider horizons of the subject.

Throughout, this paper builds on contributions in the prior literature of the resource-based view, going back to Penrose (1959). As suggested above, the discussion here is narrower in focus than most of the resource-based literature, emphasizing resources and processes that are closely related to themes in evolutionary theory. The hoped-for benefits of this narrowed focus include a sharper view of certain issues, and the establishment of the clearest possible connections to the treatment of the corresponding issues in evolutionary economics.

Routines and Resources

The definitions of key theoretical terms are often rather broad and hazy; ample room is left for pragmatic adjustment as new problems are addressed. This pattern is well illustrated by the cases "resources" and "routines." Wernerfelt (1984) explains that the term "resources" embraces "... anything that could be termed a strength or weakness of a given firm ...." — "... (tangible or intangible) assets which are tied *semi-permanently* to the firm...." Subsequent discussion in the literature has emphasized the resources that underlie competitive advantage ("strengths"), and has sought to identify the characteristics such resources must have if success is to be sustained. The term "routine" has been used in evolutionary economics in a similarly expansive fashion. Nelson and Winter (1982) say that "... most of what is *regular and predictable* about business behavior is plausibly subsumed under the heading "routine," especially if we understand that term to include the relatively constant dispositions and strategic heuristics that shape the approach of a firm to the non-routine problems it faces" (p. 15).

Given the expansiveness of these definitions, the existence of a substantial overlap should come as no surprise. At a micro level, a routine in operation at a particular site can be conceived as a web of coordinating relationships connecting specific resources; without those resources it could not exist. Considered as an abstract activity pattern, however, "that same routine" may be in operation also at a different site, where a different but similar set of resources is coordinated by a very similar web of relationships: the routine has been replicated. This suggests that the routine *per se*—the abstract activity pattern—is itself a resource.[2]

In the context of strategic decision making, the two terms have different connotations. "Resources" suggests an inventory of items whose relationship to decision options requires definition through strategic analysis. By contrast, "routines" connotes a menu of previously learned patterns of action. Typically, some of these patterns have acquired the status of default options: they are carried out in the absence of an explicit decision to the contrary. Deliberate decision making (when it occurs) often takes the form of a choice from the prevailing menu of routines. It can, however, take less structured forms as well, such as the development of an intention to expand the menu in a particular direction.

Diversity of resources and management challenges

The preceding paragraphs attempt to capture what can be said about the general conceptual relationships between "resources" and "routines." This paper, however, aims not at a comprehensive treatment of these relationships, but at a careful examination of some of the issues that are specific to the overlap between the two concepts. Some types of resources are more relevant than others in this connection, and a preliminary task is to pick out from the broad array of "resources" the types that are most closely linked to "routines."

In the literature of the resource-based view, a broad range of resource types has been mentioned by way of illustration. There is a corresponding diversity in the managerial tasks required for the effective development and exploitation of the different resources. Defending the intellectual property represented by a patent position is quite a different undertaking from defending the team-embodied skills of the professionals in the R&D lab, which is in turn quite different from defending the team-embodied skills and specialized assets of the assembly line. When

---

[2]In a helpful conceptual discussion, Amit and Schoemaker (1993) narrow the term resources to refer to "stocks of available factors owned or controlled by the firm," most if not all of which are tradable. "Capabilities, in contrast, refer to a firm's capacity to deploy *Resources*...." (p. 34). Routines, not explicitly mentioned by Amit and Schoemaker, are among the organizational processes underlying capabilities. However, since routines are not just a way of deploying, but deploy*able* in their own right, they arguably belong under the resources rubric as well.

reputation is at stake, it is not so much the legal context as pragmatic understanding of human nature and of the media environment that is the issue. Also, while a reputation for toughness may be generally valuable, it must be developed and exercised quite differently with respect to rivals, suppliers and workers. Different types of resources thus pose quite different managerial challenges, and may be strategic or "critical" to quite different degrees (Wernerfelt, 1989)

Although the specific challenges differ widely across resources, they typically involve both a static aspect and a dynamic aspect. The static aspect consists of employing the resource to generate a flow of quasi-rents in the near term. In the explanation of interfirm profitability differences at given point in time, it is this static aspect of differing resource endowments that dominates the picture. The most interesting strategic issues, however, involve the dynamic aspect—the challenge of leveraging the existing resource position into a more favorable future position (Dierickx and Cool 1989; Kogut and Zander 1992). This challenge in turn has different components, among which the following three may be identified: (i) the *speculative* component, where superiority involves a better eye for resource value, (ii) the *developmental* component, where advantage inheres in a superior ability to amplify the contributions of present resources and expand existing lines of activity, and (iii) the *creative* component, which consists of the ability to combine resources in novel ways and establish new activities. It is in addressing the dynamics of resource exploitation that one finds the strongest complementarities between the resource-based view and evolutionary economics—and also between those two and the synthesis dubbed the "dynamic capabilities approach" by Teece, Pisano and Shuen (forthcoming).

Montgomery (1992) provides a good illustration of the static-dynamic distinction in an exposition featuring the Disney cartoon characters as a key resource of Walt Disney Company; her example also serves well to illustrate the role of creativity.

From the static viewpoint, the value of this type of resource is fundamentally a matter of intellectual property law. If there were no way to prevent rivals from doing a knock off copy of any Mouse-related product, then there might be esteem but there would be little profit in the claim to offer the One and Only Original Mickey Mouse. In fact, however, the law does protect the profit potential of that claim and the corresponding claims with respect to other characters. Given the protection of that institutional frame, however, the Mouse and his friends cannot merely reproduce indefinitely in the form of any given product, but also mutate

151

into entirely new forms.[3] This possibility illustrates the dynamic aspect of the profit opportunity inherent in the Disney characters: how can human creativity be applied to exploit these profit potentials in ways that are ever-new in detail, and responsive to ever-changing circumstances?

Montgomery's example nicely illuminates the subtlety of this dynamic aspect. On the one hand, it is clear that the Disney characters are a very valuable resource indeed. On the other hand, just how valuable it is probably depends fundamentally on the effectiveness with which human creativity is mobilized to expand its applications. Because of the inherent uniqueness of creative achievement, the amount that analysis from the strategic management viewpoint can contribute much to such an undertaking is open to question. At the same time, the example also serves well to illustrate the point that the concerns of the resource-based view are broader than those addressed in this paper: here, more attention is given to the relatively prosaic developmental component of resource dynamics than to the creative component.

Team-embodied skills as the focal example

The type of resource to which this discussion relates most directly is team-embodied skills, and the corresponding routines are the activities in which the team exercises those skills repetitively. Illustrative settings might include an assembly line, the back office operations of a financial institution, a fast food counter, a construction site, an airport gate, or a football field, to name but a few. There are several related propositions about these situations that derive from the basic understanding of skills and routines developed in evolutionary economics; all touch on the central point that routines and supporting skill packages are a key repository of knowledge in the firm: the firm "knows how" to do something because it commands the appropriate routines.

Organizational command of a routine is not reducible to the level of individual skills, because the context of each individual performance includes the performances of other members; learned patterns of interpersonal coordination are the basis of team performance.

---

[3]Biologist Stephen Jay Gould wrote a fascinating essay in recognition of the "50th birthday" of Mickey Mouse. He identifies interesting parallels between the transformation of Mickey's image by cultural evolution (i.e., creative resource dynamics) and the evolutionary development of the human species (Gould, 1980, Chapter 9).

By the same token, command of the routine does not reduce to the resource "team-embodied skills" because there is more to the context of individual performance than just the performances of other team members. Heading the list of these other contextual features are the equipment and facilities (appropriately arranged and installed) that establish the physical setting; next come the information flows from the environment that trigger particular performances. But the list of possible context dependencies continues more or less indefinitely.

The fact that the appropriate details of individual performance are linked to highly specific contexts implies that the required constituent resources are not available as such in the marketplace. The requisite mutual consistency of individual contexts is the product of organizational learning and other processes that reshape the skills of individuals after they have joined the organization. "Generic labor is rented in the market; firm-specific skills, knowledge and values are accumulated through on the job learning and training." (Dierickx and Cool 1989: 1504).

The knowledge and information-related aspects of inputs joined in a productive routine represent territory that is largely unexplored by economic analysis. Following the classic exposition of information economics by Arrow (1962), most scholars have recognized that information is not an ordinary economic commodity subject to ratio-scale measurement, but something with an economic logic of its own. Central to this logic is the contrast between high costs of initial creation or acquisition and costs of reproduction that are so low as to be considered negligible. At the opposite conceptual pole from Arrow-type information are service flows of generic inputs, whose potential for contributing information to the production process is left implicit in their definition, description or index number. For these inputs, ratio-scale measurement is thought to be non-problematic. Team-embodied skills occupy an intermediate position between these poles. They do embody significant information and their initial creation involves corresponding up-front costs—characteristics of Arrow-type information. On the other hand, like ordinary inputs, they are required in production on a continuing basis in some ratio to the level of activity, and the costs of additional units do not become negligible after the first unit is acquired. As for ratio-scale measurement, it is certainly feasible to measure the service flows in terms of the time put in; economically significant ambiguity nevertheless arises because the definition, observation and measurement of the relevant skills are all problematic. This ambiguity may result in significant transactional hazards because of the buyer's inability to ascertain what he or she is buying.

153

Resources with these characteristics occupy a central position in evolutionary economics and the resource-based view of the firm; team-embodied skills provide the most straightforward illustration of the general analytical issues involved. One issue in particular is central to the discussion of replication that follows—the character of the process by which new members acquire their skills, or by which new similar teams are created. Frequently, this instruction process places demands on the time of individuals already possessing the skills, and thus involves a short-term sacrifice in terms of the availability for current production of skills of the very type that the firm seeks to expand. More generally, the instruction process relies on some resources idiosyncratic to the firm, if not literally on the members of some "template team."

Replication and Rents—and Monopoly Returns

Because appropriately specialized input resources cannot simply be purchased on markets, the firm's use of a profitable routine is limited in the "short run" by its available stocks of those resources, if by nothing else. The mix of activity may be subject to routine adjustment, but individual activities are always subject to upper bound constraints set by the availability of the input service flows containing coordinating information. Over time, however, the firm can typically augment its stocks of all of the requisite resources. It can acquire and install new units of specialized equipment, or produce these itself. Most importantly, it can develop new supplies of the team-embodied skills capable of coordinating the routine. It can therefore replicate existing activity patterns on a larger scale. In the conceptually simplest case, this means starting up a new plant with capabilities that are intended to be substantially identical to those of the original, "template," plant. Such a replication effort involves not merely the establishment of the appropriate physical setting, but also the replication of a hierarchical structure of organizational routines. Of course, even if exact replication is aimed at, it will never be fully achieved in practice, and a number of variables will affect its actual precision. In many actual cases the objective is not exact replication but partial replication, accompanied by adaptive or innovative change in some routines.

The analysis of replication presents a number of interesting and challenging issues. In the strategic management literature, most of the illumination of the subject has been indirect, reflected from inquiries into the problems facing a rival who aspires to imitate a profitable performance where productive knowledge is not codified (Lippman and Rumelt 1982;

Barney 1986, 1991; Reed and DeFillippi 1990). Less severe versions of the same problems confront the effort to replicate a productive performance within the boundaries of the same firm, but these have received less attention. It has been noted, however, that there are subtle and important considerations linking imitation, replication and the problem of sustainable advantage (Winter 1987; Kogut and Zander 1992; Zander and Kogut forthcoming). And recently, the problem of replication of routines has been closely studied in its own right, under the heading "intra-firm transfer of best practices" (Szulanski 1994).

Here, the focus is on the point, noted above, that the replication of routines typically requires support from the firm's existing stocks of idiosyncratic resources. This requirement arises because productive knowledge is not fully codified and the generic labor inputs available on the market do not command the coordinating information specific to an individual firm's routines. For example, the design of a new production line may draw on the expertise of engineers whose normal duties consist primarily of trouble-shooting and incremental adaptation of the prevailing routine. The latter role is likely to endow them with just the sort of tacit knowledge needed to create a good design for the new line, knowledge that is not likely to be possessed by newly hired engineers.[4]

There are implications of two related kinds. First, the availability of idiosyncratic resources constrains the rate at which routines can be replicated, and also imposes opportunity costs of replication. These considerations bear on the technically feasible and economically appropriate rate of growth of the firm as a whole. Penrose (1959) emphasized this causal nexus but focused almost entirely on managerial resources. Rubin (1973) provided a formal statement of the problem in the framework of the economic theory of production, and related theoretical issues were addressed at a more abstract level in the adjustment cost theory of investment (Lucas 1967; Gould 1968; Treadway 1970).

Second, the value of idiosyncratic resources to the firm—i.e., the present value of their future rent streams—is affected by the fact that their possible uses include development of more idiosyncratic resources. In simple cases this involves production of more resources of same type, but analogous issues arise when resources are creatively applied to extend the

---

[4]See the HBS case "Altoona Corporation: Consumer Products Division" for an interesting account of an organization stressed by these sorts of competing demands on its key engineers.

155

capabilities of the firm (Kogut and Zander 1992; Teece, Pisano and Shuen forthcoming). In many cases this source of value may greatly outweigh the present value of directly productive service flows; such situations illustrate most strongly the role of idiosyncratic resources as explanations of long-term advantage. In a hypothetical world of fully codifiable knowledge and costless replication, this additional value would be associated with the knowledge *per se* (the ability to supply a flow of Arrow-type information), and the competitive advantage obtained would depend on the effectiveness with which the firm could protect this intellectual property. In the world of uncertain imitability and costly replication, the ability to conduct the activity on a large scale in the future depends on the scale at which it is currently conducted, and the rents to superior knowledge are assignable to the underlying scarce resources. The extent to which these idisosyncratic resources may be tradeable, and the characteristics of the markets for them (if any), becomes an important factor in the equation governing the sustainability of competitive advantage (Dierickx and Cool 1989; Peteraf 1993).

To avoid the need to allocate its existing idiosyncratic resources to support replication, the firm might attempt instead to repeat the original learning process underlying the routine. Because of the context and path-dependent character of learning, what this would create would not be a copy of the template but a new routine that might, with luck, serve the same purposes (Levinthal 1994). In almost all cases, such an approach would involve substantially higher costs: the basic distinction between the first and subsequent copies in Arrow-type information economics argues for replication; in a similar sense, so do the sunk investments in learning that the firm made in moving from its initial trials to a functioning routine. Further, reinvention would involve the acceptance of greater uncertainty regarding the time at which the new capacity would be available, as well as uncertainty regarding operating costs, output quality, and similarity to the existing routine.

These latter uncertainties imply that, quite apart from the costs of reinvention *de novo*, the economic considerations that would typically motivate replication may simply not apply to reinvention. The profitability and quality performance of the existing routine are not likely to be predictive of the reinvented one; and the latter is likely to require accommodating changes in complementary routines that would not be needed under replication. In short, while reinvention may be a plausible alternative to *abandoning* the activity accomplished by an existing routine, it is not generally a plausible alternative to replication when the goal is to seize a larger share of an extant profit opportunity successfully exploited by the prevailing routine.[5]

To explore the role of replication in the history of an individual firm, consider a hypothetical business that has attained, for the moment, a competitive advantage over its rivals. This advantage derives from an innovative product or process that the firm has successfully embodied in a stable routine; the routine is in operation at an initial scale at some particular geographical site.[6] The operation is earning above normal returns in the following specific sense: if the operation could be continued indefinitely into the future, and current price relationships continue to prevail, the net present value of the resulting future cash flow stream would be positive (and substantial relative to the assets committed) when discounted at the firm's cost of capital. Implicit in this calculation is the assumption that the firm is capable of *temporal* replication of the routine at the initial site: it can replace equipment when appropriate, it can also hire new employees (up to an including the CEO) to replace those who quit or retire, and impart to them the skills required for them to play their roles in the continuing routine. (Note that any one-time costs of the original creation of the routine are sunk and do not affect this calculation; profitability in this forward-looking sense is therefore compatible with an overall loss when those one-time costs are included.)

The question is, what might happen next? From the initial position just described, a number of different scenarios might follow. In each scenario, a range of interrelated analytical issues are illustrated; different scenarios give different prominence to the various issues. Among these are (i) descriptive issues: which scenarios are most likely, or best typify how the economy generally works? (ii) prescriptive/normative issues at the firm level: what guidance can be offered to the firm if it is seeking the largest possible returns attainable from this initial position? (iii) normative issues at the societal level: what contribution to society is the firm making, and

---

[5]This appraisal needs to be qualified, however, when rapidly advancing technology has greatly enriched the design options available for the creation of a new routine.

[6]An empirically important possibility is being set aside here: initial success may prove to be a transient phenomenon; no stable routine may emerge that is capable of sustaining the success over time. One common explanation for this outcome is that the initial success was crucially dependent on the roles played by particular individuals, and was not sustainable when some of those individuals left the scene or lost their enthusiasm for the cause.

how might that differ according to the particular actions of the firm, or the policy context in which it operates?

So far as the descriptive issues are concerned, the evolutionary economics view in its simplest terms emphasizes the following scenario: profitability is likely to be reflected in growth; growth is likely to involve a substantial component of replication or partial replication of the routine underlying the initial success, and that growth will ultimately end, quite possibly because excess returns are competed away by imitating rivals. Although there are many other possible scenarios, that one is focal.

The prominence given to this scenario reflects an implicit judgment that information-embodying idiosyncratic resources are typically a key factor in success. If the initial success were a matter of arranging untutored generic inputs according to a fully codified success formula, one would expect imitation to appear promptly, unless the formula can be protected by intellectual property law or secrecy. On the other hand, if the underlying resources that account for initial success have *no* component of (Arrow-type) information to them, then replication is not a way to leverage the initial success because the initial position confers no informational advantage over rivals. (Perhaps, in fact, there is no way to leverage that success). The normative advice that evolutionary economics derives from this descriptive account is this: when successful, copy yourself before others copy you.

Further, evolutionary economics suggests that a firm with a profitable routine in hand has an inherent advantage in pursuing this strategy, by virtue of its superior access to the successful "template" example (Nelson and Winter 1982: 118-124). This advantage is particularly significant when the existing routine involves tacit skills or otherwise resists codification. To the extent, however, that the tacitness derives from the limited "causal depth" of knowledge or "causal ambiguity" of the original success, contextual differences between the template and the new site may impede replication (Nelson and Winter 1982; Lippman and Rumelt 1982; Winter 1982).

The resource-based view offers normative suggestions that are more comprehensive than the evolutionary view, but also less focused. It would suggest that the profitability of the firm in the initial position is attributable to its ownership of some resource, but the resource need not be a replicable routine. At one extreme, the resource might be something like the Disney characters; the most profitable form of "replication" requires a substantial dose of added creativity. At the opposite (mundane) extreme, the resource might be a unique physical asset—a high-grade ore deposit, for

158

example. Whatever opportunities may exist for leveraging this resource cannot take the form of replication, since it is non-replicable by definition.

The resource-based view also stresses the point that imitation by rivals poses a threat to long-term profitability, and urges reliance on resources that are not susceptible to such imitation. Partly because such defenses are rarely perfect, the initial competitive advantage may not be sustainable indefinitely—but that is no reason to refrain from exploiting it vigorously in the medium term. In this sense, the emphasis the strategy literature gives to *sustainable* advantage may have the unintended consequence of diverting attention from the effective pursuit of transient rents.[7] Finally, there is the possibility that the profitability of the initial position is derived from market power. This would have implications for the answer to the "what next?" question; in particular, it might eliminate replication as an approach to leveraging profitability. And it obviously bears also on the normative assessment of the situation at the societal level.

Analytics of scarcity rent and market power

These various strands can be pulled together with the aid of a simple analytical framework illustrated in Figure 1. The diagram portrays the cost and demand conditions facing the profitable firm posited at the start of this section. Assume that the firm produces output by combining N different inputs in fixed proportions. If all inputs were increased by the same percentage, output would increase by that percentage: constant returns to scale prevail so far as production technique is concerned. All but one of the inputs is available in the market at given prices, in whatever amounts the firm might desire. Taken together, these N-1 inputs account for costs of C per unit output. The analytical focus is on the Nth input, which is available to the firm in a strictly limited amount. For convenience, call this Nth input the "constraint input."

The diagram is subject to different interpretations according to the nature of the constraint input. Suppose initially that the constraint input represents the classical type of rent-earning resource—specifically, land with attributes uniquely appropriate to the production of the output whose

---

[7]Barney defines a sustained advantage as one that "continues to exist after efforts to duplicate that advantage have ceased." (1991: 102). On this definition, very significant and long-lasting profit opportunities are outside of the scope of the "sustained advantage" analysis.

demand curve D is shown in the diagram. Suppose also that the diagram portrays a "long run" analysis: the N-1 inputs may include facilities that are fixed in the short run, as well as short-run variable inputs, but in the long run all these inputs are variable. The firm in question owns the entire world supply of this unique resource, and is on that account a monopolist in the output market. Its profit-maximizing course of action is to fully utilize the constraint input, which suffices for Q_A units of output. Up to that level, the

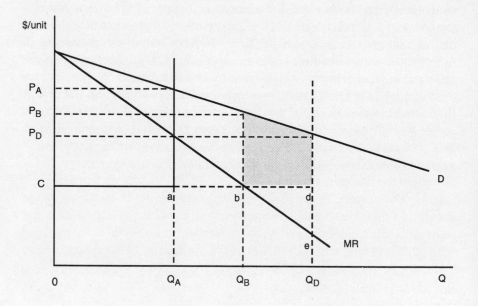

Figure 1. Scarcity Rent vs. Output Restraint

additional revenue obtained from production and sale of another unit, given by the MR curve, exceeds the marginal cost C, and beyond that level it is impossible to go. By producing at that level, the firm obtains revenue of $(P_A - C) Q_A$ in excess of the amount required to pay for the first N-1 inputs. If the firm is equity financed, it can use those funds to pay dividends. An efficient capital market will price the firm's stock so that those dividends represent normal returns.

What is the economic nature of this surplus? The firm clearly has market power: it is a monopolist in the output market, based on its "sustainable advantage" in the form of exclusive control of an essential input, and it could restrict output and raise price. What it does not have, however, is an *incentive* to restrict output. Its profit-maximizing output is the same as a competitive industry would choose. If the control of the constraint input were divided among numerous atomistic competitors, their competition would bid the price to $P_A - C$. At that price, the circumstances of the availability of the constraint input would look the same to an individual competitor as those of any other input; any amount it might (practically) want would be available at the market price.

Monopolistic market structure and "sustainable advantage" notwithstanding, the foregoing considerations point clearly to the following conclusions: (i) the difference $P_A - C$ is properly interpreted as a scarcity rent, (ii) the maximized *economic* profit is zero since the scarcity rent is simply the normal flow return on the properly calculated value of the asset. (iii) there is no efficiency loss from monopoly in this case.[8]

Consider now a situation differing from that just described in a single respect: the amount of the constraint input is large enough to support output Q_D. In this case, the monopolist does have an incentive to restrict output, specifically, to Q_B. This restraint increases the excess of revenue over cost by the amount equal to the excess of $(P_B - C) Q_B$ over $(P_D - C)$

---

[8]Some theorists may object that the absence of an efficiency loss is attributable to the sharp corners in the diagram: if marginal cost rose continuously as output approached an upper bound, there would be at least some efficiency loss. While this is true, it is also true that there are continuous examples that lie as close as one likes, in quantitative terms, to the Figure 1 case. Thus, continuity itself is not the issue. The example of Figure 1 captures the analytical connotation of "rent" and dramatizes the distinction between a scarcity rent and a monopoly return.

Q_D.[9] The profit from output restraint is attended by an "efficiency" (total surplus) loss corresponding to the shaded area; output units potentially producible at C and valued by buyers in the range P_D to P_B are foregone. Thus "market power" is a real factor in the situation: it both augments net revenues relative to a competition-mimicking result and imposes an efficiency loss. As a matter of terminology, however, it seems appropriate to identify only the net revenue increment from output restraint as a monopoly profit, since the scarcity rent $(P_D - C) Q_D$ would also accrue under competitive organization of the industry.

For a second interpretation of Figure 1, suppose now that the constraint input is a firm-specific idiosyncratic resource, such as the team-embodied skills that underlie the firm's capability to produce its product. The different quantities of the constraint input now correspond to different *short run* situations with respect to the availability of these skills. There may perhaps be other inputs that also involve durable commitments, but it is the skills package that imposes the significant constraint on the rate at which output can be adjusted. Assume the firm can replicate the skills; it is simplest to assume here that although this replication is costly and time-consuming it does not impose an opportunity cost in foregone output. At a point in time when the available skills supply supports output level Q_A, the skills earn a quasi-rent for the firm. And here again, although symptoms of market power are clearly present, the return is not affected by output restraint and in that sense is not a consequence of the market power in the output market.

Over time, the firm could replicate the skills and, if it wished, produce output level Q_D. But if the situation remains as displayed in the diagram, it obviously will not want to move beyond Q_B. In fact, it will stop somewhere short of that output level because of the positive costs of replicating the constraint input. Thus, in this "dynamized" interpretation of the diagram, the firm starts in an initial region where output restraint is no issue, replication is focal and the returns are plainly scarcity rents, and moves over time to a region where further replication is not desired, accurate assessment of demand conditions is focal, and returns are a mix of scarcity rents and monopoly returns.

---

[9] That this difference is positive follows directly from the fact that the equation of marginal revenue and marginal cost identifies the profit maximizing position. The difference corresponds, in fact, to the area of triangle **bde**.

The foregoing account neglects the first phase of this stylized historical episode, the period when the initial level of the constraint input was acquired through development of a new routine, purchase of a piece of land, or whatever. To assess the overall profitability including that first phase, one would need to know not only the information implicit in the diagram, but also the original investment costs that gave rise to this idiosyncratic resource, the replication costs, the time rates at which everything happens, and the relevant cost of capital.

Another variant of the story arises if the process is so esoteric or context-dependent that profitable replication is costly or impossible. For example, the effectiveness of the process might depend on features of its original location that are unique, or inadequately understood, and the market might be geographically segmented. In such a case, one might expect the operation to become sized relative to its original local market in a way that exploited some market power there, and perhaps transferred to a few other favorable locations. This is a more complex form of leveraging the key resource underlying the profitable initial position. Here, the absence of larger scale replication is not a reflection of monopoly restraint but of natural barriers to replication.

Missing from the above stylized account is the strategically important question of how long the situation depicted is likely to last. Various things can happen on the way from Q_A to Q_B, and a sensible firm will want to consider these scenarios as it chooses a path. Other firms may succeed in imitating the process or coming up with a substitute product; the demand curve shifts down and flattens, costs become focal and the mirage of a future regime of output restraint fades away. Alternatively, knowledge of the firm's product diffuses and the demand curve shifts to the right, with the result that the regime in which replication is the key activity is extended (although an output restraint regime may remain visible in the distant future). Or, the firm itself may extend the duration of the replication regime if it succeeds in lowering C.

Classification of returns

The foregoing analytical exercise indicates that the economic and strategic issues surrounding idiosyncratic resources involve an interweaving of themes emphasized in evolutionary economics, the resource-based view, and standard economic analysis. The resulting picture is complex, especially considering the highly stylized nature of the initial framework. The various mechanisms alluded to in the analysis are quite general, but

163

others were passed over because they do not fit easily into the stylized picture presented by Figure 1. This section presents a more comprehensive and qualitative summary of the issues, schematically organized in Figure 2.

A slightly amended version of the premise of the preceding analysis serves to organize this summary. Whereas the discussion of Figure 1 proceeded by contrasting a "team-embodied skills" interpretation with other interpretations of the constraint input, this section acknowledges that multiple obstacles to leveraging a profitable position may be present simultaneously.

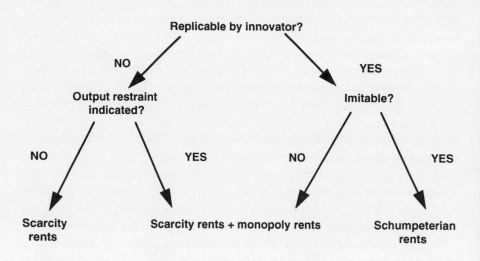

Figure 2. Classification of Returns

The first question to be asked is whether the innovator possesses a replicable routine. The answer may be no—a situation corresponding to the left branch of Figure 2. The reasons may be (i) characteristic of the site (an ore deposit of distinctive quality and other attributes, or a resort locale in a unique natural setting). Alternatively, (ii), the obstacles to replication may lie in the cognitive and motivational characteristics of the routine considered as a problem solution—complexity, tacitness, lucky outcomes in highly path-dependent organizational learning, a strong high-performance culture, and so on. Or, (iii), interactions of the routine with its site may be involved: the features of the routine that resist replication may be the determinants of its effectiveness in coping with the particular flow of micro-problems characteristic of the site—short-term variations characteristic of the site's particular raw material sources, environmental contaminants, labor pool, or customer population.

Whatever the reason for the lack of replicability, the consequence is that the innovative routine is of determinate scale. Demand conditions then determine whether this scale is small or large relative to the market, and, closely related, whether demand elasticity is large or small. If *product* attributes are not unique, and if transportation costs are not a major factor, the likely case is that the scale is small and the demand highly elastic. At the extreme, this is one output source out of many in a world market. The economic outcome is of the type illustrated by Q_A in Figure 1: there is a flow of return that is of the nature of a Ricardian rent to the scarce resource represented by the routine. The presence of this source of supply may affect the price, as it does in Figure 1, but not to the point where output restraint becomes an issue.

If product attributes are sufficiently unique or other considerations limit the extent and elasticity of demand, it is conceivable that the initial scale might exceed the long run profit-maximizing level. This is illustrated by the position of Q_D in Figure 1. Considerations of output restraint come into play in the sense that incentives for down-sizing exist. A response to those incentives might well present hazards for the stability of the routine, since, for example, different task allocations would be required in a smaller workforce. Also, an adequate analysis of the economics of such a situation would involve attention to the distinctions among variable, fixed and sunk costs, and also to the possibilities of price discrimination. (Consider a new resort hotel in a unique location, built and staffed at so large a scale that it cannot be kept full at a profit—a potential "white elephant.") Thus, it is not entirely obvious that the ultimate outcome closely approximates the one illustrated by Q_B in Figure 1. If the returns realizable (on a forward-looking basis) are sufficient to make the operation viable with some room to spare, they are interpretable as a mix of scarcity rents and monopoly returns.

These two outcomes correspond to the left-hand branch of Figure 2, with output restraint involved only in the second. The structure of the diagram reflects a basic proposition of evolutionary economics that was mentioned previously: replication of an established routine is much easier than imitation, because the imitator does not have the advantage of full access to the template (assuming the imitatee is not cooperating with the effort). Thus, it is assumed that a "no" answer on the feasibility of replication implies the same answer for the feasibility of imitation. By contrast, on the right hand of Figure 2, the "yes" answer on replication poses the imitation question as the follow-on.

Figure 2 presumes that, if replication is possible, it continues until the economic incentives for it have been eliminated. The elimination of these incentives can occur by two basic mechanisms, leading to two end conditions that are distinguished by the different returns received by the innovating firm. At one extreme, on the right hand side of the diagram, imitation sooner or later produces something approximating textbook competition, and hence zero economic profit from a forward-looking point of view. Looking forward, the once-innovative routine and the techniques for replicating it become known sufficiently widely so that this knowledge, *per se*, no longer commands a significant scarcity rent. Resources that are routine-specific continue to be involved, perhaps to an even greater degree than in the early days of the innovation. But since the nature of these resources and the methods for creating them are sufficiently widely understood, the logic of investment in these routine-specific capabilities is entirely conventional.

It should be emphasized again that this analysis say nothing at all about how the innovator fared in the episode as a whole. Looking backward, the balance between initial investments and the pace of imitation are key determinants of the temporary excess returns received by the innovator (the level of Schumpeterian rents). Given the size of the initial advantage the innovation confers, low investment in creating it and slow imitation spell greater financial success for the innovator.

The other possibility is that imitation does not occur, at least not in such a way as to leave the innovator with a future prospect of only normal returns. In this case, the innovating firm has significant control over the scale at which the innovation is implemented in the long run. Failure to take account of the limits of the market when exercising this control would be tantamount to the firm's competing with itself to bring its own economic

166

profit level to zero. Thus, the innovator will want to approach a result represented by Q_B in Figure 1. This stylized representation hardly suggests the complexity of the problem, however. In typical cases where geography and transportation costs matter, and there are significant differences in the local economic environments at the different sites where the routine might be established, the replication of the routine will typically involve its adaptation as well. The problem of appropriate scale may be faced many times over in isolated markets, or, more complex still, in a series of markets that are distinguishable but interconnected. The aggregate scale achieved through replication may itself induce change because of the managerial challenges it presents and the new scale-related innovative opportunities it reveals.

In the end, as concluded in Figure 2, the assumed absence of multiple competitors willing and able to do the same thing implies an element of output restraint and monopoly returns at the long-run position to which the firm is headed. An analysis of the full episode in present value terms might well reveal, however, that these persistent monopoly returns are a minor factor compared to the scarcity rents received in earlier phases of the replication path (Q_A-type conditions).

Assessing Profitability: Concepts and Measures

Although the field of strategic management has been informed increasingly from economics over the past two decades, surprisingly little attention has been paid to the basic question of what "profitable" really means. Economists worked hard for a couple of centuries to arrive at analytically useful meanings of terms like "cost," "rent," and "profit." Although this protracted effort produced something short of a full consensus regarding appropriate theoretical terminology, it certainly generated a sophisticated understanding of many of the issues involved. That understanding has infiltrated the strategic management literature only recently, however.[10]

In general terms, at least, there seems to be a strong consensus that profitability is central to what the strategic management field is about. Many would endorse the statement that "The fundamental question in the

---

[10]Peteraf (1993) provides the most careful statement thus far of the theoretical connections between the rent concepts of economics and the concerns of strategic management. The present paper concurs with her analysis on a number of key points.

field of strategic management is how do firms achieve and sustain competitive advantage" (Teece, Pisano and Shuen 1994: p. 1). "Competitive advantage" is typically defined as superior financial performance. Beyond this point, however, conceptual clarity starts to fade. The idea of superior financial performance may be evoked by a range of phrases such as "above normal returns," "high quasi-rents," "value creation" and other near-synonyms for "making money." For empirical work, a more operational definition of "making money" is needed. Numerous alternatives are available and have been selected in one study or another (sometimes with little discussion of their appropriateness): for example, returns on assets, return on equity, total return to investors, Tobin's q,[11] and others.

To develop a stronger theoretical grounding for the discussion of profitability, it is important to note first that economists have developed a relatively clear idea of what an economic *cost* is: it is an opportunity cost in one sense or another. There is less terminological clarity regarding returns in excess of costs, such as profits or rents, partly because different perspectives on the opportunities referenced in opportunity cost lead to different perspectives on whether a return is "excess." For example, the return measured by $(P_A - C) Q_A$ in Figure 1 is a "rent from the point of view of the industry" when the industry is competitively organized, but certainly is not an excess return at the individual firm level; the firm has to pay the market price, reflecting the foregone opportunity to use the resource in another firm.

The importation of profitability concepts from economics into strategic management faces three substantial difficulties. The first problem is that an abnormally high return in economic theory is generally measured against a social opportunity cost standard—a standard that has little relation to the business world's meaning of profitability. For example, a monopoly acquired at a price reflecting the present value of its future returns is still a profitable monopoly by the economist's standards. The fact that it yields only a normal return to its investors has nothing to do with the economic case, but everything to do with the strategic management case (cf., Barney 1986). The second problem is that those economic concepts reside most comfortably in the abstract world of those regions of economic theory characterized by complete and perfect markets, optimization and equilibrium. They are somewhat alien to the world of flux, uncertainty and

---

[11]Tobin's q is defined as the market value of the company's assets (from the liabilities side) divided by the replacement cost valuation of those assets (assets side).

strategic moves that the strategic management literature seeks to address. Finally, the available quantitative measures of financial performance, based either in accounting data or securities markets valuations, generally lack a coherent rationale in terms of the analytical needs of either economics or strategic management.[12] (Of course, some measures are better than others: "earnings per share" is little more than a trap for the unwary; measures like total return to investors and Tobin's q have problems, but of far smaller magnitude.)

Among the specific conceptual issues evoked but not thoroughly discussed in the previous section, the first that deserves scrutiny is whether ownership of a resource that earns a Ricardian scarcity rent should be considered, by itself, to confer competitive advantage. (This situation corresponds to the first interpretation offered for Figure 1, and to the far left-hand branch of Figure 2.) Many authors suggest an affirmative answer. For example, Porter's (1980) discussion of barriers to entry includes the following:

- Favorable access to raw materials: established firms may have locked up the most favorable sources and/or tied up foreseeable needs early *at prices reflecting a lower demand for them than currently exists.*

- Favorable locations: established firms may have cornered favorable locations *before market forces bid up prices to capture their full value.*
  —Porter (1980: 11)
  (emphasis supplied)

Similarly, Ghemawat says:

- Access (to resources or customers) will lead to a sustainable advantage if two conditions are met: *it must be secured under better terms than competitors will be able to get later, and the*

---

[12]Merging aspects of the second and third points, Beaver and Demski (1979) argue convincingly that income measurement can be well defined only in the context of complete markets. Outside of this hypothetical context accounting rules can be rationalized only on pragmatic cost-benefit grounds.

advantage has to be enforceable over the long run. Enforceability can come from ownership. . . ."

—Ghemawat (1986, p. 55)
(emphasis supplied)

These statements suggest that sustainable advantage can be generated by the combination of some past speculative coup with historical cost accounting. Buying low and selling high is certainly a way to make money, and buying resources low and selling the derived products high is a variant of that basic formula. However, if the speculative success occurred a long time ago, and if the rent-earning asset could be sold at a current market value, it is not clear why possession of such a rent-earning asset is any more a source of advantage than possession of the corresponding amount of well-invested cash. Under these circumstances, a management that prides itself on its ability to generate "above normal returns" as reflected in (book) ROA is a management that may be inviting a takeover bid.

The second issue has to do with the historical path of profitability in a particular firm as it grows by replicating its routines and the associated idiosyncratic resources. As it grows, such a firm is investing in a variety of intangible assets, transforming generic inputs by imparting to them the particular information, skills, locations and relationships that make these assets capable of carrying out the firm's routines. Particularly in the case of the firm-specific human capital imparted to employees, the firm cannot own these intangible assets, though it may have good reason to expect that it can draw on their services in the future. Accounting conventions typically yield a distorted economic picture of such a growth phase, under-reporting economic earnings by failing to recognize that some portion of what is designated as current cost is actually investment. As the firm's growth slows to the point where new investments of this type are approximately balanced by renewal of old ones, the earnings picture becomes more accurate. The accounting distortions of the past live on, however, in a new form: rates of return on assets are overstated because of the understatement of the asset base. Historical cost accounting produces a similar but more correctable form of this distortion; for example, in the calculation of Tobin's q the valuation of assets at replacement cost provides such a correction. This adjustment cannot, however, compensate for the fact that some important types of assets are missing from the accountants' lists in the first place.

170

If "sustainable advantage" is something that is supposed to be reflected in accounting measures like ROA, then it appears that there is a relatively straightforward way to achieve it: invest in long-lasting assets that do not show up on the balance sheet, a prime example being the initial learning that gives rise to new, replicable routines. In a hypothetical world in which everyone else's assets are fully reflected on the balance sheet, outstanding performance in terms of ROA might even be achievable by a series of investment projects with zero net present value, provided the shareholders are patient enough to put up with the understated earnings of the early years.

At the level of the firm as a whole, reliance on stock market- based valuations might appear to offer an escape from the range of measurement errors just discussed. According to the (semi-strong) efficient markets hypothesis, publicly available information about the future earning power of the firm's assets will be fully reflected in the prices of its securities. There are, however, three significant shortcomings to stock market-based performance measures: (i) they presume that the shareholders are the only claimants whose interests are at stake;[13] (ii) they do not provide valuations at the level of individual resources or conveyable packages, but only of the firm as a whole; (iii) they necessarily rely on the presumption that the relevant information is public, although keeping secrets is often an important part of effective strategic management. (Indeed, the resource-based view suggests, following a path blazed by Hirshleifer (1971), that maintaining secrecy about its own future plans is one way that a company might obtain resources at prices below their future market values.) But at least the stock market provides a valuation untainted by accounting conventions or other artifacts of historical measurement.

Where stock market valuations and derived performance measures are concerned, the famous list of five forces enumerated by Porter (1980) needs to be supplemented by a sixth: investor expectations. If the other five forces do not whittle away abnormally high returns, investors will happily get used to them. The market will certainly learn to discount systematic, sustained earning power, even if the sources of that power are not fully understood. Once this happens, any superiority disappears so far as stock

---

[13]Aside from employees, customers, suppliers and other familiar entries on the extended list of stakeholders, there is top management. Castanias and Helfat (1991) argue, in effect, that a "managerialist" interpretation of the corporation may be economically sound, at least in the sense that managers are more likely to be providing idisosyncratic rent-earning resources than the providers of financial capital.

market-based measurement is concerned. Imagine the frustration of a (hypothetically) perfect profit-maximizing CEO, fully capable of implementing every bit of valid strategic advice available from any source, who has the misfortune to lead a company that has been managed to that same high standard for decades on end. Pure good luck aside, it will be impossible for this superlative manager to look more than ordinary on stock market-based measures. The advantage goes to the manager who inherits a rich fund of strategic mistakes that can be corrected, provided that the market's awareness of the correctability of the mistakes does not precede her accession to office.

None of the foregoing should be interpreted as implying skepticism about the existence of real differences in financial performance, or as denying that available operational measures capture some of those differences. It does suggest, however, that both the resource-based view and evolutionary economics need to contribute more to the conceptualization and measurement of profitability than has been the case thus far. Attention to this agenda is particularly urgent when the questions under examination involve comparing the performance of the same firm at different points of time. It is judgments on these questions that are most likely to be distorted because the available data contain little clue as the actual timing of key speculative successes or key developmental investments in idiosyncratic resources.

Social Implications of Competitive Advantage

When a business succeeds in obtaining "competitive advantage" over its rivals, are the consequences for society at large generally favorable or unfavorable? There is, course, no general answer. It all depends, and in particular it depends on the nature of the advantage, how it was obtained, and how it is maintained. Recent commentary has pointed out, however, that different approaches to strategic analysis seem to imply different general orientations to this question. Since there is presumably no dispute about the observation that real cases vary across a wide spectrum, it is probably useful to think of these differences as relating to "first approximations" or "rebuttable presumptions about the typical case."

In particular, the competitive forces approach pioneered by Porter (1980) is seen as one in which the typical source of superior profitability is some form of market power. Forceful comments to this effect have been offered by Teece, Pisano and Shuen (1994):

This approach, rooted in the structure-conduct-performance paradigm of industrial organization, ... emphasizes the actions a firm can take to create defensible positions against market forces....

Economic rents in the competitive forces framework are monopoly rents.... Firms in an industry earn rents when they are somehow able to impede the competitive forces (in either factor markets or product markets) which tend to drive economic returns to zero.

—Teece, Pisano and Shuen
(1994: 4)

By constrast, the resource-based view of the firm, the dynamic capabilities approach, evolutionary economics, the Chicago school view in industrial economics (e.g., Demsetz 1973) and the Schumpeterian tradition (1934, 1950) are all seen as emphasizing that profitability may derive instead from superior efficiency (Teece, Pisano and Shuen 1994; Rumelt, Schendel and Teece 1991; Foss, Knudsen and Montgomery 1994).

The analytical scheme presented earlier in this paper lends some detail, and hence some complication, to this broad-brush contrast. An innovating firm seeking to operate on a larger scale, but temporarily constrained by its stock of idiosyncratic resources, may be highly profitable. By some tests it may have "market power," but this is no way implies that it is exercising socially undesirable retraint over its output: such restraint is the furthest thing from its management's mind. The happiest version of the story is that the innovator collects sufficient Schumpeterian rents to cover its initial costs and offer some encouragement to other innovators, but ultimately settles into an essentially competitive relationship with its rivals, while its innovation is applied at socially efficient levels. Of course, if imitation is successfully blocked, the episode may end in a period of output restraint. But even that persists only until the next gale of Schumpeterian creative destruction passes through.

Although the happy version of the story is only one case, it certainly provides an uplifting contrast to the static barriers-to-entry story offered by the competitive forces approach. Unfortunately, a cloud of complexity must be added to this carefully-selected sunny picture. There is a another form of output restraint to be considered: the restraint imposed by the innovator's ability to restrain imitation. Even in the early stages of an innovator's growth, the returns earned by the innovator can only be said to be untainted by output restraint, *given* the imitation barriers that restrain the outputs of other firms. These barriers may be partly "natural" reflecting the intrinsic difficulty of imitation, but there are also important institutional barriers. These include patent and trade secret protection, but also a more fundamental institutional barrier that crucially fortifies the natural ones: the absence of an affirmative legal obligation of the imitatee to cooperate with the imitator. The notion that the innovator might have such an affirmative obligation is of course quite remote from institutional reality; nevertheless, in principle the absence of cooperation from the imitatee is a potential source of inefficiency just as other imitation barriers are.[14] Finally, of course, the innovator is likely to take strategic action to enhance the effect of the natural and institutional barriers.

When posed in a realistic institutional setting, and with due recognition of the importance of innovation incentives, the problems of social welfare assessment raised here lead into deep analytical waters. As Rumelt (1984) has suggested, it is fortunate and liberating for analysts in the strategy field that rendering sharp verdicts on these difficult problems is not among our central concerns (p. 561). There seems to be merit in the general idea that the quest for profit is appraised more favorably by evolutionary economics and the resource-based view than by the competitive forces approach. We can leave the details for someone else to work out.

Conclusion

This paper has explored a piece of intellectual territory that is common ground for the resource-based view and evolutionary economics: a firm can effectively leverage a profitable initial resource position represented by superior routines and its associated team-embodied skills, and this leveraging is accomplished by replicating the routines. In this area, evolutionary economics provides a relatively detailed account of one part of the dynamic aspect of strategic management. It is an important part of the total problem, but, as was noted more than once, only a part.

---

[14] For a good, concise statement on this issue see Koopmans (1957, pp. 64-66.)

Aside from its importance, what recommends it for careful discussion is that it is a comparatively *simple* part of the total problem. The "speculative" and "creative" components of the problem of dynamic resource exploitation were mentioned but left aside. The complications of replicating routines in novel contexts received even more casual treatment. Corporate-level capabilities and management issues were left implicit, although the corporate level is the arena of the great managerial challenges of scale and scope described by Chandler (1991). These simplifications made possible a clearer view of some central issues in the descriptive and normative analysis of the quest for profit. The issues thus revealed may be obscured but certainly do not go away when more realistic complications are added to the picture. Like the quest for profit itself, the quest for better understanding of profitability can be expected to continue for a long time to come.

References

Amit, R., and Schoemaker, P. 1993. "Strategic assets and organizational rent." *Strategic Management Journal* 14 (January): 33-36.

Arrow, K. 1962. "Economic welfare and the allocation of resources for invention." In R. Nelson, ed., *The rate and direction of inventive activity*: 609-625. Princeton, NJ: Princeton University Press.

Barney, J. 1986. "Strategic factor markets: expectations, luck and business strategy." *Management Science* 32 (October): 1231-1241.

Barney, J. 1989. "Asset stocks and sustained competitive advantage: a comment." *Management Science* 35 (December): 1511-1513.

Barney, J. 1991. "Firm resources and sustained competitive advantage." *Journal of Management* 17 (October): 99-120.

Beaver, W., and Demski, J. 1979. "The nature of income measurement." *The Accounting Review* 54: 38-46.

Castanias, R., and Helfat, C. 1991. "Managerial resources and rents." *Journal of Management* 17 (October): 155-171.

Chandler, A. 1990. *Scale and scope: the dynamics of industrial competition.* Cambridge, MA: Harvard University Press.

Demsetz, H. 1973. "Industry structure, market rivalry, and public policy." *Journal of Law and Economics* 16 (April): 1-10.

Dierickx, I., and Cool, K. 1989. "Asset stock accumulation and sustainability of competitive advantage." *Management Science* 35 (December): 1504-1511.

Foss, N., Knudsen, C., and Montgomery, C. 1995. "An exploration of common ground: integrating evolutionary and strategic theories of the firm." In C.A. Montgomery (ed.), *Resources from an evolutionary perspective: towards a synthesis of evolutionary and resource-based approaches to strategy*: 1-17. Norwell, MA: Kluwer Academic Publishers.

Ghemawat, P. 1986. "Sustainable advantage." *Harvard Business Review* (September-October): 53-56.

Gould, J. 1968. "Adjustment costs in the theory of investment of the firm." *Review of Economic Studies* 35: 47-55.

Gould, S. 1980. *The panda's thumb: more reflections in natural history.* New York: Norton.

Hirshleifer, J. 1971. "The private and social value of information and the reward to inventive activity." *American Economic Review* 61: 561-574.

Kogut, B., and Zander, U. 1992. "Knowledge of the firm, combinative capabilities, and the replication of technology." *Organization Science* 3: 383-397.

Koopmans, T.C. 1957. *Three essays on the state of economic science.* New York: McGraw-Hill.

Levinthal, D. 1994. "Adaptation on rugged landscapes." Unpublished manuscript. Wharton School, University of Pennsylvania.

Lippman, S, and Rumelt, R. 1982. "Uncertain imitability: an analysis of interfirm differences in efficiency under competition." *Bell Journal of Economics* 13: 418-438.

Lucas, R. 1967. "Adjustment costs and the theory of supply." *Journal of Political Economy* 75 (August, Part I): 321-334.

Montgomery, C. 1992. "Resources: the essence of corporate advantage." Teaching note. Boston: Harvard Business School.

Nelson, R. 1991. "Why do firms differ, and how does it matter?" *Strategic Management Journal* 12: 61-74.

Nelson, R., and Winter, S. 1982b. *An evolutionary theory of economic change.* Cambridge: Harvard University Press.

Penrose, E. 1959. *The theory of the growth of the firm.* New York: John Wiley & Sons.

Peteraf, M. 1993. "The cornerstones of competitive advantage: a resource-based view." *Strategic Management Journal* 14: 179-91.

Porter, M. 1980. *Competitive strategy.* New York: The Free Press.

Reed, R., and DeFillippi, R. 1990. Causal ambiguity, barriers to imitation, and sustainable competitive advantage. *Academy of Management Review* 15: 88-102.

Rubin, P. 1973. "The expansion of firms." *Journal of Political Economy* 81: 936-949.

Rumelt, R. 1984. "Towards a strategic theory of the firm." In R. Lamb, ed., *Competitive strategic management.* Englewood Cliffs, NJ: Prentice-Hall.

Rumelt, R. 1987. "Theory, strategy and entrepreneurship." In D. Teece, ed., *The competitive challenge: strategies for industrial innovation and renewal*: 137-158. Cambridge: Ballinger.

Rumelt, R., Schendel, D., and Teece, D. 1991. "Strategic Management and Economics." *Strategic Management Journal* 12: 5-29.

Schumpeter, J. 1934 (Orig. in German, 1911). *The theory of economic development.* Cambridge: Harvard University Press.

Schumpeter, J. 1950. *Capitalism, socialism and democracy*, 3rd ed. New York: Harper and Row.

Szulanski, G. 1994. "Intra-firm transfer of best practices project: executive summary." INSEAD and International Benchmarking Clearinghouse.

Teece, D., Pisano, G., and Shuen, A. Forthcoming. "Dynamic capabilities and strategic management." *Strategic Management Journal.*

Treadway, A. "Adjustment costs and variable inputs in the theory of the competitive firm." *Journal of Economic Theory* 2: 329-347.

Wernerfelt, B. 1984. "A resource-based view of the firm." *Strategic Management Journal* 5: 171-180.

Wernerfelt, B. 1989. "From critical resources to corporate strategy." *Journal of General Management* 14 (Spring): 4-12.

Winter, S. 1982. "An essay on the theory of production." In S. Hymans, ed., *Economics and the world around it*: 55-91. Ann Arbor. Michigan: University of Michigan Press.

Winter, S. 1987. "Knowledge and competence as strategic assets." In D. Teece, ed., *The competitive challenge: strategies for industrial innovation and renewal*: 159-184. Cambridge: Ballinger.

Zander, U. and Kogut, B. Forthcoming. "Knowledge and the speed of transfer and imitation of organizational capabilities: an empirical test." *Organization Science*.

8

THEORIES OF THE FIRM, STRATEGIC MANAGEMENT, AND LEADERSHIP

Christian Knudsen
Institute of Industrial Economics and Strategy
Copenhagen Business School

1. Economics and Strategic Management

Economics and strategic management have, for many years, been developing relatively independently of one another, and they have only to a limited extent mutually stimulated one another. One reason is that economists have focussed little attention on the individual firm and its specific competencies. Indeed, although economists have for a long time been occupied by something they called "the theory of the firm," the purpose has never been to enable them to say something about the individual firm. On the contrary, the theory of the firm has merely been a sub-theory of a more general theory of prices and markets. A more important explanation of the absent collaboration between economists and strategic management theorists is probably that for many years economists have based their work on a conceptual model which actually excludes the very existence of the phenomenon which is the raison d'etre or the justification for the field of strategic management. By basing their theorizing on the assumption that firms within the same industry are subject to identical cost and demand conditions, economists have actually assumed a world in which heterogeneity among firms cannot occur. However, this heterogeneity is the very precondition for the domain of strategic management.

179

The most important cause of improved relations between economics and strategic management in recent years is the emergence of a series of new research traditions within economics. These paved the way for introducing new research perspectives and simultaneously eliminated some of the issues that impeded collaboration with the field of strategic management. First of all, the emergence of a series of new research traditions has turned the single firm into a significant explanandum of economic theory instead of merely viewing it as a "logical atom" within a more comprehensive theory of prices and markets. Second, these new theories have broken with the assumption that firms are fundamentally identical thereby eliminating one of the most important obstacles to collaboration between economics and strategic management.

These economic theories have facilitated quite new relations with the field of strategic management by replacing the orthodox neoclassical conception of the firm as a "production function" and a "maximizing" decision-maker. This has happened by making the firm the primary level of analysis: the firm is viewed as a complex institution which has emerged with the purpose of mediating collaboration between resource owners. Thus, completely new "metaphors" for what constitutes a firm have found their way into economics. Therefore, today, economists have access to a set of alternative theories based on different metaphors which facilitate the analysis of highly distinct aspects of firm behavior.

The purpose of this discussion is thus to examine the existing stock of theories of the firm within economics and, secondly, to examine what kind strategy understanding and perception of leadership these theories imply. The first step is to identify the different metaphors or ways in which the various research traditions conceive of the firm. Identifying the various metaphors used by these different theories should make it possible to determine what sort of conceptions of strategy and leadership they imply. Finally, this analysis enables us to identify a series of lacunas in our typology which must be filled in, before we can say that we have established a genuine "strategic" theory of the firm capable of understanding leadership and strategy from an analytical point of view.

2. A Typology of Research Traditions Within the Contemporary Theory of the Firm

The characteristics of inertia and limited possibilities for flexibility apply not only to firms but also to the world of research. Just as firms demonstrate great inertia in adapting to new conditions, many research

180

traditions are based on frameworks that demonstrate limited flexibility in formulating and subsequently solving empirical problems. Within the world of research, inertia primarily appears as a commitment to certain explanatory principles and heuristics, i.e., methods for problem solving. Therefore, inertia will be an invariable quality of any system that has as its goal the generation of new and deeper knowledge in order to create new and more sophisticated capabilities for solving future problems. Therefore, like many firms, individual researchers have been forced to sink large investments in the generation of specific competencies and heuristics. If these researchers, for one reason or the other, decided to solve problems in a new way, investments would be wasted, and new investments would have to be made in order to generate a different heuristic and an alternative set of basic hypotheses. The assumption of complete flexibility is dubious, not only as a description of how research is conducted but also as a norm for how to act. In the world of research, we are fully aware of the fact that "theories capable of explaining everything explain nothing." Theories demonstrate complete flexibility precisely because they merely incorporate previous falsifying instances into new theories which is why they never produce any genuinely "new" or "deeper" knowledge. Popper refused such ad hoc strategies with the comment that new theories must "proceed from some simple, new, and powerful unifying idea" (1963:242). The purpose of this rule was to avoid adhocery and thus ensure that an area of research does not disintegrate and become fragmented. A similar interpretation can be applied to the norm within strategic management prescribing the pursuit of maximum coherence (Dosi, Teece, Winter 1992) in a firm's activities with a view to secure continuous accumulation of knowledge and resources. In this case, too, the demand for coherence must be viewed as an attempt to avoid fragmentation and disintegration of the firm and to maintain adequate momentum in further developing the firm's capabilities.

If we now focus on the theories of the firm, the "inertia" demonstrated by various research traditions as to problem solving capacity, is often justified by referring to how restrictive or spacious a "metaphor of the firm" the given research tradition rests on. Therefore, within the theory of the firm, the criteria for appraising a research tradition is rarely its predictive capability, but rather what has been called its *resilience*. It is its capability to avoid anomalous problems in a creative and innovative way, and to fit phenomena of apparently widely different natures into the same theoretical structure. For example, if one is to assess a theory of the firm, one must start out by identifying the basic metaphor of the firm on which the given tradition rests, and then attempt to assess the theory's capability to solve a number of various conceptual and empirical problems.

The following analysis examines the metaphors applied by various theories of the firm and how these metaphors effect the theories' capacities for problem solving. The underlying assumption of this paper is that the development of the economic theory of the firm has been cumulative. This derives, among other things, from the fact that when new metaphors are constructed—and hence new research traditions within the theory of the firm emerge—these metaphors stem from attempts to overcome those restrictions encountered by previous metaphors and theories of the firm. When one metaphor of the firm is replaced by another, this is usually justified by referring to the new metaphor as being more spacious. The new theory is thus characterized by a larger problem-solving capacity or greater resilience, relative to existing theories. Thus, in the following I will attempt to identify the "problems" within an existing theory that have led attempts to introduce more "general" or "more spacious" metaphors of the firm.

Accordingly, this analysis differs from similar analyses of the various theories within organizational sociology, such as that conducted by Morgan (1986). In *Images of Organization*, Morgan attempts to identify the metaphors and analogies underlying the various research traditions within organizational theory. He goes to far as to argue that the different metaphors or organizational theories have been developed in order to solve different problems. He suggests that it would be outright meaningless to attempt to compare organizational theories which rest on different metaphors since they typically represent incommensurable and incomparable images of reality. Morgan's aim, therefore, is to produce as complete a catalogue as possible of the most important metaphors within organization theory. In contrast, the following analysis views the theory of the firm from a more cumulative perspective. It attempts to understand how each new theory emerges from the problems encountered by previous theories and metaphors.

Table 1 illustrates a typology of some of the most important theories of the firm. This multitude of theories have risen out of two more-or-less interdependent development trends. The first of these trends involves a series of attempts to fill in the neoclassical tradition's "black box" representation of the firm as a decision-making unit characterized by a homogeneous goal. A number of more recent theories have attempted to view the firm as an institutional arrangement between a number of input or resource owners. The conception of the firm as a production function has thus been replaced with a series of alternative metaphors which, among

Table 1 A Typology Of Theories Of The Firm

Unit of analysis	Transaction		Decision-maker	
Theoretical perspective	Economic–political	Economic–legal	Economic–technological	Economic–organisational
Level of analysis	Society	Firm	Industry	Firm
Type of explanation and concept of rationality:				
Equilibrium model and maximization rationality		Principal-agent theory	Neoclassical theory	Managerialism
Functionalist model and either: a) "as if" maximization		Nexus-of-contract theory (positive agency theory)		
or: b) bounded rationality		Williamson's transaction cost theory		Behavioralism I
Change-oriented model of explanation and Rule-governed (procedural) rationality	Constitutional theory of the firm: Selznick, Vanberg		Evolutionary programme	Behavioralism II/ Evolutionay theory of the firm; Penrose's resource-based theory of the firm

Knowledge-based theory of the firm

other things, view the firm as an adaptive coalition, a contractual arrangement, a political constitution, etc. Along with this development, there have been various attempts to expand the behavioral foundation of the theory of the firm beyond the maximization principle. Today, maximization is supplemented with a series of theories based on bounded rationality or procedural rationality (rule-following). This trend is an expression of attempts to view the firm from a more process-oriented perspective, and therefore to view it as an entity which exists in a historical context. New metaphors have emerged to characterize the firm as, for example, a "hereditary mechanism" which functions as a repository of the firm's accumulated knowledge and capabilities. As a result of these two trends, we are currently facing a multitude of theories of the firm whose total theoretical and empirical capacity for problem solving greatly exceeds that of neoclassical microeconomics. In order to map out the potential of this research field in relation to strategic management, the various metaphors employed within economic theories of the firm are examined below.

3. The Firm as a Production Function and Unitary Decision Maker: From Neoclassical Economics to Modern IO-analysis

Not only within orthodox microeconomics, but also within large parts of modern game theory and IO-analysis (Industrial Organizational Analysis), the firm is perceived as a unitary decision maker with a homogeneous goal (often profit), that it is capable of pursuing optimally. Or in the words of David Kreps: "...the firm is of the category of an individual" (1990:93). Thus, it has almost been deemed self-evident that firms—like individuals—could be ascribed goals and preferences. In spite of the fact that neoclassical economists typically have argued in favour of the principle of methodological individualism, organizational goals are claimed to exist. Consequently, one treats a super-individualistic entity as if its existence and behaviour were totally independent of the behaviour of the organizational members.

Despite criticism, orthodox theory has persistently adhered to this view of the firm, arguing that the firm does not constitute an independent explanatory object; the primary intellectual task has been to explain the formation of prices within different market structures (cf., Machlup 1967). Thus, the level of analysis within neoclassical theory has been the industry rather than the single firm. And precisely because neoclassical economists, game theorists, and modern IO-analysts see the industry as their primarily level of analysis, they argue in favour of conceiving of the firm as an anonymous ideal type, ignoring that firms within the same industry may be unique, have different histories, and thus may have developed specific identities.

In keeping with the orthodox view, firms within an industry are viewed as fundamentally uniform, having access to exactly the same pool of knowledge. The firms in these models are therefore assumed to have identical cost and demand curves. "Variations" among firms within the same industry are further assumed to be non-existent. Thus, it is assumed that the market structures within which the firms operate are historically invariable and that all changes within such systems are exogenous and only temporary. In the terminology of the biologist Mayr (1982), one could, therefore, say that neoclassical theory basically views the market from a typological rather than a populational perspective. The population type of approach stresses the uniqueness of individuals and ascribes a key role to the "variations" within a system. Such a system is described as the distribution of properties possessed by a population of individuals (firms). Contrary to the typological conception, the population perspective focuses on those endogenous and cumulative changes which imply changes in the distribution of those properties possessed by the individuals (firms) within a population (industry). Within economic theory, Schumpeter (1942, and see Section 8), with his dynamic and evolutionary concept of the economy, has applied such population thinking within economics.

Apart from viewing the firm as a unitary and maximizing decision-maker, neoclassical theory conceptualizes firms as if they were "production functions." Therefore, firms are primarily viewed from a technological perspective and described as production units that efficiently transform a series of homogeneous inputs into a series of outputs.

Combining the "production function" perception of the firm with the above mentioned typological perception of industries, one can, in keeping with Nelson (1991), characterize the neoclassical theory in terms of a "cookbook metaphor." Just as the cook who has access to a various recipes, neoclassical economists assume that the firm immediately and without any costs has access to a whole menu of capital intensive and labour intensive production techniques. It is further assumed that the firm's choice of concrete techniques matches the present, relative factor prices. And when these relative factor prices change, the firm is assumed, without any costs, to replace one type of technique with another to suit its new environment.

In addition, the "production function" perception of the firm rests on a series of implicit assumptions about the character of productive knowledge. First of all, any firms within an industry are assumed to have access to exactly the same pool of productive knowledge. In keeping with the typological conceptions of industries, knowledge about production techniques is assumed to emerge as inexplicable, exogenous shifts in the firms' production functions, rather than as an endogenous experience-based learning process within the individual firm. Therefore, neoclassical theory portrays the firm as an "entity without history." Secondly, no firms will be better at absorbing new productive knowledge than others (cf., Cohen and Levinthal 1990) as they are all assumed to have access to the same cookbook and hence to possess identical background knowledge. Thirdly, it is assumed that there is a sharp distinction between what the firms know and what they do not know, since their production sets are assumed to be strongly constrained. Thus, within neoclassical economics one ignores the essential fact that a large proportion of technical knowledge is tacit and experience-based.

It was this theory of the firm which Caves and Porter imported into strategic management in the mid-seventies. On the basis of Bain's entry-barrier model, they attempted to explain the existence of above-normal profits as an expression of the firm's market power. Bain described his theory of the firm in a way that suggests that it is identical with the one outlined above:

> I am concerned with the environmental setting within which enterprises operate and in how they behave in these settings as producers, sellers and buyers: By contrast, I do not take an internal approach, more appropriate to the field of management science, such as could inquire how enterprises do and should behave in ordering their internal operations and would attempt to instruct them accordingly...my primary unit of analysis is the industry of competing group of firms, rather than the individual firm or the economy wide aggregate of enterprises (1956: 7-8).

This emphasis on the external rather than the internal conditions of the firm also underlies Michael Porter's (1980) contribution to strategic management. The SCP-paradigm was originally formulated to support the anti-trust politicians in their efforts to reduce or totally remove barriers to entry. By turning it upside down, Porter attempted to demonstrate how firms could utilize appropriate market positioning to exploit the very same market imperfections. However, because he departed from a theoretical tradition which perceived the industry as the primary level of analysis and the firm as a "black box," Porter's notion of strategy could not be linked to the "strengths and weaknesses" component, but exclusively to the "opportunities and threats" component of Andrews' classical SWOT-framework.

Applying game theory to modern IO-analyses has not decisively changed the neoclassical perception of the firm and its understanding of strategy (cf., Saloner 1991 and Shapiro 1989). Even though the concept of parametric rationality has been replaced by a concept of strategic rationality, modern IO-analysis retain the industry as their dominant level of analysis. Furthermore, game theory maintain the typological perception of industry rooted in the neoclassical analysis. This perspective treats all firms (players) as fundamentally uniform and therefore excludes by definition that firms within the same industry may be heterogenous. For example, when defining what constitutes rational behaviour individual players is assumed to observe a "principle of symmetry" implying that he has to ascribe the same form of rationality to his opponent that he apply himself (maximizing expected utility). By applying this principle, Schelling (1961) argues that game theorists ignore information about the type or identity of opponents that real world agents typically will use to make "rational" decisions. Schelling exemplifies his argument:"if a man knocks at a door and says that he will stab himself on the porch unless given 10 dollars, he is more likely to get the 10 dollars if his eyes are bloodshot." To signal what type of an agent one is—or one's identity—is therefore of great importance to the outcome of the social processes studied by game theorists. The more certain values have been internalized by an agent, i.e., the more they shape his whole personality, the greater is his credibility of being a certain type of agent.

However, a condition for conceptualizing firms within the same industry as having different identities is that we reject the typological type of analysis and its perceptions of "heterogeneity" and "variations" as non-existing. One approach is to broaden the behavioral foundation of the theory, allowing firms to be capable of forming their own identity by a set of pre-commitments. This implies that the perception of the firm as an invariant entity in neoclassical economics and game theory is replaced by a theory in which firm-specific history is important for understanding differences in firm behaviour within the same industry.

4. The Firm as an Optimal Contractual Arrangement: From Managerialism to Principal-Agent Models

The conception of the firm in orthodox or standard microeconomics has been exposed to numerous criticisms since the 1930s. Empirical studies by Hall & Hitch (1939) and Berle & Means (1932) were particularly important, since they resulted in the emergence of two new heterodox traditions in the 1960s: managerialism and behavioralism. It was characteristic of these two traditions that they were involved in undermining the profit and the maximization parts of the profit maximization hypothesis, respectively. They were, as well, important precursors to the "exchange perspective," in which the decision-making unit was replaced with the transaction as the basic unit of analysis. It was within this perspective that the principal-agent model emerged in the 1970s, which lead many mainstream economists to look for ways to replace the neoclassical "black box" view of the firm.

Managerialism emerged primarily as a result of Berle & Means' study of how the diffusion of ownership in large U.S. corporations had led to a separation of ownership and control. Managerialism was particularly engaged in modelling the effects of separating ownership and managerial control on the firms' goals. Concrete examples of such models are Baumol's (1959) model of revenue maximization and Williamson's (1964) generalized utility-maximization model of managerial behavior. These two models did not, fundamentally, imply any decisive break with the neoclassical tradition, as the firm was still viewed as a goal-seeking and maximizing unit. The only difference was that profit was replaced with other goals in order to be able to model the "discretionary" behavior of managers.

However, because of the importance of managerialism to a long-term perspective, this tradition has had a far greater impact on the development of the theory of the firm than its own, relatively modest contribution immediately seems to suggest. First of all, by demonstrating that ownership can affect economic conditions, managerialism has created a legitimate place for a legal perspective. Secondly, studies within managerialism of managers' discretionary behavior have clearly pointed toward the introduction of more general concepts such as asymmetric information characterizing moral hazard and adverse-selection problems.

In the seventies, with the emergence of principal-agent theory, the two perspectives mentioned above were combined. Unlike their counterpart in managerialism, principal-agent theorists do not accept the idea that firms and organizations can be ascribed goals or that firms are capable of making decisions. Instead, they replace the image of the firm as a "goal-seeking," decision-making unit with a view of the firm as "a nexus or a set of contracting relationships amongst individuals." The firm is thus reduced to a "legal personage" that enters into a number of bilateral, contractual relations with the firm's various interest groups. The advantage of this view is that it avoids "a personalization of the firm," in that the firm is no longer seen "as if" it were an individual or a single decision-maker to whom a definite "objective function" can be attributed (cf., Jensen & Meckling 1976). Rather, the firm is now analyzed as a complex set of relations and viewed as the outcome of a complex equilibrium process. Contrary to the neoclassical tradition, which viewed the firm as the unit of analysis and the industry as the most important level of analysis, the principal-agent model's unit of analysis is the transaction and its dominant analytical level is the firm. In Georgious' (1973) terminology the "goal paradigm" of neoclassical microeconomics was replaced by the "exchange paradigm" of the principal-agent model.

The principal-agent theory nevertheless continued to accept the fundamental behavioral assumptions of neoclassical theory. The principal-agent theory thus persisted in using maximization rationality as its basic behavioral foundation. Accordingly, it was assumed that the principal delegated some of his decision-making authority to another individual, the "agent," authorizing him to make decisions on his behalf, typically in situations of asymmetric information. The main theoretical problem of the principal-agent theory was to design a contract that provides the agent with the incentive to act in the interests of the principal. That is, how to design an incentive compatible contract that stimulates such behaviour.

In the principal-agent model, the view of leadership is closely linked to the view of the firm as a contractual structure, and to the role of a "central agent." This implies that the manager's role is to enter into a series of bilateral contracts with the firm's various interest groups. Leadership is thus concretely linked to the role of designing incentive compatible contracts, minimizing the need for control.

Both neoclassical theory and the principal-agent theory build on a traditional maximization model which assumes the single firm or the contractual agent to be capable of anticipating the consequences of each alternative and of choosing the alternative with the best consequences. However, if one makes the decision-making problems increasingly complex and uncertain, it will, accordingly, become increasingly difficult to identify optimal solutions. Alchian has pointed out that "the ... approach, which

189

starts with certainty and unique motivation, must abandon its basic principles as soon as uncertainty and mixed motivations are recognized" (1950: 34-35). This implies that certain phenomena cannot be explained as if they were a result of rational decisions by human beings; rather, they must be understood as the end-result of an evolutionary process. Viewed from this perspective, the existence of firms cannot be explained in terms of human design, but rather as the outcome of an evolutionary process. An economic institution such as the firm must therefore be explained as adaptations or solutions to a social problem of coordination or collaboration. In many cases it will be impossible to specify an optimal solution to such a situation. The final solution must rather be assumed to have materialized as a result of selection among various alternative solutions.

One could argue that the existence of institutional arrangements is inseparable from the existence of "genuine" uncertainty. Institutions therefore only emerge in decision situations in which "unforeseen" contingencies could take place and which the economic agents cannot handle in a perfectly rational way merely by formulating "state-contingent contracts." The firm therefore has to be explained as an institutional response to such an "open" decision situation in which orthodox equilibrium models and the concept of perfect rationality are replaced with an adaptive explanatory model and either a concept of "as if" maximization or bounded rationality.

5. The Firm as an Adaptive Institution and a Political Coalition: Behavioralism

The behavioralist theory of the firm was developed at the Carnegie Institute of Technology (later called Carnegie-Mellon University) at the end of the fifties. In 1963 Cyert and March published their book *A Behavioral Theory of the Firm*. While managerialism criticized the profit component of the profit maximization hypothesis, the behavioralists found the assumption of maximization problematic in itself. The behavioralists based their perception of the firm as a political coalition and an adaptive institution on Barnard and Simon's "inducement-contribution" schema and Simon's theory of bounded rationality, respectively.

In keeping with, but completely independent of, the principal-agent theorists, the behavioralists found the neoclassical theory's perception of the firm as a decision-making unit to be an unacceptable break with the principle of methodological individualism. Cyert and March formulated this idea very precisely: "People (i.e., individuals) have goals; collectivities of people do not" (1963:26). However, the principal-agent theorists chose to make the "transaction" the basic unit of analysis, whereas Cyert and March persisted in viewing firms from a decision-making perspective. They thus argued that in the creation of "a theory of organizational decision-making, we seem to need something analogous—at the organizational level—to individual goals at the individual level" (1963:26). The impossibility of this task is evident from the fact that the challenge faced was to "identify some concept of organization goals that is consistent with the apparent denial of their existence" (1963: 26). Thus, contrary to principal-agent theory, behavioralism remains within the "goal paradigm," since it upholds the view of organizations as decision-making units, albeit in a more moderate form. However, contrary to neoclassical theory, which took the firm and its profit maximizing goal for granted and which focused on explaining phenomena at the industry level, behavioralism wanted to establish a theory of the firm. This implied being able to explain how the goals of the firm emerged as a result of bargaining between single individuals or groups.

Cyert and March's basis for solving this task was Barnard (1938) and Simon's "inducement-contribution" schema. According to this model, organizing a number of individuals into a coalition should be possible if the individual members are given appropriate inducements, thus motivating them to remain loyal to the coalition. From this perspective, the situation of the firm could be described as a "truce" between the individual organizational members, but one obtained at the constant risk of latent conflicts of interests turning into manifest conflicts. Cyert and March (1963) nevertheless perceived such a truce as relatively stable since many goal conflicts are in fact avoided through sequential attention to goals, i.e., solving one problem at a time. Another such mechanism was *slack* resources which, particularly in connection with major changes in the environment, contributed to the stability of the truce between the members of the coalition.

Cyert and March furthermore suggested replacing the neoclassical view of the firm as a decision-making unit with a perception of the firm as an adaptive institution. There were several reasons for this. First of all, firms are often confronted with unpredictable and uncertain environments. Secondly, when solving problems, firms are subject to restrictions resulting from the above-mentioned difficulties in ensuring a stable coalition. Thirdly, any decision-maker's capacity for collecting, storing and using information is limited. Given these restraints on rational decision-making, the firm is characterized as an *adaptive rational system* rather than as a *perfect rational system*. When Cyert and March (1963) stress that the firm is an adaptive *rational* system, they are emphasizing that it is possible for firms to adapt actively—and not merely passively—to their environment through learning. They are therefore critical of Alchian's and Schumpeter's views that, over the long-run the behaviour of the individual firm is formed by the "environment" through market selection processes. However, giving priority to process analyses over equilibrium analyses, and short-term studies over long-term analyses, Cyert and March found it reasonable to focus on situations of imperfect adaptation to new environments.

As an adaptive institution, the firm is characterized by short-term behaviour that is determined by a series of behavioral rules which Cyert and March (1963) term "standard operating procedures." These rules constitute an organizational memory since they represent solutions to a series of "standard" problems previously encountered and solved by the firm. In other words, the firm's knowledge about how to solve various problems is "embedded" in such procedures. Thus, understanding the short-term behavior of a firm should consist in identifying the set of rules in operation.

However, if the firm is viewed not only from a short-term perspective but also from a somewhat longer perspective, the behavioral rules of the firm must be assumed to be subject to a series of changes as a result of organizational learning. The behavioralists characterize this search-and-learning process as *problem governed*. That is, something is not perceived as a problem until the organization is unable to fulfill its goals. Therefore, the organization will continue to search for alternatives until it finds an alternative which "satisfies" the goal or the organization adjusts the goal to a level within which acceptable alternatives exist. The search is, furthermore, "simple minded," implying that one typically searches for alternative solutions close to existing solutions and that relatively simple "cause-and-effect" relations are assumed in the search process. Finally, the search is "biased," i.e., the search for new alternatives is directed toward particular areas which may be determined by the organization's history. Nelson and Winter's research program, which is discussed in Section 8, develops a view of the firm as an adaptive institution. Their program incorporates the more long-term perspectives of learning, and aspires to turn "the theory of the firm" into a "micro-foundation" of a more comprehensive theory of markets and their evolution.

Within strategic management, the behavioralists' perception of the firm has primarily led to a confrontation with what Selznick (1957) termed a "technical" conception of management. According to Selznick, the "rational" manager could wield the organization as a simple instrument to handle the firm's external market behavior and to achieve an exogenous goal. The behavioralists view management as much more a question of handling the firm's "internal" issues by, for example, being able to conduct "political" negotiations with potential coalition partners with the aim of identifying and maintaining a "viable" coalition. Instead of the "technical aspects," a far more important role is assigned to the "political" and/or negotiatory aspects of management. As Selznick (1957) pointed out, leadership in Simon's "inducement-contribution" schema is linked to individuals' capability to fulfill the role of "interpersonal agent": continuously securing the "truce" between the coalition partners and renegotiating the new conditions for this coalition, even when the environment is subject to major changes. And, precisely because one focuses on the manager as the bargaining agent, one tends exclusively to view the firm from an incrementalistic, "muddling-through" perspective (Quinn 1980), unlike Selznick, who views the manager as an "institutionalizing agent" that provides the organization with its basic mission, values, and identity, as Selznick did (see Section 10).

There are several reasons for the view of leadership taken by the behavioralist theory of the firm. First of all, behavioralism's interest in a short-term rather than a more long-term perspective keeps it from viewing leadership as important to the formation of the organization's basic values and identity. Secondly, like maximization rationality, Simon's concept of bounded rationality seems to constitute too narrow a behavioral foundation, since it does not allow for actions to be assessed in other ways than by their consequences. According to the so-called consequentialist view, it is meaningless to talk about the rationality of goals (and hence to discuss the basic values on which the firm acts). In combination, these two points imply that behavioralism has been unable to develop an adequate theoretical understanding of leadership and strategy that views the more short-term, operational strategies of the firm from a more long-term perspective.

7. The "Nexus-of-Contract" View of the Firm: Alchian and Demsetz

In line with behavioralism, some economists, directly or indirectly linked to the Chicago School, have argued that the firm should not be thought of as a perfectly rational agent but, on the contrary, as an adaptive institution. As the Chicago economist Alchian (1950) expressed it: "All individual rationality, motivation, and foresight will be temporarily abandoned in order to concentrate upon the ability of the environment to *adopt* "appropriate" survivors even in the absence of any adaptive behavior" (1950:21). Alchian thus argued for introducing a totally new explanatory model within economics, in which not only structural phenomena such as behavioral rules, norms, and institutions—but also the firm itself—should not be explained as the result of rational design, but—on the contrary—as the outcome of a "blind" process of selection or adaptive learning. In particular Friedman (1953) argued that if one applied a long-term perspective, selection would produce precisely the same result that maximizing agents equipped with perfect foresight would reach through an educative process. Therefore, an equilibrium state could be interpreted as the outcome of either a "blind" selection process or a learning process in which economic agents would converge towards the optimal decision-making rule. Or, in the words of Friedman: "The process of "natural selection" thus helps validate the "maximization of returns" hypothesis...or rather, given natural selection, acceptance of the hypothesis can be based largely on the judgement that it summarizes appropriately the conditions for survival" (1953: 32). Friedman talked about a concept of "as if" maximization that did not assume consciously rational agents but a perfectly functioning selection mechanism, that in the long-term ensured the survival of those firms who for one reason or another have selected optimal decision rules. Thus, a pure adaptionist (or functionalist) explanatory model had been introduced which, rather than taking structural phenomena like the capitalist firm for granted, attempted to explain its existence. One would then argue that only the optimal solution (institution) would survive in the long run. In other words, the firm should not be viewed as a rationally designed institution but rather as the efficient outcome of an unspecified selection process.

Alchian and Demsetz (1972) attempted to answer the question: why do capitalist firms exist at all? In order to answer this question, Alchian and Demsetz started by identifying the problem of social cooperation to which the capitalist firm was an efficient solution. If one assumes (as Alchian and Demsetz do) that an economy consists of a number of input or resource owners, one can, in principle, imagine that they can be organized in several different ways, ranging from autocracy over various forms of cooperative arrangements to a more centralized structure like the capitalist firm. The potential advantage of cooperation between different resource owners relates to the possibility of achieving a series of specialization gains. But, for such an arrangement to emerge and survive, each resource owner must be rewarded according to his or her marginal

194

productivity. Alchian and Demsetz justify the decisive role that they assign to this problem as follows:

> If rewards were random, and without regard to productive efforts, no incentive to production effort would be provided by the organization; and if rewards were negatively correlated with productivity the organization would be subject to sabotage. Two key demands are placed on the economic organization—metering input productivity and metering rewards (1972: 75).

Consequently, Alchian and Demsetz do not assume that the firm, as a perfectly rational agent, is able to design *ex ante* an optimal incentive system. On the contrary, they assume—in keeping with Alchian's article of 1950—that it is not the firm's perfect foresight but rather the environment's ability to select more efficient institutional arrangements which is the ultimate causal mechanism behind the emergence of particular institutional structures. However, exchanging the neoclassicists' rational design explanations for the Chicago School's adaptive explanations, leads to a reversal of cause and effect:

> We conjecture the direction of causation is the reverse—the specific system of rewarding which is relied upon stimulates a particular productivity response. If the economic organization meters poorly, with rewards and productivity only loosely correlated, then productivity will be smaller; but if the economic organization meters well productivity will be greater (1972: 77).

Alchian and Demsetz explain the difficulties of solving the metering problem by referring to the characteristics of team production. This type of production is characterized by the following features: 1) several resources are used; 2) products are not the sum of the separable outputs of each cooperating resource; and 3) not all resources used in the team-work process belong to one individual. Under such conditions, it would be very difficult and costly to determine the contribution of a particular resource to the total production and reward it according to its productivity. Team production thus places the individual resource owner in a "contribution dilemma" or "free rider dilemma" in which there is no incentive to invest a great deal of efforts, since the return will not be allotted to the single individual but to the resource owners as a group. Consequently, one will end up in a sub-optimal situation characterized by "shirking." Alchian and Demsetz' basic hypothesis is that "the costs of metering or ascertaining the marginal product of the team's members are what call forth new organizations and procedures" (Alchian and Demsetz 1972: 79). That is, experiments will be conducted with various institutional arrangements, in order to find a solution to the metering problem. The arrangement which best solves this problem is assumed to the one which (in the end) will emerge as the winner of the competition between all the tested alternatives. Therefore, the winner is the most efficient suggestion for a solution, the one which minimizes the costs of metering.

Alchian and Demsetz then argue that the optimal institutional arrangement to solve the metering problem and to minimize metering costs is the capitalist firm. This institution consists of a contractual arrangement which is defined by the following bundle of rights: (1) one of the team members specializes in controlling the others; (2) the team production assigns to this member the residual rights; (3) he or she takes the position of a "central agent" in a series of bilateral contracts with the other resource owners; (4) he or she has the right to alter the membership of the team; and (5) this individual can sell his or her rights that define ownership of the firm.

In their characterization of the capitalist firm as the "nexus of contract" between the "firm" and some independent resource owners, Alchian and Demsetz emphasize its voluntaristic nature. The capitalist firm is thus claimed never to consist of anything else but spot contracts, and consequently it does not differ at all from a network of market relations. Therefore, the contractual relationships between employer and employee is claimed to be identical with the relationship between the grocer and his customers. Alchian and Demsetz thus claim the employment contract to represent the following: "The relationship of each team member to the owner of the firm is simply a "quid pro quo" contract. Each makes a purchase and sale. The employee can terminate the contract as readily as can the employer, and long-term contracts, therefore, are not an essential attribute of the firm" (1972:85). This clearly brings Alchian and Demsetz in conflict with the transaction cost conception of the firm. According to transaction cost theory, the firm is by and large identical with the employment contract, which is both a long-term contract, and one that implies a relationship of authority.

Alchian (1987) as well as Demsetz (1988) have, however, subsequently distanced themselves from their original nexus-of-contract

196

conception of the firm, recognizing that it would be very difficult to identify the distinct characteristics of a firm if its institutional arrangement consisted exclusively of short-term spot contracts. Therefore, the employment contract must be perceived as a long-term and incomplete contract ascribing a certain authority to the employer over the employee within non-specified "acceptance zones." It is precisely the incomplete nature of the contract which makes the firm an efficient adaption to situations characterized by unpredictable events. Moreover, the nexus-of-contract-theory description of the firm as a contractual structure with a "central agent" who contracts with individual resource owners is hardly sustainable. The firm's contractual structure can hardly be characterized as a series of bilateral contracts; rather, it is a multilateral contract which specifies the conditions of a long-term collaboration between a multitude of resource owners. As pointed out by Alchian, the aim of this comprehensive contract is to "restrain opportunism and "moral hazard" by individual owners, each seeking a portion of each other's firm-specific, expropriable composite quasi-rent" (1987: 234). The social contract thus—like a constitution—specifies the set of rules of the game in order to enable single resource owners to invest their resources in a firm without being exposed to opportunistic rent-seeking. We shall return to this co-called constitutional view of the firm in Section 10.

But which view of strategy and leadership does the nexus-of-contract theory imply? Within the field of strategy, the nexus-of-contract theorists have been very critical of the SCP-paradigm's "market-power" perspective and its view of strategy as a question of appropriate positioning. The nexus-of-contract theorists do not view the creation and exploitation of entry barriers, etc. as a "sustainable" competitive advantage since they will be eliminated over time by more efficient firms. The size and scope of a firm will, according to nexus-of-contract theorists, be determined exclusively by its efficiency. If the firm becomes increasingly efficient, it will grow, whereas reduced efficiency implies that previously-achieved competitive advantages will gradually erode.

Nexus-of-contract theory's view of the firm is similar to behavioralism's view of the firm as a political coalition, albeit the former ascribes greater importance to contractual and legal aspects. However, one decisive dimension distinguishes nexus-of-contract theory from behavioralism: the former applies a long-term equilibrium perspective rather than a more short-term process perspective. This implies that while behavioralism has focused on the firm's capacity to adapt to new environments via organizational learning, the nexus-of-contract theory has almost exclusively focused on the environment's ability to form efficient long-term firm structures. Thus, nexus-of-contract theory presents a much more passive or reactive image of the managerial role than does behavioralism.

8. The Firm as an Institutional Adaptation to Market Failures: Transaction Cost Economics

Transaction cost theory can be traced back to Coase's classic 1937 article, *The Nature of the Firm*. It was this article which formed the basis for Williamson's elaboration of the transaction cost paradigm in the 1970s. Transaction cost theory can be described as a continuation of the nexus-of-contract theory's view of the firm as an adaptive institution, even though Williamson has modified it with insights from behavioralism and, in particular, Simon's contribution of the theory of bounded rationality.

The central thesis of the transaction cost paradigm was that there are different ways of organizing transactions, and that these are associated with different costs. In Williamson's words: "transactions are assigned to and organized within governance structures in a discriminating (transaction-cost economizing) way" (1981:1564). This implies that Williamson does *not* explain different "governance structures" as resulting from a rational plan, intention, or design, but rather as emerging from the "beneficial consequences" of a specific governance structure in economizing on transaction costs. A governance structure like the firm, for example, will thus be viewed as an efficient solution to a problem of social interaction; it is thus perceived as an adaptive institution.

Contrary to the nexus-of-contract theory with its roots in the methodology of the Chicago School, Williamson maintains that adaptive (or functionalist) explanations are an expansion and correction to orthodox "maximization-cum-equilibrium" explanations. This view can be contrasted with that of nexus-of-contract theorists who, on the basis of Milton Friedman's article of 1953, argued that the selection mechanism functioned as an "optimizing agent," implying that adaptive explanations could be reduced to orthodox equilibrium explanations. In keeping with Herbert Simon (1983), Williamson's "weak selection" principle implies that the selection mechanism does not necessarily ensure "survival of the fittest" but merely "survival of the fitter." In line with this, competition between alternative institutional solutions to a certain problem of coordination or cooperation would not necessarily lead to institutions which minimized transaction costs but only economized on such costs. Further, Williamson argued that the adequate behavioral foundation for transaction cost theory was not the "as-if" principle of maximization used within the nexus-of-contract theory, but rather Simon's concept of bounded rationality. Williamson wanted to stress that adaptive explanations transgressed the domain of "maximization-cum-equilibrium" models by explaining the existence of the institutional framework which equilibrium models took for granted. Finally, Williamson argued that adaptive explanations had been introduced into economics to facilitate the handling of "open" decision-making situations of structural uncertainty (cf., R. Langlois 1984). Such decision situations occur when the decision-maker cannot specify *ex ante* the optimal choices for each single decision situation. For example, if there is a high degree of uncertainty about future conditions in contractual negotiation, it will be impossible and too costly for the parties to specify a complete "state contingent contract." Nevertheless, it can be argued that a rational response to situations involving a high degree of uncertainty would be for the contractual partners to specify a method or procedure for solution of conflicts or disagreements in the future. Rationality, thus, is no longer related to the substance of a single action but is, on the other hand, a question of whether or not the procedure for making decisions is sensible.

According to Williamson (1975, 1985), the firm should be analyzed as a governance structure emerging in response to a situation in which bounded rational and opportunistic agents must enter contracts characterized by a high degree of uncertainty and asset specificity. In such situations, it will be impossible, or at least very costly, to formulate a state contingent contract specifying how the parties should react in any imaginable future state. On the contrary, an efficient adaption to a situation in which "surprises" can occur will be to formulate an incomplete contract. That is, a contract that does not specify what action should be taken in every imaginable situation but merely one, which *ex ante* specifies which method that the parties should apply when adapting the contract to new circumstances.

Both Coase (1937) and Williamson (1975; 1985) view the "firm" or the "hierarchy" as by and large identical with the employment contract. This contract between the "firm" and the employee is partially open-ended because the employee—in return for a certain salary—agrees to grant the employer authority to decide which tasks the employee is required to perform within a certain "acceptance zone." This open-endedness of the employment contract is understood to enable the firm to adapt efficiently to unpredictable events. By viewing the firm as essentially identical with the "authority relation," transaction costs theory departs from the nexus-of-contract conception of the firm as a pure market arrangement.

In spite of these conceptual differences, nexus-of-contract theory and transaction cost theory both use the same adaptionist model of the firm. Within the field of strategic management, the most significant consequence is that, like nexus-of-contract theory, transaction cost theory is based on an "efficiency" perspective. This perspective is very critical of Porter's (1980) "market power" and "strategizing" perspective. Williamson perceives "efficiency" considerations as being much more important than market positioning, arguing that "all the clever ploys and positioning, aye all the king's horses and all the king's men, will rarely save a project that is seriously flawed in the first-order economizing respect" (1991: 75). Thus, from the perspective of the transaction cost theory, strategic management primarily consists of determining a firm's efficient boundaries by making a whole series of separate "make-or-buy" decisions. These decisions entail finding out whether or not to undertake certain activities internally or to outsource them. The purpose of these individual decisions is to attain a perfect "fit" between the environment of the firm and its organizational structure.

In conclusion, behavioralism, nexus-of-contract theory, and transaction cost theory can be said to share a view of the firm as an adaptive institution. Their primary difference lies in whether it is sufficient to view the firm only as an institutional arrangement that is the outcome of a selection process, or whether the analysis should focus on the process or mechanism that has produced this arrangement as well. Being rooted in the Chicago School, nexus-of-contract theory argued that the selection mechanism functioned as an "optimizing" agent, obviating the need to incorporate the process into the analysis. On the other hand, behavioralism focused on the internal decision and bargaining processes by which an "organizational" goal emerges. Transaction cost theory represented a kind of compromise. Like nexus-of-contract theorists, transaction cost theorists viewed the firm as the outcome of an unspecified selection process. However, in keeping with behavioralism, Williamson expressed a willingness to expand his theory to include a more processual component:

> The argument [the transaction cost analysis] relies in a general background way on the efficacy of competition to preserve a sort between more and less efficient modes and to shift resources in favour of the former. This seems plausible, especially if the relevant

outcomes are those which appear over intervals of five or ten years rather than in the very near term. This intuition would nevertheless benefit from a more fully developed theory of the selection process (1985: 22-23).

The risk is that transaction cost analysis will incorporate these evolutionary processes in an ad hoc way, merely adding them onto the basic theory itself instead of integrating them into its assumptions. An illustrative example of such an *ad hoc* approach to "process" analysis is Williamson's analysis of "the fundamental transformation" in which an originally atomistic relation is gradually transformed into a bilateral relation in which both parties have invested assets of a high degree of specifity, thus creating a lock-in situation. Even though Williamson here incorporates a "processual" element into his theory this is not allowed to effect the basic behavioral assumptions of the transaction cost paradigm. A better way of building "processes" into the theory would have been to either modify or replace its behavioral foundation. One could replace Williamson's interpretation of the assumption of "opportunistic" behavior as "self interest with guile" with the original interpretation of opportunistic behavior as "myopic" or "short-sighted" behavior. As we shall argue in Section 10, this would facilitate an emphasis on the firm as a political institutions rather than as an contractual arrangements, and it would more clearly portray the firm as an entity existing in a historical context.

In the following sections, we will look into some theories of the firm which, in a far more consequent and non ad hoc way, have tried to incorporate the processual elements into their behavioral foundation. In relation to strategic management this a series of understandings of the firm have emerged, which focus on a dynamic rather than static concept of efficiency, thus directing attention towards the firm as a knowledge "accumulating" entity.

9. The Firm as a Repository of Knowledge: Nelson and Winter's Evolutionary Paradigm

As Cyert and March have clearly pointed out, the behavioralist theory of the firm was not meant as a theoretical alternative to the neoclassical research tradition with its focus on industry analysis; it was rather designed to contribute to understanding the firm itself—the firm viewed as an institution:

Ultimately, a new theory of firm decision-making behavior might be used as a basis for a theory of markets, but at least in the short run we would distinguish between a theory of microbehavior, on the one hand, and the microassumptions appropriate to a theory of aggregate economic behavior on the other hand. In the present volume we argue that we have developed the rudiments of a reasonable theory of firm decision-making (1963:16).

The behavioralist theory of the firm did not expand from being "a theory of microbehavior" to include "microassumptions appropriate to a theory of aggregate economic behavior" until Richard Nelson and Sidney Winter presented their "evolutionary" research programme. They developed the behavioralist theory of the firm beyond its origin as a short-term analysis of firm behavior, into a more long-term analysis of how the firms within an industry adapt to new environments through a stochastic process of search for new and more profitable routines. The principal goal of Nelson and Winter's evolutionary research programme was not to construct a new theory of the firm, but to create a microfoundation for modelling a Schumpeterian or a dynamic theory of competition. They shifted the focus from a neoclassical study of behavior within given market structures to situations in which new structures were continuously created and former structures destroyed. As a consequent interest shifted to studying how dynamic rather than static efficiency was achieved: that is, how to construct economic structures which, to the greatest possible extent, allow for accumulating knowledge and capabilities. The focal problem of such a change-oriented analysis is how to secure a trade-off between static and dynamic efficiency that will ensure a "sustainable" growth process. As discussed below, the shift from a static to a dynamic concept of efficiency has significant implications for the nature of strategy within a change-oriented and evolutionary framework.

Although evolutionary theory, like neoclassical theory, views the firm primarily as a "production unit," Nelson and Winter is very critical of the latter's "cookbook metaphor":

...it is quite inappropriate to conceive of firm behavior in terms of deliberate choice from a broad menu of alternatives that some external observer considers to be 'available' opportunities for the organization. The menu is not broad, but narrow and idiosyncratic; it is built into the firm's routines, and most of the "choosing" is also accomplished automatically by those routines (Nelson and Winter 1982: 134).

Evolutionary theory conceptualizes the firm as a bundle of routines containing and passing on rather idiosyncratic knowledge about how various activities should be performed. Moreover, evolutionary theory describes the firm as a historical entity, because its productive knowledge is the result of an endogenous, experienced-based learning process. To understand the present behaviour of the firm, one needs to reconstruct the firm's accumulation of capabilities. As Veblen emphasized, we must uncover the cumulative process leading to the firm's current ways of doing things: "the process of cumulative change that is to be accounted for is the sequence of change in the methods of doing things—method of things dealing with the material means of life" (Veblen 1899: 70-71). The firm of neoclassical theory is, on the other hand, characterized as being an entity without any history since changes in its productive knowledge are entirely the result of exogenous shifts in its production function. Consequently, from an evolutionary perspective, firms are seen as having developed different capabilities and will thus be perceived as having different identities, whereas neoclassical theory views firms within the same industry as identical because they possess knowledge of the same production techniques.

By viewing the firm as an historical entity, the evolutionary research programme not only clashes with neoclassical theory but also with nexus-of-contract theory and transaction cost theory which jointly view the firm as the efficient outcome of a selection process. In a genuine, change-oriented perspective, one would view the firm as a result of a cumulative causal process of which the result of each period constituted the initial conditions for the subsequent period. Viewed in terms of such a cumulative causal model, it is impossible to assume that the selection process necessarily ensures that each individual component or economic transaction is organized most efficiently; the selection process would always have to rest on existing structures and, as a result of reconfigurations, its existing organizational structures, would be adapted to perform new functions. Or, in the words of Sidney Winter:

> In the evolutionary view—perhaps in contrast to the transaction cost view—the size of a large firm at a particular time is not to be understood as the solution to

some organizational problem. General Motors does not sit atop the *Fortune* 500 because some set of contemporary costs minimization imperatives require a certain chunk of the U.S. economy to be organized in this way. Its position at the top reflects the cumulative effect of a long string of happenings stretching back into the past, *among which* were the achievement of relatively good solutions into the past to various technological and organizational problems.... In short, a position atop the league standings is not a "great play." It does not exclude the possibility that there were also several not-so-great plays (1988: 178).

This argument can be interpreted as a critique of the "atomistic" research strategy of adaptionist models. For instance, transaction cost theory decomposes the firm into a series of independent transactions; it is then assumed that each transaction can be analyzed independently, further assuming that firms organize transactions in a way which economizes on the transaction costs. Since a complex network of interdependent transactions occurs within the firm, the totality of transactions, and not the individual transactions, are subject to a "market test" of efficiency. We must thus assume that if a firm is characterized by such a bundle of interdependent transactions, some of the transactions will prove to be inefficient.

The evolutionary theorist therefore advocates a more holistic perspective of the firm, arguing that complex organizations and their capabilities emerge through a cumulative process in which the first solutions constituted the building bricks of the subsequent, more complex, organizational forms and capabilities. This implies that the selection mechanism will not affect the structures de novo, but mold those that are already the result of the evolutionary process. Therefore, changes in a firm's capabilities will consist of incremental adaptations to a complex, interdependent system. According to Winter the selection mechanism will therefore "produce progress, but...not...an "answer" to any well-specified question or list of questions about how activities should be organized" (1988:177).

Viewed from a strategy perspective, evolutionary theory of the firm and industry theory are evidently weak on a series of dimensions. For example, Winter points to the fact that the evolutionary paradigm is rooted in a "weak" concept of rationality which leaves no room for proactive actions of a strategic nature:

204

In the theoretical world [of evolutionary economics], strategic analysis in the sense defined here has no place, although of course there is abundant scope for *ex post facto* discussion of which habits and impulses proved successful. As a response to a need for guidance in the real world, this fatalistic perspective has obvious and severe limitations (Winter 1987: 161-162).

A possible explanation of the relatively modest impact of the evolutionary paradigm on the strategy discipline is that is has only to a limited extent focused on the individual firm; its dominant level of analysis has been the industry. And from this perspective it is only natural to explain "success" in terms of "blind luck" rather than superior knowledge, competencies, capabilities, etc. However, since the publication in 1982 of *An Evolutionary Theory of Economic Change,*" Nelson and Winter have gradually shifted focus from industry level to firm level making the evolutionary paradigm increasingly relevant to the strategy discipline. One example is Dosi, Teece & Winter (1993), who have suggested that the concept of coherence should be ascribed a central role as the perception of strategy . In order for a firm to secure continuous accumulation of its capabilities, they suggest that the major aim of the firm must be to secure "coherence" between existing and new activities. If this condition is not met, the knowledge structure risks becoming fragmented, which in the long run may undermine its innovative capabilities.

9. The Firm as a Bundle of Resources: Penrose's Theory of the Limits to the Growth of the Firm

Contrary to Nelson and Winter (1982), who had primarily been interested in developing an evolutionary theory of market and competition, Penrose (1959) was interested in building a theory of the individual firm and its growth process. However, both Penrose's and Nelson and Winter's contributions represented a clash with the traditional price theory in that their theories support a Schumpeterian and dynamic understanding of competition. However, contrary to Nelson and Winter's explicit ambition to model Schumpeterian competition at the industry level, Penrose's goal was just to build a theory of the firm which could constitute a "microfoundation" for, or at least be compatible with, Schumpeter's theory of dynamic competition. Therefore, Penrose based her theory on what she described as an "unfolding perspective": to use the gradual unfolding of an organism as an analogy for studying the firm's growth processes. That is, Penrose attempted to focus on the way in which the firm's resources and capabilities were gradually created through an irreversible and cumulative causal process. However, Penrose (1952) was very aware of the weaknesses of applying biological analogies within a field in which human motivation constitutes a significant driving force behind social change processes. In the controversy with Alchian (1950) over biological analogies in the early fifties, she argued thus: "an alternative growth approach which, in common with the biological variant, insists that a predisposition to growth is inherent in the vary nature of firms, but which, in contrast, makes growth depend on motivation—in the usual case on the businessman's search for profits" (1955: 531). Compared to both Alchian's (1950) and Nelson and Winter's (1982) evolutionary models, Penrose attempted to base her theory on a considerably stronger concept of rationality. This has several significant implications for the potential application of her theory within the field of strategic management.

Stressing that neoclassical theory was not originally conceived as a theory of the firm but as a theory of prices within different market structures, Penrose argued for the need for a new understanding of the firm, instead of "tortuously trying to force an adaptation of the (neoclassical) theory of the firm merely because it has proved to be a valuable concept for a different purpose" (1959: 14). Being occupied with understanding the limits to a firm's growth, she advocated that the neoclassicists' "production function" concept be replaced with a view of the firm as a heterogenous bundle of resources and as an entity for accumulating knowledge. According to this view, the firm consists of a bundle of heterogenous resources which—depending on the experienced-based knowledge developed within the firm—could yield a wider or more narrow range of productive "services." Or in the words of Penrose:

> It is the heterogeneity, and not the homogeneity, of the productive services available or potentially available from its resources that gives each firm its unique character. Not only can the personnel of the firm render heterogeneous variety of unique services, but also the material resources of the firm can be used in different ways, which means that they can provide different kinds of services (1959: 75).

By stressing the heterogeneity rather than the homogeneity of the firm's productive services, it immediately becomes possible to understand the firm in a way far more adequate to the field of strategic management. Neoclassical theory assumes that all firms within an industry have access to the same "cookbook" of recipes and are subject to identical cost and demand conditions. However, the neoclassical theory has difficulties in explaining why some firms have competitive advantages over their competitors. As pointed out in Section 3, within this theory the only ways to obtain competitive advantages were by having scale economies or by exploiting market imperfections or barriers to entry by a strategy of positioning. Viewed from Penrose's growth perspective, heterogeneity among firms (and hence the ability of certain firms to gain sustained competitive advantages over other firms within the same industry) could be explained by the fact that each individual firm, through its life cycle, accumulated very different and idiosyncratic knowledge. These knowledge bases determined the capability of the firm to exploit and combine its stock of resources for the production of specific "services."

Penrose's claim that the firm's accumulated pool of knowledge may be a source of "sustainable" competitive advantages is based upon two significant properties of this knowledge. Firstly, the nature of this knowledge is "experience-based" rather than "objective." This implies that it contains a vast element of "tacit" knowledge making it difficult to transfer from one firm to another, and thus making it difficult for competitors to imitate. Secondly, it is assumed that the knowledge-base of the firm does not primarily consist of human capital of which certain individuals are the carriers, but consists of what Coleman (1988, 1990) has described as "social capital" and Prescott and Visscher (1980) term "organizational capital." According to Nelson and Winter's evolutionary research programme, the competitive advantages of the firm are not linked to the individuals' skills, which can be bought in factor markets, but to organizational routines which are not readily tradeable in factor markets. Like social capital, organizational routines constitute a kind of "immaterial" capital which is the result of long-term teamwork between the various resource owners in an organization. Prahalad and Hamel's (1988) definition of what constitutes a firm's "core competences" as the "collective learning in the organization, especially how to coordinate diverse production skills and integrate multiple streams of technology" can also be characterized as "social" or "organizational" capital.... This social capital may, for instance, consist of experienced-based norms governing coordination and collaboration, such as organizational culture.

Viewed from the perspective of strategic management, another important consequence of Penrose's resource-based theory is that, contrary to orthodox neoclassical theory and Porter's theory of strategy, it emphasizes internal over external limits to growth: "the fundamental limit to the productive opportunity of the firm cannot be found in external supply and demand conditions; we must look into the firm itself" (1959: 44). There are several reasons for preferring an internal to an external perspective. First, according to Penrose's knowledge-perspective the production set is determined endogenously though the accumulation of knowledge within the firm. As a consequence, and in contrast to the neoclassical theory, the firm's size constraints may change independently of any exogenous changes in its market environment or in its production function. Secondly, another reason for shifting focus from external rather than internal conditions stems from the replacement of Porter's short-term perspective with Penrose's long-term perspective. From a short-term perspective it may seem sensible to make predictions about the environment; on the other hand, from a long-term perspective such predictions will make little sense since the environment is subject to structural changes.

Penrose's theory (1955, 1959) in particular assumes that the managerial resources, and the services they yield, determine the limits to growth of the firm. Contrary to many other resources, managerial resources cannot immediately be increased through purchase on a factor marked, because the market for such resources will be imperfect. Bearing in mind the importance ascribed earlier to a firm's social capital, the development of teamwork solutions to coordination and cooperation problems should perhaps be viewed as more important to the growth of the firm than to the development of managerial resources. For example, when a team continuously is confronted with the same problem of coordination, it will gradually develop social rules for how to solve the problem. The emergence of new social rules is often a lengthy process leading to stabilization of the team members' expectations of one another's behavior, which contributes significantly to the economization of the individual's scarce decision-making resources. And the deeper these social rules are embedded in the organization, as more or less unconscious "habits" of how to perform certain activities, the more services are released which make growth possible and which can be used to solve new problems.

An important implication of these processes is that the firm's rate of growth will be no faster than the rate at which it releases new services, generates experience and hence accumulates "social" or "organizational" capital. For example, the product markets in which the firm will be able to operate will depend on the type of social capital it has accumulated and hence the organizational capabilities which it possesses. The crucial problem that Penrose wants to address with her theory is: which is the best way of organizing the firm's development in such a way that it experiences "sustainable" growth. According to Penrose, the firm is often faced with the dilemma that the release of new services makes it profitable to expand in certain directions; however, this expansion may simultaneously undermine the firm's long-term potential for growth. That is, in isolation the firm may experience the individual single step in the growth as efficient; however, in the long-run the total outcome of the growth process may prove inefficient.

This strategic dilemma may be described theoretically in various ways. Within decision theory, this dilemma can be described as a *problem of dynamic time-inconsistency* (cf., Strotz 1956). Faced with an intertemporal decision problem, the firm will not follow its original long-term plan, but will choose the solution that appears optimal according to a short term calculation. This "self-command" problem (cf., Schelling 1984), a problem of "weakness of the will," makes it necessary for the firm to discipline its short term thinking in order to secure a consistent, long-term pattern of action.

Within evolutionary theory, the above problem is described as an attempt to ensure a reasonable balance between the emergence of new variations and selection among them. We may end up in two potential imbalances or learning traps (cf., March 1991; Levinthal and March 1993). The first occurs when a system (an organization) continuously is assailed with new variations at a speed which makes it impossible for the selection mechanism to have the desired effect; that is, to select the "fittest." The second imbalance occurs when too few variations are produced and the system (the organization) becomes stagnant and conservative.

Finally, the same problem is described in terms of Schumpeter's theory of dynamic competition as an attempt to reach a sensible balance between static efficiency—in the sense of exploitation of already existing resources—and dynamic efficiency, which focuses on the organizational learning of new routines and capabilities (cf., Ghemawat; Costa 1993). Viewed in this perspective, staking too much on static efficiency will tend to make the firm conservative, in the sense that it will ignore evident possibilities of growth; on the other hand, if the firm stakes too much on dynamic efficiency it will tend to become fragmented and, over time, its knowledge-base will be undermined.

10. What is Still Missing in our Search for a "Strategic" Theory of the Firm?

After the above mapping of the status of research within the theory of the firm, we should be better equipped to examine the limits and deficiencies of economists' analysis of the firm, viewed from the perspective of strategic management. The development of the modern economic theory of the firm has been characterized by two trends that are more or less independent. The first trend pertains to an opening of the neoclassical black box representation of the firm. As a result, the firm is no longer viewed as merely a production unit but also, for example, as an organization—or a contractual arrangement. This has led to relatively new relations between economics and such disciplines as organization theory, law, and political science. The second trend has consisted of a gradual broadening of the behavioral foundation of economics, constructing new theories of the firm, and basing these theories on alternative and less well-developed concepts such as bounded rationality and rule governed/procedural rationality. The development stemmed from an increasing desire to analyze the firm from a "process perspective" rather than an "equilibrium perspective." As a result, the perception of the firm as a "perfect rational decision-maker" has been abandoned in favour of the view of the firm as an institutional arrangement, which represents an efficient adaption to the environment, and finally in favour of the view of the firm as a unit of knowledge accumulation. Also, the view of strategy as either a rational plan or a positioning of the firm has given way to an emphasis on the static efficiency of the firm's economic organization, and to finally viewing strategy as a question of consistent behavior over time that secures a balance between static and dynamic efficiency.

Combined these two trends has led to the development of a series of new conceptions of the firm that shed more light on the multi-facetted image of the nature of the firm. And, viewed from the perspective of the field of strategic management, this development has facilitated a series of new ways in which we, within the field of economics, can analyze and give a new understanding to concepts such as strategy and leadership. However, in the remaining part of this article I shall argue that the two above mentioned development trends do not go far enough, and a sufficiently spacious metaphor is yet to be developed which can be used as an actual "strategic" theory of the firm.

In order to illustrate this assertion, I shall argue that the embryo of such a "strategic" theory of the firm can be found in Selznick's classic book

Leadership in Administration: A Sociological Interpretation. Although this book was published in 1957, it anticipated the present trends, and provides a foundation for the building of a new "strategic" theory of the firm (cf., Knudsen 1995).

In order to justify this assertion, I shall attempt to demonstrate that Selznick, in his discussion of how an organization over time establishes its own "identity," "character," or "distinctive competencies," de facto has introduced a broader concept of rationality than those concepts within the existing theories of the firm. Secondly, Selznick (1957, 1969) advocates the necessity of replacing the view of organizations as contractual arrangements with a perspective viewing organizations as political constitutions. He thus argues in favour of a view which, to a certain extent, has been suggested by theorists such as Alchian and Woodward (1988), Demsetz (1988), Gifford (1991) and Vanberg (1990) (see Section 6).

Extending the arguments of Nelson and Winter as well as Penrose, Selznick suggests that an adequate understanding of the firm "requires a genetic and developmental approach, an emphasis on historical origin and growth stages. There is a need to see the enterprise as a whole and to see how it is transformed as new ways of dealing with a changing environment emerges" (1957). For the same reason he is very critical of both a "technical" view of the firm, which exclusively views it as a means to achieve exogenous goals, and of an "opportunistic" view of the firm, which focuses on the achievement of static efficiency or a "fit" between the organization and its environment. As an alternative to these two views of the firm, he advocates one for which leadership consists of:

> accepting the obligation of giving direction instead of merely ministering to organizational equilibrium; in adapting aspiration to the character of organization, bearing in mind that what the organization has been will affect what it can be and do; and in transcending bare organizational survival by seeing that specialized decisions do not weaken or confuse the distinctive identity of the enterprise (1957:149).

This view of the firm is on several dimensions close to Penrose's resource-based theory. However, one advantage of Selznick's version is that he is far more explicit about the principles of rationality underlying his theory. By viewing the firm as an individual, the focus of analysis is on the ways in which an organization restrains its own future behavior in terms of "character-defining commitments" aimed to build its identity. Paradoxically, it is precisely by abandoning its freedom of action and tying its future behavior to a set of principles that the firm actively can shape its future role.

One way of interpreting Selznick's view would be to see it as an example of the time-inconsistency model mentioned in Section 9. It suggests that an individual should be viewed in terms of a "multiple-self" model of intrapersonal conflict between the short-term and long-term interests. Schelling (1984) refers to the problem of time-inconsistency as a *self-command problem*. According to Selznick, this problem will only be given sufficient attention if the nature of leadership is "institutional" rather than "technical." Technical leadership implies "the pursuit of immediate short-run advantages in a way inadequately controlled by considerations of principle and ultimate consequences," whereas "institutional leadership" implies that one should "look to the long-run effect of present advantage ... and how changes effect personal or institutional identity" (1957: 143). Thus the aim of the individual must be the construction of a coherent and cumulative character. Therefore, strategy and leadership are primarily a matter of "linking" the development of the firm to a series of "precommitments" by which one actively shapes the "role" of the firm and defines its underlying "mission." This is a cumulative process in which the identity of the firm is shaped in the same way as an individual actively moulds his or her own identity through conscious career planning.

In terms of the principle of methodological individualism, it may be problematic to view the firm from the perspective of a clinical psychologist. The firm is not an individual with a single goal; on the contrary, it is an institutional arrangement between a multitude of individuals. The challenge is to explain how such a arrangement can act as a relatively well-coordinated unit and can exist as a "going concern" which is gradually capable of constructing a set of "distinctive competencies." Selznick characterizes the firm as a *political constitution*. This implies that the firm is a cooperative arrangement between a number of resource owners which is established with the aim of realizing those specialization returns that long term, team-work almost always yields. But in order for the individual resource owner to risk investing in and handing over his or her resources to such a cooperative arrangement, the firm must, qua an institution, be able to guarantee the individual resource owner freedom from exploitation by the others' rent-seeking behavior. The guarantee is a social contract or a constitution between the resource owners that restricts the collectivity's, and hence the firm's, future freedom of action; The constitution specifies a series of procedures for how to decide on behalf of the collectivity and for how to distribute the mutual output among the individual resource owners.

From the constitutional perspective, the firm is an institutional arrangement whose primary task is to counteract the rent-seeking behavior of the single resource owner and thus facilitate the long-term accumulation of capabilities within the firm. The existence of the firm is explained in terms of an institutional solution to the problem of time-inconsistency. That is, each resource owner in a cooperative arrangement may have an inclination to take a short-run rather than a long-run view. In order to inhibit such behavior, which may result in the firm being unravelled as a "going concern," all resource owners must be "committed" to take a long-term view of their behavior within the constitutional framework of the firm. Contrary to transaction cost theory, which interprets "opportunistic" behavior as "self-interest with guile," the assumption of opportunism within constitutional theory is that it is "myopic" or "short-term" behavior.

Conclusion

It is often argued that the more theoretical pluralism a discipline harbours, the stronger is competition between various theoretical schools and the greater are the chances of theoretical breakthrough (cf., Popper 1963). Or as applied by Seth and Thomas (1994: 185) in their thesis on the relationship to strategic planning: "Our broader prescription for continued development of the field is for theoretical pluralism."

However, this thesis does not seem to be generally valid as it completely ignores how the knowledge of the discipline is organized. If , for example, we take as a point of departure Whitley's (1984) analysis of how various disciplines are organized, we can distinguish between two basic types: applied science such as management science, the knowledge of which is organized in a very fragmented and adhoc way, and more basic scientific disciplines such as physics which are much more hierarchically organized. The thesis on the relationship between theoretical pluralism and scientific progress specifically seems to aim at the latter type. On the other hand, increase in theoretical pluralism does not necessarily result in the same positive effects within the former type. If, for example, theoretical pluralism increases significantly within a fragmented adhocracy, the result is rather a "vicious circle" or "learning trap" which Levinthal and March describe as:

Organizations [intellectual fields] are turned into frenzies of experimentation, change, and innovation by a dynamic of failure. Failure leads to search and change which leads to failure which leads to more search, and so on. New ideas and technologies fail and are replaced by other new ideas and technologies, which fail in turn (1993:105-6).

In fragmented adhocracies researchers typically seem to have great difficulties in "absorbing" new contributions into the already existing knowledge structure. Most often they merely they tack on new threories to the existing structure as pure ad hoc appendixes. The effect of this deficient ability to integrate new knowledge is that it becomes increasingly difficult to produce new and more "profound" knowledge (i.e., scientific progress) as the knowledge structure becomes increasingly fragmented and incoherent.

Attempts to counteract the "vicious circle," and thus avoid further fragmentation of the knowledge structure, are of decisive importance to securing a certain minimum of coherence and hence the possibility for producing scientific progress in the future. Probably the most important means to achieve a certain coherence within relatively fragmented disciplines is to attempt to integrate and, in this way, synthesize theories that so far have been separated. This does not necessarily involve constructing a superior paradigm capable of resolving all future problems. Merely attempts to reduce the variability threatening to undermine the discipline's coherence and future potentials for progress.

As implied in Figure 1, one of the most significant attempts of integration within modern theory of the firm involves exploring the possibility of bridging the perception of the firm as a "productive unit" within evolutionary and resource-based theory and the perception of the firm as an "exchange structure" within transaction cost theory and constitutional theory of the firm. The purpose of such a synthesis: a "knowledge-based" theory of the firm, would be to "transgress" some of the limitations characterizing each of the two perspectives, respectively.

References

Alchian, A. 1950. "Uncertainty, evolution, and economic theory." *Journal of Political Economy* 58:211-221.

Alchian, A. 1987. "Property rights." *The New Palgrave* 3:1031-1034.

Alchian, A., and Demsetz, H. 1972. "Production, information costs and economic organization." *The American Economic Review* 69:777-795.

Alchian, A., and Woodward. 1988. "The firm is dead: long live the firm." *Journal of Economic Literature* 26:65-79.

Bain, J.S. 1956. *Barriers to new competition.* Cambridge, Mass.: Harvard University Press.

Baumol, W.J. 1959. *Business behavior, value, and growth.* New York: MacMillan.

Barnard, C. 1938. *The functions of the executive .* Cambridge: Harvard University Press. Reprinted 1962.

Berle, A.A. Jr., and Means, G.C. 1932. *The modern corporation and private property.* New York: The Macmillan Co.

Coase, R.H. 1937. "The nature of the firm." *Economica* 4.

Cohen, W.M., and D.A. Levinthal. 1990. "Absorptive capacity: A new perspective on learning and innovation." *Administrative Science Quarterly* 35:128-152.

Coleman, J.S. 1988. "Social capital in the creation of human capital." *American Journal of Sociology* Suppl. 94:95-120.

Coleman, J.S. 1990. *Foundation of social theory.* Cambridge, Mass.: Harvard University Press.

Cyert, R., and March, J.G. 1963. *A behavioral theory of the firm.* Englewood Cliffs NJ: Prentice Hall,Inc.

Demsetz, H. 1988. "The theory of the firm revisited." *Journal of Law, Economics and Organization* 4:141-162.

Dosi, G., Teece, D. and Winter, S.G. 1992. "Toward a theory of corporate coherence: preliminary remarks." *Technology and Enterprise in a Historical Perspective*, edited by Dosi, Giannetti, and Toninelli. Oxford: Clarendon Press.

Friedman, Milton. 1953. "The methodology of positive economics." In M. Friedman (ed.), *Essays in positive economics.* Chicago: University of Chicago Press.

Georgiou, P. 1973. "The goal paradigm and notes towards a counter paradigm." *Administrative Science Quarterly* 18:291-310.

Ghemawat, P., and Costa , J.E.R. 1993. "The organizational tension between static and dynamic efficiency." *Strategic Management Journal* 14:59-73.

Gifford, A., Jr. 1991. "A constitutional interpretation of the firm." *Public Choice* 68:91-106.

Hall, R.L., and Hitch, C.J. 1939. "Price theory and business behavior." *Oxford Economic Papers* (2):12-45.

Jensen, M. and Meckling, W. 1976. "Theory of the firm: Managerial behavior, agency costs, and capital structure." *Journal of Financial Economics* 3:305-360.

Knudsen, C. 1995. "The competence view of the firm: What can modern economists learn from Philip Selznick's sociological theory of leadership." In W.R. Scott and S. Christensen (eds.), *Advances in the Institutional Analysis of Organizations: International and Longitudinal Studies*. London: SAGE.

Kreps, D.M. 1990. *A course in microeconomic theory*. New York: Harvester Wheatsheaf.

Langlois, R. 1984. "Internal organization in a dynamic context: some theoretical considerations." In Jussawalla and Ebenfield (eds.), *communication and information economics*. Elsevier Science Publication: 23-49.

Levinthal, D.A and March, J.G. 1993. "The myopia of learning." *Strategic Management Journal* 14:95-112.

Machlup, F. 1967. "Theories of the firm: marginalist, managerial and behavioral. *American Economic Review* 57:1-33.

March, J.G. 1991. "Exploration and exploitation in organizational learning." *Organization Science* 2:1-19.

Mayr, E. 1982. *The growth of biological thought: diversity, evolution, and inheritance*. Cambridge, Mass.: Harvard University Press.

Morgan, G. 1986: *Images of organizations*. London: SAGE.

Nelson, R. 1991. "Why firms differ, and how does it matter?" *Strategic Management Journal* 12:61-74.

Nelson, R., and Winter, S. 1982. *An evolutionary theory of economic change*. Cambridge: Harvard University Press.

Penrose, E.T. 1952. "Biological analogies in the theory of the firm." *American Economic Review* 52:804-819.

Penrose, E.T. 1955. "Limits to the growth and size of firms." *American Economic Review, Papers and Proceedings*: 531-543.

Penrose, E.T. 1959. *The theory of the growth of the firm*. Oxford: Oxford University Press.

Popper, K.R. 1963: *Conjectures and refutations*. London: Routledge.

Porter, M. 1980. *Competitive strategy*. New York: Free Press.

Prahalad, C.K. and Hamel, G. 1988. "The core competence of the corporation." *Harvard Business Review* 66:79-91.

Prescott and Visscher. 1980. "Organization capital." *Journal of Political Economy* 80:446-461.

Quinn, J.B. 1980. *Strategies for change*. Homewood,Ill: Irwin

Saloner, G. 1991. "Modeling, game theory and strategic management." *Strategic Management Journal* 12:119-36.

Schelling, T. 1984. *Choices and consequences: perspectives of an errant economist.* Cambridge, Mass. Harvard University Press.

Schumpeter, J.A. 1942. *Capitalism, socialism and democracy.* London: Unwin.

Selznick, P. 1957. *Leadership in administration: a sociological interpretation.* Berkeley: Harper and Row.

Selznick, P. 1969. *Law, society and industrial justice.* Berkeley: Russell Sage Foundation. With the collaboration of Philippe Nonet and Howard M. Vollmer.

Seth, A., and Thomas, H. 1994. "Theories of the firm: Implications for strategy research." *Journal of Management Studies* 31:165-191.

Shapiro, C. 1989. "The theory of business strategy." *Rand Journal of Economics* 20:125-137.

Simon, H. 1983. *Reasons in human affairs.* Stanford: Stanford University Press.

Strotz, R.H. 1956. "Myopia and inconsistencies in dynamic utility maximization." *Review of Economic Studies* 23:165-180.

Vanberg, V. 1992. "Organizations as constitutional systems." *Constitutional Political Economy*, 3:223-53.

Veblen, T. 1899/1961. "Why economics is not an evolutionary science." In *The place of science in modern society.* New York: Rusell and Rusell.

Whitley, R. 1984. *The intellectual and social organization of the sciences.* Oxford: Clarendon Press.

Williamson, O.E. 1964. *The economics of discretionary behavior: managerial objectives in a theory of the firm.* Englewood Cliffs, N.J.: Prentice Hall.

Williamson, O.E. 1975. *Markets and hierarchies: analysis and antitrust implications.* New York: Free Press.

Williamson, O.E. 1981. "The modern corporation: origins, evolution, attributes." *Journal of Economic Literature* 19:1537-1568.

Williamson, O.E. 1985. *The economic institutions of capitalism: firms, markets, relational contracting.* New York: The Free Press.

Williamson, O.E. 1991. "Strategizing, economizing, and economic organizations." *Strategic Management Journal* 7: 159-187.

Winter, S.G. 1987. "Knowledge and competences as strategic assets." In D.J. Teece (ed.), *The competitive challenge: strategies for industrial innovation and renewal.* Cambridge: Ballinger.

Winter, S.G. 1988. "On Coase, competence and corporation." *Journal of Law, Economics and Organizations* 4:163-180.

9

BUSINESS STRATEGY FROM THE POPULATION LEVEL

John Freeman
Haas School of Business
University of California, Berkeley

Much of the debate in the literature on business strategy revolves around the appropriate unit of analysis. For Michael Porter (1980) and others who take a "market power" position, the issue is how *markets* are structured and how a particular focal firm can take advantage of that structure. A second position, called the "resource-based view" (Wernerfelt 1984) begins with the firm, asks what its resources are, and then considers what product markets the firm could serve so as to most efficiently utilize the array of resources at its disposal. Both of these positions take for granted the ability of managers to control what firms are doing and how. This involves both the degree to which managers (presumptively top managers) *control* the organizations they are supposed to manage and the *speed* with which adjustment can be made. Finally, both take a single firm as the strategic referent, treating strategic analysis as something done *uniquely* by that firm.

Why should one consider the level and locus of control to be worth considering when scholars formulate approaches to strategic management? The answer is simple—if the people making strategies are not also in control of the organization, then strategies will often remain unimplemented; and unimplemented strategies are irrelevant. The issue is not simply whether the firm is under control at a given moment, but also where the strategies are developed and by whom. Everyone would probably accept the assertion that sometimes the people who make the strategies fail to get them implemented, or that the strategies   are

219

implemented so slowly as to be ineffectual. The question, then, is how often managers find themselves presiding over this kind of implementation failure. If it is a common problem, managers ought to be considering various strategic moves with an eye toward the probability of implementation. It is curious that Porter's second book, *Competitive Advantage*, is intended "to bridge the gap between strategy and implementation, rather than treat these two subjects independently or consider implementation scarcely at all as has been characteristic of much previous research in the field" (1985: 3) . It does so without ever considering the control problem.[1]

Speed of implementation matters, also because the world within which firms operate is constantly changing—sometimes rapidly or erratically, sometimes more slowly or more predictably. Porter's (1980: 156-188) analysis of industry evolution notes a number of ways in which markets change, complicating the strategic problem for the focal firm. More recently (Porter, 1991), he has called for a theory of strategic dynamics, but notes that existing approaches, including the resource-based view, do not provide one. Wernerfelt (1984) employs a simple comparative static analysis to show how consideration of resources can lead to specific recommendations about which of two markets to enter first or whether to enter them simultaneously. Since both the market power and resource-based view are rooted firmly in orthodox microeconomic theory, both tend to assume markets in equilibrium, suitable for static analysis. But strategies are often conceived to deal with disequilibrium conditions, where new technologies, political upheavals, or dramatic demographic changes produce opportunities and threats. These conditions do not last forever, so opportunities and threats appear as windows in time.

If the application of scientific methods is more than just pretense, there would seem to be something fundamentally wrong with viewing the strategic problem as one of understanding what is unique about a particular firm and its situation. Science is about the replicable, about repeated events. The scientist seeks to understand the common, the ordinary so as to be able to appreciate and understand that rare, extraordinary event. If this is true, then research in business strategy ought to begin with analysis

---

[1]Chapter 11 (Porter, 1985) does discuss the organizational problems of implementing horizontal strategies. Many of these involve political problems between units and individuals. The point of importance for present purposes is that those devising the strategies often know that some of the possible strategic options available to them would be difficult or impossible to implement, and, therefore, shun them.

of the typical firm—how do business firms of a given type deal with a certain kind of problem? This suggests that a useful place to start an analysis of strategy is with groups of firms employing common solutions to general problems. After one understands such general issues, one should elaborate fundamental knowledge with the nuances facing particular firms.

Ecological Theory[2]

How should one go about developing an approach that corrects these weaknesses? We can start by noting that business firms adopt many of the features of their individual strategies as packages when the original form of organization is selected. That is to say, many of the gross features of resource configuration are implied when an entrepreneur starts a new business of a given type.

The decision to found a new bank implies possession or access to financial resources necessary to pass the minimum standards of regulators. It also presupposes knowledge of bank operations. Institutional prescriptions for organizations vary, of course, across societies and other contextual boundaries. But within those boundaries, business firms and other kinds of organizations experience substantial pressures to conform to expectations of what such an organization should look like. One can see the requisites for a business plan, demanded by venture capitalists and others with funds to invest, as a set of standards that are partly specific to the kind of business being contemplated. It is also undoubtedly true that the various forms of organization that are observable in some sphere of business activity have varying operating and competitive advantages. So there are social and economic factors at work.

The point is that the entrepreneur is not free to design his or her business with complete freedom. Were this untrue, we would see an infinite blending of organization attributes and qualities, so that it would be impossible to talk about a "bank" as distinct from a "credit union" or even a "restaurant." Every organization would be more or less one or the other. One of the points of agreement between such an ecological view of strategic issues and the resource-based view of the firm is that both agree that at any point in time, a firm's strategic position should be defined in part through reference to its existing stock of resources in the context of the environment

---

[2]For detailed literature reviews, see Hannan and Freeman 1989; Singh and Lumsden 1990; Brittain, 1980; Hannan and Carroll 1992.

in which it currently exists. As in Wernerfelt's original (1984) position and in subsequent treatments (Barney 1991), resources are understood to mean more than simply assets.

But what of implementation issues? Organizational ecology takes the position that all change occurs with friction. Redeploying resources takes effort, effort that cannot be simultaneously used for productive activity so change is doubly costly. The more fundamental the change is, the more effort it takes. This effort involves the search and decision processes involved in choosing the new course of action and the new configuration of resources. It also involves the internal struggle that generally commences when resources are deployed. A good measure of the importance of a change is the share of the firm's resources up for grabs. The bigger that share is, the more resistance there will be (Pfeffer 1981). So the more fundamental the change is, the deeper the strategic problems being addressed, the more arduous the adjustment process will be (Hannan and Freeman 1984). Because strategic changes take effort, they will take time to effect. So organizations adopt new strategies, along with other kinds of changes, with some *inertia*. That is, they tend to change slower than the world around them. So when some perturbation occurs in the markets, social environments or legal environments of business firms, one can expect a stochastic response. Some organizations adjust; other do not. Failure follows. Opportunity comes with it. That is to say, as existing organizations struggle to deal with this changing world, some succeed and make the adjustment. Others cannot adjust and disappear. As the process unfolds, pockets of resources go unexploited. New markets appear and entrepreneurs rush to fill them before the existing firms can identify them and redeploy their resources.

The ecological perspective on strategy combines features of the resource-based view and the market power view. The ecological perspective focuses on the ways in which various strategies fit in with an environment that selects for or against these strategies by encouraging foundings and discouraging failures. In doing so, it examines both the threats and opportunities that underlie the market power view and also the strengths and weaknesses that underlie the resource-based view (Barney 1991).

An example of these processes is the chaos that followed deregulation in the savings and loan business (Haveman 1993). Deregulation coincided with a surge in interest rates. Thrifts were unable to compete in part because regulations limited the rate of interest they could charge for home loans and the rate they could pay for deposits. When regulations were lifted, they were able to invest deposits in a wide range of vehicles with which they no little experience and very little expertise. Staying where they were, in the S&L organizational form, was perilous because it was not obvious that the form itself was viable anymore. Why go to a S&L when banks, stock brokerages, and other financial services companies could offer the same services at better prices? On the other hand, diversifying into real estate development and speculating in the financial markets was perilous as well, perhaps more. So a wave of strategic changes and failures swept over the population of savings and loans. If one were to perform a strategic analysis of any particular S&L, one would need to have a grasp of the changes affecting all of them before one could make judgments about how to fashion a new strategy. At least it would be useful to have this knowledge. Furthermore, one would probably benefit by concentrating attention on those trying new solutions to common problems: new thrifts opening with experimental solutions to these problems, thrifts trying different modes of diversification, thrifts in failure. What works, and what is not working? Answers to these questions are best sought at the population level.

The organizational form

Business firms and other kinds of organizations come packaged in ways that allow us to name them as types. The forms may be more or less general. Organizational ecologists have, for the most part, shied away from Linnaean schemes of classification (an exception is McKelvey 1981). So the term "form" could be used with reference electronics firms, semiconductor firms, memory manufacturers, or DRAM manufacturers, for example. Within each of these, one could also distinguish the first-to-market strategists from the followers. The reason for leaving matters at this vague level is that there is no generally-accepted basis for prioritizing variables that might serve as defining criteria. Which is most important depends on the theoretical problem at hand. So one might be interested in explaining variations in operating efficiencies and would, therefore, pay close attention to transactions costs (Williamson 1975, 1985). In contrast, the issue of interest may be innovation in technology. Appropriability issues (Arrow 1962; Teece 1989) may suggest variables to examine.

The important idea underlying the notion of a form as ecologists use the term is *shared fate*. Organizations are viewed as constituting a population when they manifest a given form, and the form is significant to the degree that those organizations employing it experience a similar set of

223

survival risks or advantages. In this sense, they share a fate based upon their common characteristics.

The relationship between such characteristics of the organizational form and business strategies is not difficult to see. The form is, in part, the strategic patterns pursued in common by some set of firms. For example, open architecture in personal computer technology opened the door to vertical disintegration. Firms specializing in direct marketing could buy copy the designs, purchase the components, and co-market the software with very little overhead. A wave of foundings swept over the industry in the 1980s as companies such as Dell, Northgate, and Gateway drew market share away from their vertically integrated competitors such as IBM. So the specialist non-integrated firm is an organizational form. It competes *as a form* with the vertically integrated generalist form in the computer industry.

The ecological niche—competing in multidimensional resource space

Most research in business strategy assumes that resources are made available to firms or denied them through market mechanisms. To be sure, researchers differ in their assumptions about how efficient those market are, but although scholars taking the resource-based approach write about such intangibles as reputation and established contacts, their theorizing tends to emphasize markets. Furthermore, they usually focus on a single "industry." This refers to a bundle of more or less substitutable goods. The problem is that from the firm's perspective, this may make little sense. Many firms are not in a single industry, nor are they participating broadly in any industry. Such a pattern is particularly likely when their current architecture results from a pattern of diversification through acquisition. As they acquire other firms for specific strategic reasons, they acquire a variety of attendant capabilities and resources that involve them in ever more complex businesses.

Business firms, even small ones, operate in a resource space that includes conventional markets, but also includes political support, information, and access to social networks. Securing the resources that are needed at any moment in time is the fundamental strategic issue for all firms. Of course some of these resources are particularly important in the sense that their variable availability impacts the survival chances of the organizations in question more than do other resource variations. This may be because they simply are more important for such firms, or because their supply is more problematical. By examining the pattern of availability of these critical resources over time, we can identify the resource levels at which a particular kind of organization prospers. This is what ecologists call the population's *niche*. Competition is partly niche-specific. It is the combination of resources and the range of availability that defines the niche.

Niches may be more or less highly specialized. Specialized organizational forms often evolve where the dense packing of generalists in the middle of some resource space has left small spaces that newly evolving forms can fill. Carroll had described the specialist strategy in these terms (1984), and developed a formal model of resource partitioning to show how populations may expand in the face of concentration. Freeman and Hannan (1984, 1989) showed how specialists can sometimes be expected to out-compete diversified firms under conditions of uncertainty. The relevance to the resource-based literature on diversification (Montgomery and Wernerfelt 1988) seems obvious.

Since we will be considering semiconductor manufacturing in some detail below, perhaps a brief example will be useful here. During the 1980s the business press was full of stories about the disappearance of U.S. dominance in semiconductor manufacturing. The largest firms in the world, measured by yearly sales volumes, were no longer American, but Japanese. Eisenhardt and Schoonhoven (1990) studied entrepreneurial semiconductor manufacturing firms during this same period and found that most of them were prospering. Few had disappeared. How could this be? The answer is that the new ventures were not in Dynamic Random Access memories (DRAMs), but in a host of other branches of the technology. They were making analog circuits, non-volatile memories and logic devices, for example. Today, the largest semiconductor firm in the world is Intel Corporation. Intel exited DRAM production at about this same time to concentrate on microprocessors. Two observations emerge from this example. First, there may be no recognizable thing as "the semiconductor industry" if industry is defined as above—a set of substitutable goods. DRAMs are not substitutes for analog devices. Second, understanding the strategic threats and opportunities in rapidly changing resource spaces can be facilitated by looking at patterns of foundings and failures in populations of organizations, because foundings occur where there are underexploited resources and failures occur where resources are drying up.

Evolution and Constraint

The term "evolution" usually refers to long term, cumulative change. Such a pattern may be seen in increasingly efficient production systems, or in escalating returns to owners, but such desirable outcomes are not presumed. The term "strategy" refers here to a firm's *characteristic way of doing business* (Freeman and Boeker 1984): the ways in which it gathers resources, and the routines it employs to use those resources. The term "resource" means funding, raw materials, labor, information, and access to political and social support. The term is used differently than it is by strategists taking the resource-based view (Barney 1991) in that ecologists usually leave out characteristics of the organization itself. Under conditions of scarcity, this characteristic way of doing business includes response to other organizations also seeking those resources.

Evolution and strategy are linked through processes of selection. The outcome of this process is not profitability, or market share, or shareholder wealth. Rather, it is firm survival. The linkage between strategic behavior of firms, or of the managers who work for those firms, and survival is taken as a subject for research. It is not assumed. "Survival of the fittest" does not necessarily mean survival of the best managed. Sometimes, the best ways for owners to maximize their own wealth is to kill the firm. Firms are often run in such a way that owners' interests are subordinated to those of managers. Finally, firms often disappear through processes of acquisition that may make top managers and owners rich, while the firm as a recognizable organization disappears. Biotechnology companies in the United States rarely disappear through disbanding. Most that disappear are acquired (Barley and Freeman 1992). They do so in part because of the very high costs of bringing human therapeutics to market. In this industry, only the best managed and most technically able firms ever get close to market. Genentech, Cetus and Syntex are among the biggest and most successful biotechnology companies, but have been acquired. Time will tell whether their organizational operations lose identity.

This tendency to confuse firms with owners/managers is particularly problematical when students of business strategy write as if the firm were a single decision maker. They borrow from orthodox microeconomics in assuming that firms are unitary, rational actors. One can, therefore, anthropomorphize with impunity. Virtually the entire corpus of organizational research recoils at such an assumption. Without belaboring the point, its seems obvious that if the dynamics of strategic processes are taken as significant, the internal functioning of organizations will matter. At the very least, it takes time for individual people to communicate, arrive at a common understanding of the problems confronting the firm, consider alternatives, and pick an intendedly efficacious strategy. So even if one wishes to take a rationalist position, it is hard to avoid the assumption that internal organization will speed up or slow down the process of strategic choice. Furthermore, if one admits that it matters when the firm does what it does, it is difficult to avoid the separation of strategy implementation from strategy formulation. A strategy that remains unrealized is worse then irrelevant, because it took effort to devise. A strategy that is formulated in the absence of some effort to estimate the time to implement is dangerous, even if it is correct at the time it is devised.

So it seems reasonable to assume that firms are filled with people who have their own ambitions, fears, and needs. These individuals compete and cooperate, devise novel possible solutions to problems, and contend for resources as they support some alternatives and oppose others, and organize to make these things happen. This leads some scholars to focus on the internal selection process (Burgelman 1983). Nelson and Winter discuss the concept of organizational routine as a form of truce (1984: 107-12). Because these individuals do not take the positions they support at random, they tend to fall into groups that support or oppose various strategic alternatives. The consequences provide them with common interests. Indeed, this is what the literature on principals and agents is all about (see Gibbons, 1993 for a discussion of how such differences of interest undergird internal organization). The point here is that an evolutionary account of strategic management does not preclude the manager from an active role. The same can be said for analyses of populations of firms.

Introducing consideration of such complexities vitiates the use of conventional performance criteria. How is profit to be apportioned when the distinction between fixed and variable costs evaporates under analysis of firm dynamics, and the current sales of one product line are sacrificed to gain long term strategic advantage in another? In addition, we know that strategic advantage is often sought by using accounting devices to send misleading information to competitors and to the capital markets as well. Return on Equity calculations would seem particularly suspect in these circumstances. One can observe less ambiguously whether a firm is in or out of business, or some line of business, than one can observe whether it is making money.

From an ecological point of view, the set of forms (with their populations) evolves, not the individual firm. This is one of the principal differences between this form of evolutionary theory and that advocated by Nelson and Winter (1982). The forms develop over time as organizations are created, or join the population through change processes, or disappear from the population. They also evolve through change of firms that make up the population. These change processes are treated well by other bodies of theory, so organizational ecologists have little to say about them.

In order for ecological approaches to strategic management to prove useful, we need to be able to show that life events through which firms appear and disappear in some population account for enough of the strategic change to be interesting (as compared with the adjustment processes most strategy researchers presume). In addition, we need to show that variations in strategically important variables come packaged in discrete groupings that are amenable to treatment as organizational forms. This is what the rest of this paper tries to do.

An Example: Semiconductor Manufacturing in the U.S.

One of the serious weaknesses in the literature on strategic management is the gulf between theory and empirical research. Much of the basic conceptual work has been done without the discipline of empirical work. So falsifiability is a common problem. The empirical work often seems theoretically impoverished. That is, the theory that is evoked often is not necessary to generate the data analysis. And anything seems to pass muster as "strategic" in the empirical literature if its dependent variable is a performance measure of some sort.

One of the virtues of research conducted at the population level is the well-developed methodological base. This involves the use of sophisticated methods to estimate the rates at which various relevant vital events occur. Most conventionally, these events are foundings and failures. Each may occur in a variety of ways. For example, foundings occur most obviously through entrepreneurship but can also occur through schism, when existing firms split or divest some part. Similarly, a merger between two or more existing organizations may yield something so new and unlike any of the forebears that one would choose to view the event as a form of founding. For failures, disbanding through such processes as bankruptcy are the obvious mode. But firms may also disappear when they are absorbed through merger. There are theoretical issues to be considered when one or more of these is selected for study. The important methodological issue is that one must be able to observe when such an event occurs, and it must result in some change in the observed population.

228

When events are observable in this way, the result is a dependent variable measured on a ratio scale. Either one is counting members of the population or one is observing whether or not an event have happened to a single organization (in which case the dependent variable can be treated as binary). It is usually the case that one can make these observations without having to depend on some self-interested actor to tell how well he or she is doing, as is often the case when performance measures such as Return on Investment are used.

In the empirical example that follows, we use participation in a technology as the rule to define whether an organization is in or out of the population. So the life event of interest here is *exiting* the U.S. semiconductor business. This is discussed below. At this point, however, it is perhaps useful to note that these firms are interesting to study because the population is large. Population analysis of business strategy may not prove very useful if the population is defined in such a way that the numbers are very small.

Semiconductor technology

The term "semiconductor" refers to the electrical properties of silicon and other substances from which microelectronic circuits are built. When carefully controlled impurities are added to these substances, their ability to conduct electricity changes. Although semiconducting materials had been used in electronics for decades, the invention of the transistor signaled the start of the electronics revolution.[3]

Tushman and Anderson have argued convincingly that technologies tend to change in fits and starts (Tushman and Anderson, 1986; Anderson and Tushman, 1990). They refer to these changes as "discontinuities." When discontinuities are sufficiently radical to render existing expertise obsolete, competence is destroyed and heightened rates of failure are to be expected coupled with the entry of new organizations designed around the new technology. The development of semiconductor electronics fits this definition because expertise in the design and production of existing electronic devices such as vacuum tubes was not helpful when it came to producing transistors and other devices built from semiconductors. In fact,

---

[3]Detailed accounts of the development of semiconductor technology and the history of the industry can be found in Tilton 1971, Braun and MacDonald 1978, Wilson et al. 1980, Borrus 1988, and Brittain 1991.

it appears that the profitability that remained in conventional electronics manufacturing, the relatively low level of uncertainty, and the bureaucratic production organization that characterized existing firms worked to their disadvantage when they tried to enter the semiconductor industry (Brittain and Freeman 1980). This technical discontinuity, invention of the transistor, opened the door to the development of a new organizational form whose structure was suited to exploiting the highly uncertain business of producing semiconductor devices—the free-standing semiconductor merchant market manufacturer.

We limit attention here to merchant market producers, organizations that sell semiconductors on the open market, as opposed to firms that manufacture only for their own use, so-called captive producers. Texas Instruments is an example of a free-standing semiconductor producer. It designs and produces a wide variety of semiconductor devices for sale all over the world. In contrast, Hewlett-Packard manufactures only for its own consumption.

Technology for producing semiconductor devices has consistently proved difficult to master. Merchant market producers are typically run by managers who know the technology intimately. Success in semiconductor production is not simply a matter of buying the necessary equipment and hiring smart engineers to design products. Rather, it involves substantial learning by doing, matching organization to technology by developing organizational routines through trial and error.

The early emergence of an organizational form set up to specialize in semiconductor production for sale on the open market can be seen as a response to uncertainty and opportunity inherent in both the development of the technology and in the market for semiconductor products. In each case, change has been cumulative and accelerating, yet erratic.

The emergence of a multibillion dollar market from virtually nothing in the late 1940s is matched by the increasing sophistication of the devices themselves. The functional capabilities of these products increase with degree of miniaturization. With the introduction of the integrated circuit in 1960, the "chip" of common parlance, a continuous decline of the size of features commenced. The smaller the feature size, the more functioning elements can be packed on a chip, which translates into increasingly complex functions. By virtually any measure, the functioning capabilities of semiconductor devices has grown at an amazing rate. The size of the market and the capability of the technology have developed in an erratic way. The market has a pronounced business cycle which results from factors mentioned above: the cost of inventories of semiconductor devices, rapid obsolescence, and the integral nature of the products of which they are vital components. When demand for final systems, such as computers, declines, manufacturers cut back orders of chips. In order not to be caught with expensive inventories of devices that may be obsolete when the market turns up again, systems manufacturers cut back their orders by amounts greater than the drop in their own demand. Similarly in growth, when demand for the final product picks up, manufacturers of these systems often increase orders for semiconductors by more than the proportionate increase in demand in anticipation of further demand increases. A shortage of components can mean loss of market share and competitive disadvantage. One can see this inventory control problem as a game between systems manufacturers and semiconductor manufacturers, each trying to place the burden of uncertainty on the other.

Semiconductor experts can usually predict the form of the next innovation. However, they do not often know which firm will make the breakthrough or what its technical specifications will be. These issues are important because the first firm to introduce a new product often sets the standard for the industry. Followers face delays in introducing a competing product because they have to redesign to fit the new standards. Furthermore, the pioneer has the advantage of a head start down the learning curve. Thus there are major advantages accruing to being early into the market.

The important point is that uncertainties stemming from the business cycle and from the innovation process itself have created turbulence in the industry. This turbulence translates into opportunities for entry. On the other hand, turbulence also represents risk.

As time went on, and the technology evolved, the industry became famous for its magnified business cycle. That is, booms and busts in the economy at large were more severe in the semiconductor business because the pace of technical change made for quick obsolescence. This meant that being caught with a large inventory of semiconductor components carried the increased cost of having obsolete components in stock when the flow of orders increased. So when a systems manufacturer experiences a drop in orders of 10%, the response is likely to be a cut in orders to semiconductor suppliers of 30%. When orders pick up, being caught short of these vital components means loss of market share and opportunity costs reflecting the substantial margins such systems usually command. As a result, the systems manufacturer increases order to the semiconductor manufacturer by amounts greater than the upswing in demand for the final product.

Figure 1a shows the rapid growth of the U.S. semiconductor market from 1946 to 1984. The uncertainty buried in this long-term pattern of grown is based in the high capital requirements of the business and the long lead times in building production capacity. If one expects 40% compound growth and only experiences 20% growth in a given year, the results can be devastating.

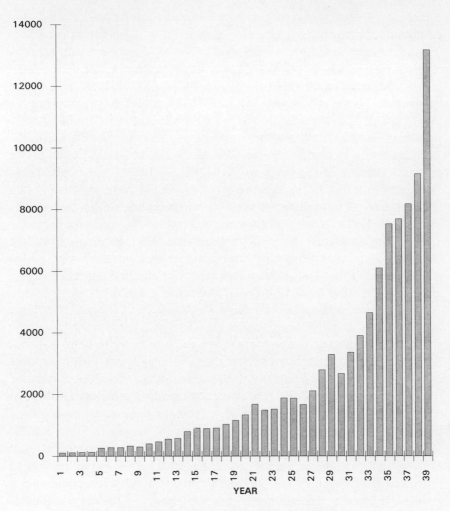

Figure 1a. North American Sales

Figure 1b shows how the number of products in the market has grown over the same period reflecting the technological side of the industry's evolution. As integrated circuits became more powerful and more versatile, some products were dropped.[4]

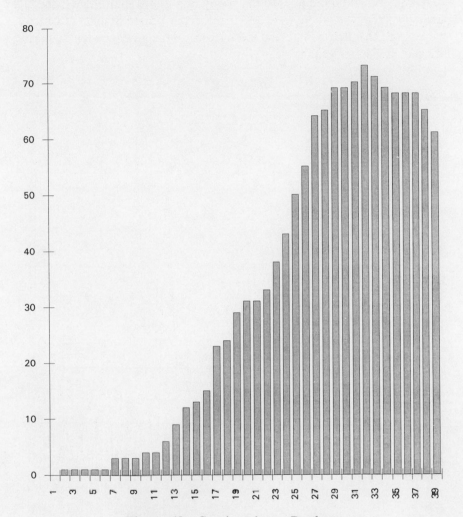

Figure 1b. Semiconductor Products

---

[4]Sources for these counts of products and the numbers of firms are reported in the next section, "Methods."

The combination of rapidly increasing sales over the history of the business is accompanied by accentuated cycles in demand, and rapidly evolving technology that changes in fits and starts, create high rates of foundings and failures in the business. In the early years, founding rates were higher than failure rates so the population grew rapidly. It reached its zenith in 1972 when there were 330 firms in the United States. In general, we can see that entries into and exits from semiconductor manufacturing tracked each other year by year.

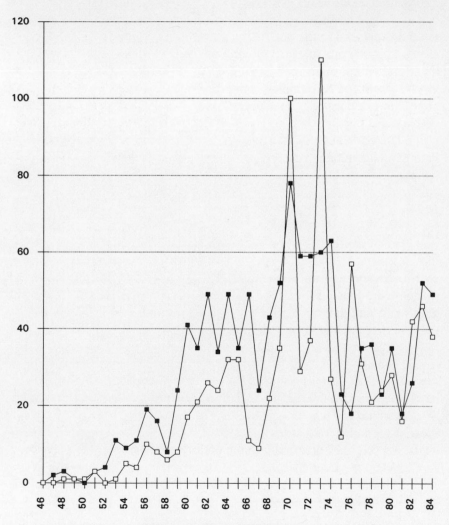

Figure 2. Entries and Exits

234

Methods

Populations can be studied empirically if one can satisfy a few simple requisites. First, one must be able to observe organizations of the form or forms under study. One needs to know at least whether they were in existence in each of a series of time periods such as calendar years. This time series should start with the first time period such organizations existed to avoid left censoring and truncation problems.[5] The more precise the information dating vital events (e.g., date the organization disappeared), the better. So one needs to be able to establish boundaries in time the tell when the firm appeared in the population and when it disappeared. The second requisite is that one must be able to distinguish organizations manifesting the form in question from those manifesting some other form. That is, one needs a rule for recognizing when an organization is in or out of the population in question. In this study the two requisites are satisfied by defining the population in terms of manufacturing semiconductor devices in the United States. We define an entry when a firm first appears in our listings of manufacturers, and an exit as when it disappears from those listings.

Data

Our data come primarily from a standard industry reference book: the *Electronics Buyer's Guide*. This annual publication lists standard electronic devices yearly, and all the companies in the United States that manufacture those devices and sell them on the open market. We coded both firms and devices for the years 1946 through 1984. This yielded a three-dimensional array: firms by semiconductor devices by years.

Our first task was to define the vital starting and ending events. We focus attention on entries and exits because some producers of semiconductor devices are subsidiaries of bigger corporations that may have been founded long before their entry into the semiconductor industry. So one would not want to use the date of founding of General Electric as the starting point for a study of semiconductor firms. Rather, one would want to use the date on which GE commenced its operations in semiconductor manufacturing. The assumption underlying our

---

[5]See Tuma and Hannan (1989) for a detailed treatment of these methods. Hannan and Freeman (1989) and Hannan and Carroll (1992) also review these applications.

operationalization is that participating in the business of manufacturing semiconductor devices for sale requires a very demanding commitment from an organization. Decisions to enter and leave the business are not made blithely, because the capital intensity is high, the expertise required is hard to come by, and the organizational routines required to make a company viable in this business take great effort to develop. Consequently, we expect strong inertial forces to affect such organizations. Indeed, such inertia in the face of great environmental turbulence is the main reason for studying this industry.

Many large corporations have multiple divisions in the semiconductor business. We aggregated over such subunits, noting when the company began to sell semiconductor devices and when it stopped. A firm-year observation is treated as right-censored if the organization continued in the semiconductor business after that year. An exiting event was recorded if the year in question was its last year.

We had to deal with the problem that mergers and acquisitions produce firm endings. We used names of the semiconductor producers and changes in their names, supplementing the information in the *Guide* with information gathered during interviews with managers of semiconductor companies, and published accounts, for deciding when a firm ceases to be an independent actor. If a company changed its name to indicate that it is a division of another company, we regard the change as an acquisition; this is an ending event for the acquired firms and as an entry for the acquiring firm (assuming it was not in the semiconductor business before).

Our coding stopped in 1984 because it was at about this time that the Japanese became dominant in DRAM manufacturing. We could not justify a focus on U.S. manufacturing after the business became truly global. Unfortunately, a redefinition of market boundaries would have to be carried backward to the appearance of the very first semiconductor firm, and comparable data worldwide are not available.

Using these data, we observe 1,197 firms active at one time or another in the U.S. semiconductor business. Of these 895 exited or disbanded. We supplement the *Guide* data with various yearly time series for the industry including such variables as aggregate semiconductor sales (in constant dollars), and Moody's AA corporate bond interest rate at year end (which we consider a cost of capital measure). We also note whether the firm was a division of a larger firm. Finally, we introduce two period effects to control for sea changes in the technology: 1960 (Period 2) for the introduction of the integrated circuit and the planar production process,

Number of Semiconductor Firms

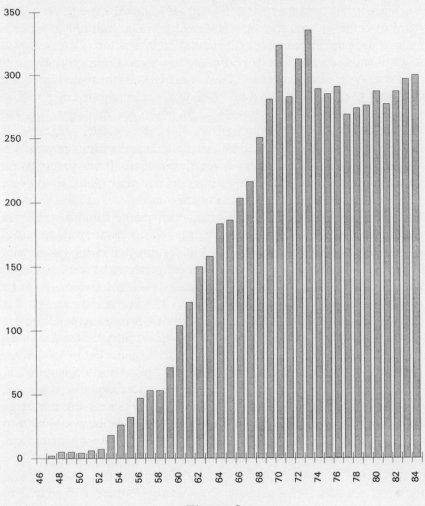

Figure 3

1970 (Period 3) for the introduction of the microprocessor. (For further details see Hannan and Freeman, 1989.)

    Our main measure of attempts at adaptive change involves changes in the mix of products offered. We use a standard set of 80 product categories. For each firm, we recorded the categories in which it offered products in its initial year and each subsequent year. For instance, one of these categories is MOS Memory-Dynamic RAMs. Offering a one megabit memory chip when a firm already produces a 256K bit chip is not counted here as a technology change. But offering a dynamic RAM when none was produced before is such a change. According to our informants, change among these products involves substantial changes in core technologies. That is, such changes impose heavy costs of investment, reorganization, and construction of new routines. Therefore, we use information of the occurrence of such changes to mark the adaptive changes that might affect life chances.

The outcome of interest is exit from the industry. In order to accommodate time-variation in covariates, we analyze firm-year spells (a standard procedure in this research tradition). Each firm's tenure in the industry is broken into yearly segments and associated with appropriate levels of all covariates for that year. The outcome in our analysis is a binary variable that tells for each firm in each year of its existence in the industry whether the firm was still operating in the industry at the end of the year. .This variable is zero for all but the last year observed for each firm. For firms whose histories are censored on the right (i.e., still sell in semiconductor devices at the end of the study), it is also coded as zero for the final year of observation.

Although it is customary to talk about the semiconductor industry, and we have used that terminology in this paper, it is not clear that this is correct. The differences among the various semiconductor devices would seem to be too great to permit such facile aggregation. Light-emitting diodes are not substitutes for microprocessors, for example. Since not all firms produce all products, it might be better to note that these products are bundled together by firms seeking advantage. These advantages range from technical complementarities in production to adaptive growth patterns through which firms grow by adding products that are similar to those already being offered.

Partitioning variation by source

We only make a start here in studying the processes by which variations in production mixes occur. Our method is to establish a baseline against which to compare firms' strategic behavior. Following Nelson and Winter's (1982) practice of thinking in terms of random draws from experience, we might define a "herd rule." Firms mimic the prevailing practice. In each year, we look at the stock of products being offered by

238

firms in the prior year, and ask what the distribution would look like if firms made choices with probabilities derived from the prior year's data. So, for example, when a firm enters the business, a baseline expectation could be derived by saying that its probability of offering a product is based on the proportion of firms offering that product the previous year. That is, "expected frequencies" are based on simple imitation. The same for changes and exits. Firms exit as a result of a short of random grim reaper. If the firms that disappear are randomly drawn from the current year's population, then the product offerings that disappear will reflect their frequency of offering in the current year. Finally, organizations adding or dropping products will follow the herd. They will drop products that few others offer, and they will add products that everyone else is offering. (We might use changes rather than counts, but space limitations preclude exploring all the nuances here.)

Analyzing mortality

Because we know only the first and last year a firm appeared in the data, and our independent variables are all yearly observations as well, most of the methods of event history analysis are not available. We employ a simple logit that treats exiting as a log-linear function of a combination of regressors. An observation is censored if the firm does not exit in the year under observation or if it is still present in the last year, 1984. So the logit model simply predicts whether a firm in the business this year is likely to exit next year.

Technical evolution

We can readily count the number of new products sold each year, and we do so at the firm level to control for both diversification and size. We would expect the effects on mortality to be negative in both interpretations (and they are). But we are especially interested in the bundles of products that firms produce and how those bundles form group-ings that shift year by year. The question is, how to study such shifting patterns.

Inspiration for an approach was drawn from social network analysis, particularly the work of Ronald Burt (1982, 1992). Usually, network analysis begins with an adjacency matrix, which presents each side of a dyadic relationship as rows and columns (if Actor 1 establishes a relationship with Actor 2, there would be a one in row one, column 2, the cell would be zero otherwise). When a firm produces a given product, there is a potential relationship between it and each firm or individual purchasing that kind of product. So resource flows can be tracked by looking at participation in a market. Burt often looks at such relationships using devices such as input/output tables, cluster analyzing the aggregate participation in industries so observed. In this case, we cluster analyze a year's set of firm-product offerings. The results tell us what combinations of products tended to be offered together in that year. The question, then, is how to apply this method over time given that both firms and products are entering and leaving.

SAS PROC VARCLUS performs a principal components factor analysis in hierarchical form. This procedure was run for each year so that its estimates were independent between years. The eighty binary product code variables were clustered so as to show the tendency for products to be manufactured and sold in combination. The minimum second eigenvalue criterion was used to limit the program's factor extraction and this criterion resulted in a maximum of seven factors extracted in any year. At the beginning of the series, when there was only one product being sold, it extracted none.

A variable of considerable strategic interest is turmoil in the industry. This is defined as the extent of change in product groupings between the current year and the year before. We would expect this to have a positive effect on the rate of mortality. That is, if a firm is active in a strategic group characterized by high levels of uncertainty—many of the products being sold in that group this year were not sold together last year—we would expect its hazard of exiting to rise.

Results

Partitioning variations in product offerings

Some years ago Hannan and Freeman (1984) theorized about inertia in organizational populations. They argued that there is a hierarchy of variables that reflect the degree to which variations would reflect fundamental changes in the organization. At the lowest level, adding or dropping the colors offered for bars of soap would happen with minimal friction. At the highest level, the fundamental values of the organization would be very slow to change and would occasion much resistance. For example, turning a religious organization, such as a synagogue, into a for-profit firm such as a horse racing track, would be so unusual, and so

240

difficult to manage, that it is ludicrous to contemplate. We consider modifying the product offering of semiconductor firms to be somewhere in-between.

Of the 1,197 organizations, 468 added a product at least once, 617 exited without introducing a new product after their initial appearance, and 112 were still active in the industry in 1984 without having introduced a new product. At the other extreme, 114 firms added products four times or more. Sometimes, firms entered with products offered by few others. In doing so, they added variability to the industry, shifting the frequency distribution of offerings. The same happened when firms that were exiting took with them unusual product offerings. Finally, evolution in the industry may occur when existing firms make adjustments to the products offerings, adding or dropping products.

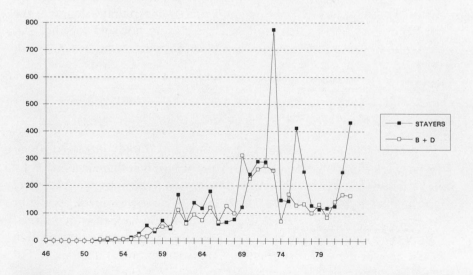

Figure 4a. U.S. Semiconductor Industry: Variations in Products (A)

This figure tracks the three processes of interest. Frequencies expected are based on the previous year's proportionate offerings in each product category. They are compared with frequencies observed in the current year. The sum of the three when added to last year's totals by product equal this year's totals by product. So the three lines represent the evolutionary process exactly.

We see that in the early years, because there are very few products, there is not much to explain. Starting in the 1960s, all three lines rise, but effects of entries rise faster than effects of exits. This shows that entries and exits add variation to the product offering in the industry. That is, firms appear for the first time with nonstandard combinations of products. Firms exit, taking with then nonstandard product bundles as well. So the evolution of the technology reflects both the adjustment process that Nelson and Winter study and the population level processes of interest to organizational ecologists. Furthermore, the relative contributions of these processes change over the course of industrial evolution. About the time of the introduction of the integrated circuit (1970), entries add more variation than exits.

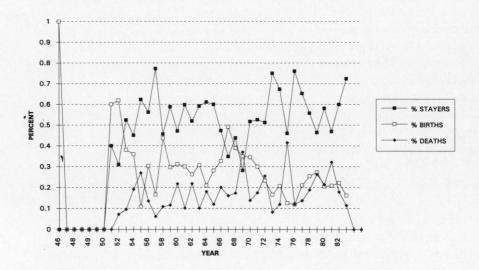

Figure 4b. U.S. Semiconductor Industry: Variations in Products (B)

In most years, the summed contributions to variability in product offerings produced by entries and exits comes close to variability contributed by adjustments. The contributions of "stayers" greatly exceeded the contributions made through entry and exit in only four years.

Of course we would expect the relative contributions of vital processes to be relatively greater when the variables of interest reflect fundamental qualities of organizations, rather than differences in technology of the kind studied here. Few strategy researchers, however, would argue that such technical changes are strategically irrelevant. The effects of entering with nonstandard bundles of products, or exiting with such bundles, are clearly substantial. Perhaps such a nonstandard combination addresses opportunities created by the rapidly developing technology. On the other hand, it may be that exiting of firms with nonstandard bundles reflects the lower viability of such combinations of products and technologies. Most important, however, is the implication that students of strategy should consider such aggregate level issues when they think about how strategy is made.

Modeling exits with effects of product groupings

Limitations of time and space preclude presentation of cluster analysis details. We can, however, examine the results of validation exercise. While coding the data, we received a copy of the annual report of the Semiconductor Industry Association. That report presented a classification of products by similarity in technology. A simplified version of that scheme is presented next, matched up with the results of our cluster analysis for 1984. Notice that these two schemes do not reflect exactly the same thing. Our cluster analysis uses market behavior—who produces and sells what—while the SIA scheme refers to similarities in technologies. Now, we would expect similarities in one, and the complementarities they represent, to be reflected in the second, but this is not necessary. Does market behavior reflect technical complementarities?

The two classifications do not match exactly, but there is a correspondence. Looking at Discrete Devices, Diodes and Rectifiers, for instance, we see that of the nine products so classified in the SIA based scheme, all are either in cluster 5 or 6. Analog/Linear IC's only include one product not in cluster 1. Without performing a rigorous analysis, we can only tentatively conclude that market behavior of these semiconductor firms corresponds well to technical complementarities. Equally important for our purposes, such correspondence validates the cluster analysis. The

DISCRETE DEVICES		INTEGRATED CIRCUITS		CUSTOM DEVICES	
1. Diodes and Rectifiers		**1. Digital Integrated Circuits**		**1. Custom ICs**	
Germanium diodes	5	Bipolar logic-ECL	2	Digital-bipolar	1
Silicon diodes	5	Bipolar logic-DTL	2	Digital-MOS	7
Microwave diodes	6	Bipolar logic-RTL	2	Linear Custom	1
High speed switch	5	Bipolar logic-TTI	2	2. Hybrids	
Tunnel diodes	5	Bipolar logic-Other	1	Dig. hybrid-drivers	3
Ref/Zener diodes	5	CMOS logic	7	Dig. hybrid-Multiplexers	3
Varactors	6	MOS logic	7	Dig. hybrid-custom	3
Schottkey bar. diodes	5	MOS mem-SRAMs	7	Lin. hybrid-analog switch	6
Glassy diodes	5	MOS mem-ROMs	7	Lin. hybrid-consumer	2
2. Transistors and Thyristors		MOS mem-PROMs	7	Lin. hybrid-converters	3
Germanium trans.	4	Other memory	2	Lin. hybrid-current regul.	3
Ger. power trans.	4	Microprocessors	7	Lin. hybrid-custom	3
Ger. audio trans.	4	Character generators	7	Lin. hybrid-instrument	3
Silicon trans.	5	Digital arrays	5	Lin. hybrid-other	3
Silicon power trans.	4	**2. Analog/Linear ICs**			
Silicon audio trans.	4	Amplifiers—Operational	1	OPTOELECTRONIC DEV.	
Field-effect trans.	4	Amplifiers—Consumer	1	Light-emitting	6
Microwave trans.	6	Amplifiers—Instrument	1	Photo-sens. diodes	6
Sensors and transd.	6	Line drivers	1	Photo-sens. trans.	6
Thyristors	5	Voltage regulators	1	Photo-sens. thyris.	4
Darlington pairs	4	Timers	1	Photo-sens. ICs	2
		Linear subsystems	7		
		Analog to digital	1		
		Digital to analog	1		

Table 1. A Priori Classification of Products and Cluster Results for 1984[6]

---

[6]19 products are missing because they were not sold by anyone in 1984.

244

cluster analysis seems to produce groupings of products as they appear in the marketplace that make sense in terms of similarities in the technology.

We turn now to the analysis of exiting in semiconductors. Table 2 presents the full model, which is built on previously published work (Hannan and Freeman 1989). Because this model has been published before, the rationale for each effect is presented concisely. First, the log of Age is introduced to estimate what has been called "the liability of newness" (Freeman *et al.* 1983). As organizations age, they learn and they establish relationships with other organizations that increase their chances of survival. So the predicted effect is negative, and the estimate fits that prediction. Second, we include a quadratic expression for the effects of density, the population's size at the start of the year. The prediction is that the rate of exiting will at first rise as the population grows more dense, due to rising legitimacy for a new organizational form, followed by a rise in exiting as competition increases (see Hannan and Freeman 1987, 1988; Hannan and Carroll 1992). The effects are negative for the main effect and the positive for the squared term, as expected. Lagged exits and entries are introduced to take the known wave-like patterns in the changes of these vital rates. In part, these are thought to reflect signaling effects. The variable DIV is binary, assuming the value of one when the firm is a division of a bigger corporation. Obviously, being part of a bigger firm will buffer the organization under study from many threats, so the effect should be negative and it is.

Two variables, Interest and Agg Sales (aggregate sales) are introduced to take into account the cost of capital and the industry's business cycle. The former should have a positive effect on exiting while the effect of the second should be negative. Both estimates fit the predictions. Period effects are not hypothesized, but are included as controls. Their exclusion does not change any of the reported effects.

Model 2 reports the additional effects of N Prods, the number of products offered by the local firm at the start of the year. As argued above, this effect should be negative and it is. This could be because it is a proxy for size, and bigger firms are less likely to exit. Or it could be that the more direct interpretation, the diversification of the firm, is the main causal process. Firms diversify to spread risk, and the effect is to lower their hazard of exiting. Other analyses, not reported in detail, control for yearly sales in a subsample for which such data were available. The effects in this

245

	1	2
Intercept	-1.404* (.274)	-1.300* (.274)
Log Age	-.109* (.010)	-.092* (.010)
Density	.029* (.005)	-.028* (.005)
Density-sq	.082* (.013)	.079* (.013)
Entries	-.004 (.003)	-.003 (.003)
Exits	-.013* (.002)	-.013* (.002)
DIV	-.663* (.010)	-.047* (.102)
Interest	.249* (.044)	.244* (.045)
Agg Sales	-.281* (.038)	-.281* (.038)
Period 2	1.537* (.395)	1.526* (.395)
Period 3	-.832* (.149)	-.813* (.150)
N Prods		-.078* (.010)
Chi-Sq	344.8	426.3
df	10	11

* $P < .05$//

Table 2 Logistic Regressions on Semiconductor Firm Exiting
(reports full model)*

analysis were the same, making the diversification explanation more persuasive. Of course the two are not mutually exclusive. Model 1 is nested within Model 2. This permits a likelihood ratio test. The Chi-square value is 81.6 with one degree of freedom, far in excess of the critical value necessary for $p < .001$.

The next question is whether diversification across product groupings has an effect on the rate of exiting. It has a negative effect, as one would expect if it is tracking diversification. Note that I am controlling for total number of products offered, so this effect concerns the distribution of products over groupings. Model 3 reports the effect of number of product groupings in which the firm participate. Even controlling for the number of products that firm offers, N Clusters has a negative effect. Spreading products out among a set of groupings lowers the hazard of exiting. Turmoil is also expected to have a positive effect on exiting. It does. So instability in the product grouping, or in the strategic grouping if one wishes to view it that way, does increase the rate of exiting.

Conclusion

What does this have to do with strategy? If we assume that firms are inert, how can they behave strategically? Of course, we are not assuming that firms are perfectly inert, only that they change with cost an effort. The search procedures so ably modeled by Nelson and Winter (1982) are assumed to be operating here, but search is expensive. So is strategic implementation. After all, if this were not true no firm would ever fail and entrepreneurship would be a very rare phenomenon. Existing firms would instantly move into new markets and technologies and would crowd out upstarts so rapidly that new firms would have no chance, or very little chance.

This analysis tells us that some of the variability in what firms produce at the aggregate level is explained by their nonrandom exiting. That is, one of the processes introducing variability is existing. And exiting is explainable, in part, by looking at the combinations of products that are usually produced together, and which of those combinations the firm in question produces.

Another way of putting this is that it matters what a semiconductor firm produces. It is more likely to be in the business next year if it sells some products rather than others. Reliable information on such an issue would probably be worth attention for any firm facing questions about where to move next, given the current combinations being offered by competitors. But firms produce products in combinations. Complementarities seem to exist, as some combinations are more likely than others. It is curious, then, that firms that spread their offerings out among these groupings have lower exit rates. This suggests that following the established practice is not likely to increase longevity. It may very well be that technical complementarities do not correspond to risk reduction. It may make sense from a resource point of view to produce technically similar products, but from the perspective of market-induced risk, the opposite is in order.

This conclusion is an appropriate one given the purposes of this volume. Analysis of evolutionary process at the population level suggests that both the market power and resource-based views have merit, but that the prescriptive advantages of each are difficult to untangle without focusing research, in part, on the strategies pursued by firms similarly situated. This is what population level analysis is all about.

References

Anderson, P., and Tushman, M.L. 1990. "Technological discontinuities and dominant designs: a cyclical model of technological change." *Administrative Science Quarterly*, 35: 605-633.

Arrow, K.J. 1962. Economic welfare and the allocation of resources for invention. In R.R. Nelson (ed.), *The rate and direction of inventive activity* (pp. 609-625). Princeton: Princeton University Press.

Bain, J. S. 1959. *Industrial organization.* New York: John Wiley.

Barley, S.R., Freeman, J., and Hybels, R.C. 1992. Strategic alliances in commercial biotechnology. In Nithin Nohria and Robert Eccles (eds.), *Organizations and network analysis.* Cambridge: Harvard Business School Press.

Barney, J. 1991. "Firm resources and sustained competitive advantage." *Journal of Management* 17: 99-120.

Braun, E., and MacDonald, S. 1978. *Revolution in miniature: the history and impact of semiconductor electronics.* Cambridge, England: Cambridge University Press.

Brittain, J., and Freeman, J.H. 1980. "Organizational proliferation and density-dependent selection." In John Kimberly and Robert Miles (eds.), *Organizational life cycles* (pp. 291-338). San Francisco: Jossey-Bass.

Burgelman, R.A. 1983. "A process model of internal corporate venturing in the diversified major firm." *Administrative Science Quarterly* 28: 223-244.

Burt, R.S. 1982. *Toward a structural theory of action*. New York: Academic Press.

Burt, R.S. 1992. *Structural holes*. Cambridge, Mass.: Harvard University Press.

Carroll, G.R. 1984. The specialist strategy. In Glenn Carroll and David Vogel (eds.), *Strategy and organization* (pp. 117-128). Boston: Pitman.

Carroll, G.R. 1985. "Concentration and specialization: dynamics of niche width in populations of organizations." *American Journal of Sociology* 90: 1262-83.

Eisenhardt, K.M., and Schoonhoven, C.B. 1990. "Organizational growth: linking founding team, strategy, and environment and growth among U.S. semiconductor ventures, 1978-1988." *Administrative Science Quarterly* 35: 504-529.

Electronics Buyers Guide. Supplement to *Electronics*, various years. New York: McGraw-Hill.

Freeman, J., and Boeker, W. 1984. "The ecological analysis of business strategy." *California Management Review* 26: 73-86.

Freeman, J.H., Carroll, G.R., and Hannan, M.T. 1983. "The liability of newness: age dependence in organizational death rates." *American Sociological Review* 48: 692-710.

Freeman, J.H., and Hannan, M.T. 1983. "Niche width and the dynamics of organizational populations." *American Journal of Sociology* 88: 1116-45.

Hannan, M.T., and Carroll, G.R. 1992. *The dynamics of organizational populations*. New York: Oxford University Press.

Hannan, M., and Freeman, J. 1987. "The ecology of organizational founding: American labor unions, 1836-1985." *American Journal of Sociology* 92: 910-43.

Hannan, M.T., and Freeman, J. 1988. "The ecology of organizational morality: American labor unions, 1836-1985." *American Journal of Sociology* 94: 25-42.

Hannan, M.T. and Freeman, J. 1989. *Organizational ecology*. Cambridge, MA: Harvard University Press.

Hannan, M.T. and Freeman, J. 1984. "Structural inertia and organizational change." *American Sociological Review* 49: 149-64.

Haveman, H.A. 1993. "Follow the leader: mimetic isomorphism and entry into new markets." *Administrative Science Quarterly* 38: 393-627.

Hawley, A. H. 1950. *Human ecology*. New York: Ronald Press.

McKelvey, B. 1982. *Organizational systematics*. Berkeley: University of California Press.

Montgomery, C., and Wernerfelt, B. "Diversification, Ricardian rents, and Tobin's q." *RAND Journal of Economics* 19: 623-632.

Nelson, R.R.., and Winter, S.G. 1982. *An evolutionary theory of economic change.* Cambridge: Harvard University Press.

Pfeffer, J. 1981. *Power in organizations.* Marshfield, Mass.: Pitman.

Porter, M.E. 1980. *Competitive strategy: techniques for analyzing industries and competitors.* New York: Free Press.

Porter, M.E. 1985. *Competitive advantage: creating and sustaining superior performance.* New York: Free Press.

Porter, M.E. 1991. "Towards a dynamic theory of strategy." *Strategic Management Journal* 12: 95-117.

Singh, J.V., and Lumsden, C.J. 1990. "Theory and research in organizational ecology." *Annual Review of Sociology,* 16:161-195.

Teece, D. 1989. *Innovation and the organization of industry.* Unpublished paper. Berkeley: Center for Research in Management.

Teece, D., Pisano, G., and Shuen, A. 1994. *Dynamic capabilities and strategic management.* Unpublished paper. Berkeley: Center for Research in Management.

Tuma, N.B., and Hannan, M.T. 1984. *Social dynamics: Models and methods.* New York: Academic Press.

Tushman, M.L., and Anderson, P. 1986. "Technological discontinuities and organizational environments." *Administrative Science Quarterly* 31: 439-65.

Wernerfelt, B. 1984. "A resource-based view of the firm." *Strategic Management Journal* 5: 171-180.

White, H.C. 1981. "Where do markets come from?" *American Journal of Sociology* 87: 517-547.

Williamson, O.E. 1975. *Markets and hierarchies: analysis and antitrust policies.* New York: Free Press.

Williamson, O.E. 1985. *The economic institutions of capitalism.* New York: Free Press.

Wilson, R.W., Ashton, P.K., and Egan, T.P. 1980. *Innovation, competition, and government policy in the semiconductor industry.* Lexington, Mass.: D.C. Heath.

10

OF DIAMONDS AND RUST:
A NEW LOOK AT RESOURCES

Cynthia A. Montgomery[1]
Graduate School of Business Administration
Harvard University

The German philosopher Hegel told us that one can understand oneself better by understanding others. By seeing what one is not, one sees better what one is. In the stream of discussions at the Copenhagen conference, I gained a new perspective on the challenge of blending evolutionary and strategic theories of the firm: the biggest hurdles are not analytical but philosophical. Evolutionary theorists and business strategists have fundamentally different world views. Although our preconference paper (see Chapter 1) duly noted the different legacies of each tradition, we missed the enormity of the ideology, the deep-seated convictions and ways of seeing that underlie the respective streams of work.

Around the table in Copenhagen, surrounded by evolutionary theorists and population ecologists, I came to see that strategists are diehard optimists: the kind of people that can be depended on to see the glass half full, not half empty. In contrast, the population ecologists and evolutionary theorists appeared rather sober (if not somber), and might be described as realists. I believe this difference is at the heart of some of the most

[1]This paper benefited from many conversations with Robert E. Kennedy and Birger Wernerfelt. Elizabeth Wynne Johnson helped to frame the issues from the venerable perspective of the liberal arts. Their insights are gratefully acknowledged.

251

significant gaps between these scholarly traditions, and underlies the differences in the ways we go about our work.

One could conceivably discover far worse things about one's self and the company she has been keeping. Nonetheless, the insight that strategists have a systematic tendency to seek the positive, to tell the uplifting story, was, in its own right, quite jarring. It is tempting to believe that one's outlook and behavior are unbiased, that one selects topics, seeks information, and orders the world without prejudice. To discover instead that there are patterns and proclivities in one's actions is once again to learn that free will is constrained by experience and conditioning. The lens through which one looks, and the direction in which that lens is pointed, fundamentally impacts what one sees.

Nelson and Winter (1982) describe the tendency of discipline-based scholars to see things through a common lens. Their discussion of orthodoxy in the field of economics highlights how a group of scholars can develop a communal way of conducting and evaluating research:

> ...there may be some who would deny that any "orthodoxy" exists in economics, apart from a widely shared commitment to the norms and values of scientific inquiry in general. Others would agree that an orthodoxy exists in the descriptive sense that there are obvious commonalities of intellectual perspective and scientific approach that unite large numbers of economists. But they would strenuously deny there is an orthodox position providing a narrow set of criteria that are conventionally used as a cheap and simple test for whether an expressed point of view on certain economic questions is worthy of respect; or, if there is such an orthodoxy, that it is in any way enforced. Our own thoughts and experiences leave us thoroughly persuaded that an orthodoxy exists in this last sense, and that it is quite widely enforced. (p.6)

Orthodox methods and standards tend to emerge around issues that are at the core of a discipline. These common practices facilitate the research process by making it easier for scholars to talk to one another, to build on each other's work, and to measure progress along a given set of dimensions. At the same time, orthodoxy also has its costs. While it promotes efficiency within a system, it makes it difficult to break out of a system or to develop new ways of approaching research. I will argue that many components of orthodoxy in the strategy field are borne of our optimism. Moreover, our orthodox approach has led us to give selective attention and inattention to a host of topics. In doing so, it has both narrowed and distorted our perspective.

The essay begins with a succinct comment on the development of the strategy field, and how it compares with that of evolutionary economics and population ecology. Next it examines the subset of the strategy literature called the resource based view of the firm, and illustrates how the field's heritage and biases can be seen in that scholarship. It then considers the roads not taken, the questions not asked, and the costs of avoiding those pathways. The essay concludes with some thoughts on *how* we might push back against our orthodoxy, and *why* doing so would be in the best interests of the field.

From Whence We Came

The modern field of strategic management has it roots in the field of business policy. By looking at the history of the field, we can better understand its present characteristics. Arch Wilkinson Shaw, publisher of *System* magazine (later renamed *BusinessWeek*), taught the first business policy course at the Harvard Business School in 1911. His intention was to help students integrate the lessons of functional courses by adopting the vantage point of the upper-level manager. To do this, Shaw asked a number of company presidents to visit the class, talk about the most critical problems facing their firms, and engage students in discussions about what could be done.

In the eighty years that followed, business policy courses have gone through a number of iterations. A focus on the problems and responsibilities of upper level management, however, has remained front and center. As Christensen, Andrews, and Bower (1978) explain:

> In Business Policy, the problems considered and
> the point of view assumed in analyzing and dealing with
> them are those of the chief executive or general manager,
> whose primary responsibility is the enterprise as a whole
> (p.3).

It is interesting to note that most strategy courses today are still taught by the discussion (i.e., case) method, even in schools where that is not the dominant pedagogy. Despite the fact that research and teaching material in the strategy field has become increasingly analytical, there continues to be a great interest in the problems of practicing managers, and an overriding concern with how things could be done better.

This role of advisor to management and the associated quest for normative prescriptions is arguably at the core of the strategy field. By its very nature, the field appears to have accepted a challenge to elevate practice and to improve company performance. Further, the fact that our students and many of us ultimately end up working as managers or as advisors to managers makes us particularly aware of the desirability of having a positive message to deliver. As one colleague wryly remarked: "Who would want to hire a pessimistic consultant?"

In contrast to the pragmatic world of management practice, evolutionary economics derives from different sources and measures its success by a different metric. Its intellectual antecedents are in Schumpeterian technology studies as well as in evolutionary biology. The latter examines the differential survival and growth patterns of species. Evolutionary economics, in turn, studies the survival and growth of industries or other large-scale units of economic organization. Its goal is to describe and model these dynamic phenomena, and to do it in such a way that it improves upon neoclassical models:

> The challenge to an evolutionary formulation then is this: it must provide an analysis that at least comes close to matching the power of neoclassical theory to predict and illuminate the macroeconomic patterns of growth. And it must provide a significantly strong vehicle for analysis of the processes involved in technical change, and in particular enable a fruitful integration of understanding of what goes on at the micro level with what goes on at a more aggregated level. (Nelson and Winter 1982: 206)

Population ecology also draws on concepts from biological evolution and seeks to explain the rise and fall of populations of firms. To this end, it focuses on selection forces in a firm's environment that favor some firms over others. It also considers the internal firm processes that encode a firm's way of doing things and impede its ability to change. (Hannan and Freeman 1977).

Note that, from the start, the objective of both evolutionary economics and population ecology has been to *describe* and to *explain*

254

macro-level changes in populations of firms. In contrast, management theory has sought to *improve* the conditions of individual firms. These differences are pertinent to our understanding of these fields and the issues that are at their respective cores. In themselves, they are not problematic.

What has become problematic in the strategy field are the practices that have evolved around its core. The strategy field has taken what amounts to a shortcut: in its attempts to help firms become more successful, it has focused almost exclusively on analyzing the experiences of successful firms. It has fallen into the rut of gazing at good fortune, while ignoring a broader range of experiences that are no less germane to firms' existence in dynamic competitive environments. These systematic practices are the substance of the orthodoxy referred to earlier.

High Hopes

The *American Heritage Dictionary* defines optimism as "a tendency to expect the best possible outcome or dwell on the most hopeful aspects of a situation." In the strategy field, this tendency can be seen in the extreme emphasis that is placed on carving out unique competitive positions for firms. In his acceptance speech for the Nobel Prize in literature, William Faulkner said that "man will not only endure, he will prevail." Thus he put to words the notion that mere survival is not enough, man can triumph. Faulkner's view of invincibility may not stir a passion in the hearts of economists or sociologists, but when applied to firms, it is a view that would have great appeal to most strategists.

The language strategists' use is consistent with this high-flung objective and is laden with auspicious terminology. At the center of it all is the concept of *competitive advantage*—not just any competitive advantage, but a *long run sustainable competitive advantage* that gives a firm an abiding edge over its competitors. With such advantages securely in place, the hope is that the firm will enjoy *sustained superior performance*. The likelihood of this increases if the firm's advantage is supported by a *distinctive competence*, and consistent with the *key success factors* of an industry.

Barney (1991) described the general framework used in many strategic management texts. As those in the field will recognize, the framework emphasizes the experiences of firms that have been quite successful:

(F)irms obtain sustained competitive advantages by implementing strategies that exploit their internal strengths, through responding to environmental opportunities, while neutralizing external threats and avoiding internal weaknesses (p. 99).

Underlying the acceptance of this ideal is somehow the notion that, if management tries hard enough and works smart enough, their firms too can be unusually successful. At the extreme, this sounds suspiciously like Garrison Keillor's fictional Lake Wobegon, where all of the men are good looking, the women are beautiful, and the children all above average.

The Crown Jewels

Recently, a number of strategy scholars have placed increased emphasis on understanding the internal capabilities that enable some firms to secure attractive competitive positions. This line of inquiry has been called the "resource-based view of the firm." From an evolutionary perspective, it is perhaps not surprising that this new endeavor shares much in common with practices that were already in place. It, too, has a penchant for the positive.

In the resource-based view, firms are characterized as collections of resources rather than sets of product-market positions (Wernerfelt, 1984). To see how optimism creeps into our work, it is interesting to consider the very name of this research stream. Wernerfelt (1984) originally used the term *resource* to refer to "anything which could be thought of as a strength or weakness of a given firm (p. 172)," much like economists use the term "fixed factor." More recent writers, however, have used the word to refer to only positive assets and attributes. Barney (1991), for example, says that firm resources

include all assets, capabilities, organizational processes, firm attributes, information, knowledge, etc. controlled by a firm that enable the firm to conceive of and implement strategies that improve its efficiency and effectiveness (p. 101).

Despite Wernerfelt's original intent, in fairness, Barney's usage of the word is more in line with the standard definition:

Resource: "Something that can be used for support or help; an available supply that can be drawn on when needed." (*American Heritage Dictionary*, p. 1536)

The name for this stream of work has come to tell a great deal about its emphasis: it focuses on a firm's positive assets and attributes. It is further notable that most of the attention in this line of inquiry has gone to an analysis of the "best of the best," the so-called "crown jewels" of a company. These are the resources that meet four criteria for sustaining a long-run competitive advantage:

(a) it must be valuable, in the sense that it exploits opportunities and/or neutralizes threats in a firm's environment;

(b) it must be rare among a firm's current and potential competitors;

(c) it must be imperfectly imitable; and

(d) there cannot be strategically equivalent substitutes for this resource that are valuable but neither rare or imperfectly imitable (Barney 1991: 106).

Resources with these characteristics are seen as the heart of a firm's competitive advantage, the source of isolating mechanisms to protect that advantage (Rumelt 1987), and the basis for a firm's diversified expansion (Montgomery and Hariharan 1991). Considerable effort has gone into characterizing these resources and documenting their presence in firms (Prahalad and Hamel 1990).

Like a Platonic Ideal, this characterization of a perfect form of resources is very useful from both a theoretical and practical standpoint. At the same time, it is important to know something about the size of the gap between the idealized version of a form and what is seen in reality. This is where the resource-based literature falls dangerously short.

Routines

The treatment of routines within the dialogue of the resource-based view is particularly noteworthy, especially when contrasted with its usage within evolutionary theory.

At the Copenhagen symposium, it soon became evident that all in attendance thought routines were a central concept in the line of inquiry they were pursuing. However, it was striking to see the difference in emphasis each tradition placed on the term. One side of the table (the population ecologists and evolutionary theorists) seemed to use the term as a proxy for inertia. Those on the other side (the strategists) used it as a proxy for inimitability. This difference is very telling.

In the resource-based literature, routines have come to embody the essence of a firm's competitive advantage. They are often used as examples of resources that meet all four of Barney's criteria: they are valuable; rare; imperfectly imitable, and have no strategically equivalent substitutes. The following passage from Grant (1991), who links resources with capabilities, is typical:

> Creating capabilities is not simply a matter of assembling a team of resources: capabilities involve complex patterns of coordination between people and between people and other resources. Perfecting such coordination requires learning through repetition (p. 122).

Dierickx and Cool (1989: 1507) provide a winsome example of why such routines, built up through time, may give a firm an uncontestable lead. Paraphrasing a dialogue between a British Lord and his American visitor:

> "How come you got such a gorgeous lawn?"
> "Well, the quality of the soil is, I dare say, of the utmost importance."
> "No problem."
> "Furthermore, one does need the finest quality seed and fertilizers."
> "Big deal."
> "Of course, daily watering and weekly mowing are jolly important."
> "No sweat, jest leave it to me!"
> "That's it."

258

"No kidding?!"

"Oh, absolutely. There is nothing to it, old boy; just keep it up for five centuries."

The resource-based view focuses on the tacit and slow-to-change aspects of routines as hurdles that stand in the way of firms seeking to imitate the successful routines of an industry leader: "Clearly, imitation of those stocks by other firms becomes next to impossible" (Dierickx and Cool 1989: 1509).

But the concept of routines as originally employed by Nelson and Winter (1982) had quite a different connotation. These authors used the term in a neutral way to describe "all regular and predictable behavioral patterns of firms:"

> We use this term to include characteristics of firms that range from well-specified technical routines for producing things, through procedures for hiring and firing, ordering new inventory, or stepping up production of items in high demand, to policies regarding investment, research and development (R&D), or advertising, and business strategies about product diversification and oversees investment. In our evolutionary theory, these routines play the role that genes play in biological evolutionary theory. They are a persistent feature of the organism and determine its possible behavior (though *actual* behavior is determined also by the environment); they are heritable in the sense that tomorrow's organisms generated from today's (for example, by building a new plant) have many of the same characteristics, and they are selectable in the sense that organisms with certain routines may do better than others, and, if so, their relative importance in the population (industry) is augmented over time (p. 14).

True to its roots in natural selection, Nelson and Winter's theory of economic evolution emphasizes that routines are embedded in a firm and change slowly over long periods of time. In this view, routines enable a firm to do its work, but also limit its ability to change. Population ecology, particularly work in the tradition of Hannan and Freeman, tends to emphasize the latter, linking organizational routines with structural inertia:

There are a number of obvious limitations on the ability of organizations to adapt. That is, there are a number of processes that generate structural inertia. The stronger the pressures, the lower the organizations' adaptive flexibility and the more likely that the logic of environmental selection is appropriate (1977: 930-931).

These different interpretations of routines are quite revealing. While recognizing that tacit knowledge and organizational routines can be an important source of competitive advantage, the strategy field has been slow to acknowledge the obverse. In contrast, population ecologists have tended to emphasize the dark side of things, and have taken a less detailed look at the positive role routines can play. In their present state, both traditions lack a sense of their counterpart.

Breaking Free of Orthodoxy

If a *de facto* orthodoxy has developed in the strategy field such that a preoccupation with the optimistic side of things has overshadowed a more balanced consideration of a wider range of issues, it should be possible to identify a series of topics and perspectives that have been systematically overlooked or avoided. In this section, I will introduce several topics that merit consideration in this regard. Although it is likely that the practices described here developed as a means of addressing questions at the core of the field, they ultimately have constrained our vision and effectiveness in handling just those issues.

Acknowledging the full spectrum of resources:
The good, the bad, and the boring

As discussed above, in a relatively short amount of time, the strategy field has learned a great deal about identifying and using positively valued resources. These insights have had a substantial impact in both the academic and practitioner realms. It is also fair to say, however, that the field's near-exclusive focus on the crown jewels of a corporation has created a kind of tyranny of the minority: we know a lot about a few resources, and very little about a lot of resources.

As a field, we must acknowledge that if we understand only the uppermost tail, the bulk of the resource distribution remains beyond our purview. It simply belies credibility to conclude that resources can be

260

meaningfully characterized by only two categories: the extraordinarily valuable (about which we have talked at length) and all the rest. It is impossible to draw meaningful observations across such a huge residual category.

Consider first what might be called the pedestrian resources of a corporation: cash, buildings, telephone systems, and so on. In themselves, these prosaic resources are not at the heart of a firm's competitive advantage because they can be purchased through reasonably effective market exchanges. At the same time, their common nature does not mean that their assembled presence has no consequence. Indeed, this kind of resource constitutes the majority of resources in all firms.

Further, many firms earning normal returns can claim nothing other than pedestrian resources. An evolutionary analysis would recognize the important fact that such firms are survivors. The strategy field, in its search for superstars, all but ignores their existence. For an area that exudes optimism, it is odd that the distinction between life and death is of such little consequence. One could easily conclude that our preoccupation with the uppermost echelon of firms has overshadowed our appreciation of many more.

Moving to the other end of the spectrum, consider the impact of negative endowments: resources that destroy rather than build advantage. Leonard-Barton's (1992) characterization of the process through which "core capabilities become core rigidities" begins this journey. However, the story of good resources gone bad is just the tip of the iceberg, and should not be the end of our journey to the dark side of the resource spectrum.

Special note should be made of those resources and capabilities that, *in toto*, have a negative impact on the firm. These may include such things as a reputation for fraudulent behavior, an inept marketing department, or financial obligations that exceed the firm's ability to pay. Most firms have examples of such liabilities in their resource inventory; and inheriting a bundle of them in a turnaround situation would not be uncommon. Existing theory not only fails to offer advice about such matters, it barely acknowledges that they exist.

One may be tempted to conclude that organizational liabilities can simply be characterized as the opposite of highly valued capabilities. A closer look, however, will reveal that the relationship is unlikely to be symmetric. Whereas highly valued resources may be built slowly over long periods of time, gross liabilities can be established with lightning speed. More generally, the challenge of rebuilding from deficit can dwarf that of building from a fresh start.

If we are seeking to develop a theory that interprets the success of a firm through the lens of its resource endowment, we cannot limit our focus to one tail of the distribution. Recall that Andrews characterized the firm as a collection of strengths *and weaknesses*. A theory that steadfastly overlooks half the spectrum will not stand the test of time.

Confronting the dynamic nature of resources

Just as the resource-based view has given selective attention to a narrow range of resources, it has also given selective attention to a narrow window of time. This period may be called the "golden age" of a firm, not as a designation for old age, but as a characterization of the period in time when the firm's capabilities are in sync with and support its competitive advantage. The question left unexamined, however, is what happened before and after that period?

The resource-based view has little to say about entrepreneurs, those whose inventory of resources is remarkably thin. On closer examination, one may argue that these firms lack the large scores of pedestrian resources we associate with established firms (but also overlook in their analysis), but have, in fact, a jewel in the form of an idea, or a vision of how things might be done. This line of inquiry, however, has not been developed, and it is difficult to suggest how far it could be taken.

A static look at the golden age has diverted our attention from resources that do not fare so well over time. Given the optimistic outlook that is prevalent in the field, and the preoccupation with highly-valued resources, it is not surprising that this stream of research has focused on Ricardian rents—rents that accrue to the presence of fixed, scarce factors and can persist in static equilibrium (Rumelt 1987: 142):

> In sum, four conditions must be met for a firm to enjoy sustained above-normal returns. Resource heterogeneity creates Ricardian or monopoly rents. *Ex post* limits to competition prevent the rents from being competed away. Imperfect factor mobility ensures that valuable factors remain with the firm and that the rents are shared. *Ex ante* limits to competition keep costs from offsetting the rents. (Peteraf 1993: 185)

The analysis of Ricardian rents has added considerable sophistication to our understanding of resources and competitive advantage.

It is regrettable, however, that these developments have not been balanced by a closer consideration of Schumpeterian rents, and resources and advantages that erode through time. For example, from a theoretical as well as practical perspective, we know little about the decay rates of valuable resources. Further, by focusing on imitability as an either/or condition, we have failed to address the dynamics of competition and the processes through which innovations are diffused and economic profits driven down.

In an excellent article comparing the resource-based view and five schools of economic thought, Kathleen Conner highlighted these words of Schumpeter:

> The essential point to grasp is that in dealing with capitalism we are dealing with an evolutionary process.... The fundamental impulse that sets and keeps the capitalist engine in motion comes from the new consumers' goods, the new methods of production or transportation, the new markets, the new forms of industrial organization that capitalist enterprise creates ....[T]his kind of competition is as much more effective than [price competition over existing products] as a bombardment is in comparison with forcing a door. (Conner 1991: 127)

The Schumpterian view of competition figures prominently in evolutionary theory, but has taken a distant backseat in the resource-based view of the firm. Like a quixotic quest for eternal youth, the resource-based view's fixation on forever has overshadowed the far more common situation where advantages are a matter of time and degree.

Nelson (1991), Dosi, Winter, and Teece (1992), and others have begun to address this gap. However, as a paper by Teece, Pisano, and Shuen (1992) exemplifies, inching the strategy field away from its preoccupation with never-ending profit will not be easy. In the spirit of Schumpeterian competition, Teece *et al* recognize that any given set of resources is subject to competition, and that its value will diminish as imitation sets in. They also recognize that if a firm's competitive advantage is dependent on one set of resources, in time it too will be lost. In the end, however, the authors have included a powerful escape clause in the form of higher order resources called dynamic capabilities that renew a firm's distinctive competences by generating new routines and resources.

The distinction between static and dynamic routines is an important one from both a scholarly and practical perspective. Nonetheless, in its present state, the argument has a "happily ever-after" quality, as if dynamic capabilities are the "push-back" firms need against mortality. But surely the answer is not so simple. Now that the need has been articulated, can it be met? Are dynamic capabilities free for the asking? Do they rest upon the presence of organizational slack? Do they involve a tradeoff between flexibility and commitment? Why don't all firms follow this advice, and live on in perpetuity?

The good news is that the strategy field has begun to move from a static to a dynamic treatment of resources and competitive advantage. It is here that strategists can benefit most from the insights imbedded in the evolutionary theory of the firm and its antecedent, Schumpeterian studies of competition.

Recognizing the limits of managerial prerogative

Although it addresses issues inside the firm, the reasoning behind the resource-based view is primarily economic, and shares its roots with parts of the field that have traditionally addressed strategy formulation rather than strategy implementation. Unfortunately, the resource-based view also shares a weakness with that tradition: it overemphasizes the power of managerial prerogative.

Discussions of resources often proceed with little consideration of factors that are beyond management's direct control. The role of the firm's competitive environment is one example; it will be discussed in the coming section.

A number of internal forces are also beyond management's direct control, and these too have received little attention in the resource-based literature. Leonard-Barton (1992) and others have acknowledged the "dark underside of resources," but their admonishments, while carefully argued and well recognized, remain as adjuncts to the dialogue. This is not surprising: research on strategy content hinges on optimism and has a history of blocking or marginalizing insights that might challenge managerial authority. Nevertheless, as Rumelt's discussion of inertia (see Chapter 5) and the evolutionary theorists' treatment of routines show, organizations often have a deep and broad power of their own. In such cases, this fact must be recognized and duly addressed.

Many of these issues come together in the question of what normative advice can be given to a firm that lacks scarce resources but wishes to develop some. Schoemaker (1990) and Amit and Schoemaker (1993) recognize this dilemma. These authors have modelled resource allocation decisions as high stake choices taking place in environments that are too unstable and complex to be optimized. Their research blends tenets of behavioral decision making with resource-based thinking. The strength of this kind of work is that it recognizes cognitive and behavioral limitations on individuals and collections of individuals but does so in a competitive context. In a similar vein, Nelson and Winter (1982) argued that

> . . . it is neither difficult nor implausible to develop models of firm behavior that interweave "blind" and "deliberate" processes. Indeed, in human problem solving itself, both elements are involved and difficult to disentangle (p. 11).

A recognition of which elements in the firm's internal and external environments are more or less controllable over shorter or longer periods of time is an important distinction for scholars of management. By giving elements that are beyond immediate management control the accord they are due, management, and scholars of management, should be able to attend better to the elements that are subject to their discretion.

Seeing the system: interactive firm behavior

As noted above, in its zeal to elevate firm level analysis, the resource-based view has tended to treat individual firms as if they operated in a state of competitive isolation. The folly of this practice lies in the fact that external forces largely determine the value of the firm's resources. Changes in the competitive equilibrium can produce wide swings in the value of a firm's resource portfolio. (Porter 1991)

Historically, the resource-based view has given careful consideration to the resource bases of individual firms, often focusing on the industry leader. Without denying the value of firm-by-firm analysis, it is important to recognize that the fortunes and challenges of individual firms must be evaluated in a relevant strategic context.[2] We not only need to identify *relative* resource positions, but to consider how to defend them, or how to challenge those of others. To date, this systemic quality of

---

[2]Foss and Eriksen (Chapter 3) have taken this a step forward to include a consideration of resources shared by industry incumbents, and Ghemawat (1991) has addressed the impact of commitment by one firm on the fortunes of others.

competitive interaction has been missing from most resource-based analyses.

The emphasis evolutionary theory has placed on industry-level analyses and the rise and fall of populations of firms can be instructive in this regard. At the same time, it is likely that that tradition's relative lack of experience with strategic interactions will ultimately limit the upside potential of that particular cross-fertilization. Instead, this may be an instance where the resource-based view would also benefit from further incorporation of recent game-theoretic work.

Summary

The strategy field has experienced a burst of energy and insight in the recent development of the resource-based view of the firm. One can see, however, that the field's ever-present optimism has deeply influenced the unfolding of this work. Its systematic bias has been reflected first in the choice of topics for analysis, and further in the ways these topics have been addressed.

A call for greater balance moving forward is not motivated by a simple desire for intellectual symmetry. Rather, it reflects a belief that a faithful representation of reality is the best foundation on which to base both scholarly and pragmatic advances. As it has been said, one is well advised to be a meliorist, not an optimist.

Chorus:	Did you perhaps go further than you have told us?
Prometheus:	I caused mortals to cease foreseeing doom.
Chorus:	What cure did you provide them with against that sickness?
Prometheus:	I placed in them blind hopes.
Chorus:	That was a great gift you gave to men.

—Aeschylus, *Prometheus Bound*

References

Aeschylus, *Prometheus Bound.*

Amit, R., and Schoemaker, P.J. 1993. "Strategic assets and organizational rent." *Strategic Management Journal* 14: 33-46.

Barney, J. 1991. "Firm resources and sustained competitive advantage." *Journal of Management* 17: 99-120.

Christiansen, C.R., Andrews, K.R., and Bower, J.L 1978. *Business Policy: Text and Cases.* Homewood, IL: Richard D. Irwin, Inc.

Conner, K.R. "A historical comparison of resource-based theory and five schools of thought within industrial organization economics: do we have a new theory of the firm?" *Journal of Management* 17: 121-154.

Dierickx, I., and Cool, K. 1989. "Asset stock accumulation and sustainable competitive advantage." *Management Science* 35: 1504-11.

Dosi, G., Winter, S.G., and Teece, D. 1992. Towards a theory of corporate coherence: preliminary remarks. In G. Dosi, R. Giannetti and P.A. Toninelli (eds.), *Technology and enterprise in a historical perspective.* Oxford: Clarendon Press.

Ghemawat, P. 1991. *Commitment.* New York: Free Press.

Grant, R.M. 1991. "The resource-based theory of competitive advantage: implications for strategy formulation." *California Management Review* 33: 114-135.

Hannan, M.T., and Freeman, J. 1977. "The population ecology of organizations." *American Journal of Sociology* 82: 929-64.

Keillor, Garrison. "Prairie Home Companion." National Public Radio.

Leonard-Barton, D. 1992. "Core competencies and core rigidities: a paradox in new product development." *Strategic Management Journal* 13: 111-125.

Montgomery, C.A. and Hariharan, S. 1991. "Diversified expansion by large established firms." *Journal of Economic Behavior and Organization*: 71-89.

Nelson, R.R. 1991. "Why do firms differ and how does it matter?" *Strategic Management Journal* 12: 61-74.

Nelson, R.R. and Winter, S.G. 1982. *An evolutionary theory of economic change.* Cambridge: Belknap Press.

Peteraf, M.A. 1993. "The cornerstones of competitive advantage: a resource-based view." *Strategic Management Journal* 14: 179-91.

Porter, M.E. 1991. "Towards a dynamic theory of strategy." *Strategic Management Journal* 12: 95-117.

Prahalad, C.K., and Hamel, G. 1990. "The core competence of the corporation." *Harvard Business Review*, May/June: 79-91.

Rumelt, R.P. 1987. Theory, strategy and entrepreneurship. In D. Teece (ed.), *The competitive challenge* (pp. 137-58). Cambridge: Ballinger.

Schoemaker, P.J. 1990. "Strategy, complexity, and economic rent." *Management Science* 36: 1178-1192.

Teece, D., Pisano, G., and Shuen A. 1992. "Dynamic capabilities and strategic management." Working paper, Consortium on Competitiveness and Cooperation, University of California at Berkeley.

Wernerfelt, B. 1984. "A resource-based view of the firm." *Strategic Management Journal* 5: 171-180.

Index

Innovations: and imitability, 11
Interdependencies among firms: 44-45
Investments: coordinated across firms in an industry, 61-63, 67

K

Kauffman, S.: 26
Kirzner, Israel: 85
Knight, Frank: 82-85
Knowledge: firm as a repository of, 201-205

L

Lawrence, Paul: 26
Leadership: 113-14, 210-13; failures, 113-17
Learning: *see* organizational learning
Leonard-Barton, Dorothy: 261, 264
Level of analysis: 4-6, 13, 20, 219; benefits of population-level analysis, 248; selection and, 32; *see also* unique firms
Levinthal, Daniel: 26, 28, 31, 61, 213-14
Lippman, S.A.: 7
Loasby, Brian: 73, 76n, 81
Locus of control: 219
Lorsch, Jay: 26

M

Mahoney, J.T.: 74
Managerial prerogative: 6, 219; recognizing the limits of, 264-65
March, James: 25, 28, 190-92, 201-02, 213-14
Market failure(s): *see* transaction cost economics
Marshall, A.: 48, 76n
Means, G.C.: 188
Meyer, M.: 34

Milgrom, Paul: 128
Montgomery, Cynthia: 7, 66, 143, 151
Morgan, G.: 182

N

Nelson, Richard: 3, 5, 24, 105, 135, 149, 158, 185, 202-05, 247, 252, 254, 259, 263, 265
Neoclassical economics: 102-03; transition to modern IO analysis, 184-87
Nexus-of-contract: view of the firm, 95n, 193-98

O

Opportunism: 78
Optimism: and the strategy field, 251-66
Organizational form: differences in, 26, 223-24
Organizational learning: 25, 31, 92-94
Organizational search: 25-27
Orthodoxy: heuristics in the research process, 180-184; in the strategy field, 251-53
Ownership of assets: 84-87

P

Pandian, J.R.: 74
Path dependency: 3, 5, 91-92
Penrose, Edith: 9, 11, 36, 155, 205-09; Penrosean growth of the firm, 90-91
Peteraf, Margaret: 8, 167, 262
Pisano, Gary: 31, 172-73, 263
Plasticity: 101, 103; *see also* inertia
Political structure of a firm: 31; deadlocks, 111-13
Population ecology: 104-05; benefits of population-level analysis, 247-48; compared to

evolutionary economics, 228;
compared to resource-based
view, 214-18, 253-55, 258-60
Porter, Michael: 8, 30, 51-53, 169-
72, 186-87, 200, 219-20, 265
Positioning: in resource and
capability space, 58-60
Prahalad, C.K.: 207
Price-system: use of, 72-74
Profit-seeking behavior, social
implications of: 172-74
Profitability: performance
differences across firms, 24;
sources of, 102; concepts and
measures, 148-49, 167-72, 227
Putterman, Louis: 86
Pyke, F.: 49

R

Rents: and competitive advantage,
169-72; and market power,
159-63; Ricardian, 8, 262;
versus Schumpeterian, 162-71,
262-64; *see also* replicability
Replicability: and rents, 148, 154-
67
Resources: changes in value, 12;
characteristics of valuable
resources, 257; as competitive
barriers, 65; in context of an
industry, 24, 27, 30, 44-48;
defined, 256-57; firm as a
bundle of, 205-09; firm-level
differences, 22; hierarchy of,
120-22; idiosyncratic, 155-59;
process of developing, 7, 13;
static vs. dynamic perspective
on, 262-64; stocks and flows, 7;
supporting Ricardian rents, 8;
those that are not
acknowledged, 260-62;
valuation of, 8; *see also*
routines, dynamic capabilties

Resource-based view of the firm:
compared to evolutionary
economics, 4, 9-15, 134-36,
253-55; compared to industrial
organization economics, 4, 143;
compared to population
ecology, 219-28, 259-60;
compared to transaction cost
approach, 144; history of, 6-10;
theoretical weaknesses, 8, 260-
66
Retention: 35-36
Richardson, G.B.: 73
Routines: and inertia, 114; and
resources, 148, 149-154; in
resource-based view vs.
evolutionary economics, 258-
60; *see also* coherence
Rumelt, Richard: 7, 91, 95, 262

S

Saxonian, A.: 49
Schoemaker, Paul: 7, 12, 47n, 150,
264-65
Schon, D.: 27
Schoonhoven, C.B.: 225
Schumpeter, Joseph: on dynamic
efficiency, 209; Schumpeterian
competition, 11, 163-72, 263-
64; Schumpeterian integration,
87-90
Search: *see* organizational search
Selection: level of analysis, 32;
natural and artificial
environments, 33-35; pressures,
34-35
Selznick, P.: 192-93, 210-12
Semiconductor manufacturing in the
U.S., example of population-
level analysis: 228-247
Sengenberger, W.: 49
Shuen, Amy: 31, 172-73, 263
Silver, Morris: 88

Simon, Herbert: 25, 190, 198-99
Stage of development: of the firm, 14-15
Stochastic shocks: resource-based approach in the context of, 133-134; *see also* technology, transformation
Stopford, John: 127
Strategic interaction: 265-66
Strategic management field: content vs. process perspectives, 21; and economics, 1-4, 178-79; history of, 1-2, 253-55; pragmatic nature of, 253-54; key terms, 255; optimism in, 246-60; *see also* orthodoxy
Strategy: in evolutionary economics, 3; managerial definition, 6; definition in population ecology, 226; SWOT framework, 1, 7, 43-44.

T

Technology: and disequilibrium, 11-12
Teece, David: 31, 91, 95, 172-73, 205, 263
Telser, Lester: 45
Theory of the firm: 71-72; 180-84; *see also* nexus-of-contract
Transaction costs: 14, 198-201; compared to resource-based view, 144; contracting costs and contractual hazards, 78-79; role in defining firm boundaries, 73-74
Transformation, organizational: 117-27; *see also* organizational learning
Tushman, Michael: 229

U

Uncertainty: caused by shifts in technology, 12
Unique firms: problem of focusing on, 220-21
Unitary actors: 226-28

V

Variation: 25

W

Wernerfelt, Birger: 7, 65, 149, 219-20, 256
Williamson, Oliver: 144, 198-201
Winter, Sidney: 3, 5, 24, 91, 95, 105, 135, 149, 158, 202-05, 247, 252, 254, 259, 263, 265
Woodward, S.: 78

Z

Zucker, L.: 34